Dead People I Have Known

Dead People
I Have Known

SHAYNE CARTER

Victoria University Press

TE WHARE WĀNANGA O TE ŪPOKO O TE IKA A MĀUI

VICTORIA
UNIVERSITY OF WELLINGTON

VICTORIA UNIVERSITY PRESS
Victoria University of Wellington
PO Box 600 Wellington
vup.victoria.ac.nz

A catalogue record is available from the National Library of New Zealand

ISBN 9781776562213

Published with the assistance of

ARTS COUNCIL OF NEW ZEALAND *TOI AOTEAROA*

Printed by 1010 Printing International

for Ricci, Jimmi, and Tony

Contents

Part One

'Nyah nyah nyah'

I'm in the town hall with my head in a pot full of serotonin. About me is the full scent of perfume, freshly pressed jackets, fear, alcohol. I have taken a pill, a very strong pill, and the first effect of it just dropped. My bandmates all wear baffled looks that probably mirror my own.

Half an hour ago we opened the show with two of our favourite tunes, and when our last chord died, it lifted skywards and stayed in the rafters like an old-school victory banner.

Straitjacket Fits are fresh from a tour where we've regrouped for a short reunion, and it's our last stop tonight. We thought we should celebrate, naughtily, a bit illicitly—but back in our seats the wisdom of this may have died.

It's the bNet New Zealand Music Awards, an evening to honour New Zealand's edgiest musicians. Half of Auckland is here, turned out in their town hall gear.

There's a roar. The Prime Minister has come out on the stage. Helen Clark is popular with loser musicians because she's the Arts Minister, and she has been for six years. She seems to genuinely care about people no one else cares about.

She starts a speech that I'm too far off to hear, her voice low and buried, like a shovel. Slowly, key words wander in from the haze.

'High school punk band . . . Dunedin . . . the Doublehappys . . . Straitjacket Fits . . .'

It is now apparent that her speech concerns me. There is no joy in this realisation, just an immense dread, brought on by the potent E.

'And the bNet Lifetime Achievement Award goes to Shayne Carter,' the Prime Minister says, confirming my fears.

The audience claps and starts to stand, and I stand too, like I've been sent to the gallows.

I set out on a lonely walk.

As I take the stairs to the podium, I risk a quick peek at the crowd and I can see that it goes back forever. People are peering down from the balcony.

The Prime Minister waits at the rostrum, clutching a statuette, and she wears a dark blue pant suit and red lipstick. She looks different in real life, but maybe that's just me.

With no real plan, I charge across the stage. Best to get this over.

'Heh heh heh,' the PM says as I press her into my chest.

She takes a short step backwards and hands me my award, smoothing the front of her top.

'Congratulations, Shayne,' she says.

'Thanks, Helen,' I reply, as casually as I can.

I turn to face the mob.

'Thanks,' I say, and my thanks slaps back.

'I wasn't expecting this, so thanks,' I go, repeating myself.

This is the whole of my speech.

The Prime Minister makes small chit-chat as we walk backstage, but I don't listen because I'm busy plotting an escape route, any escape route, one that is as fast as possible.

I'm now aware of the two men hovering around us in understated suits, both of them blending with the walls. Wires curl up from their collars and into white plastic pieces in their ears, and when I catch the eye of one of them he gives me a lift of his eyebrow as if to say, 'Tied one on, eh matey?'

This is my cue to run. I touch the Prime Minister gently on the elbow. 'I'm feeling a bit overwhelmed, Helen. I think I'm going to have to go away and compose myself.'

Without waiting for her response, I turn and stride off down the hall.

The drama with the Prime Minister set the tone for the rest of that night. I bounced around stupidly from one drama to another. I went to the foyer at the interval—I don't why—where I was spotted by a woman who was drinking at the bar. She lurched right over. No time for pleasantries.

Did I know my girlfriend was having an affair in New York, and that she'd already moved in with her new lover?

No, I knew none of that, but it was annoying now that I did.

The woman went on.

Perhaps I should give her my number, so she could pass on any more news?

I stumbled back into the hall and repeated all of this to my bandmates. They were curious and empathetic, as people on E often are.

'Why would she tell you that right now?' said John, which was a fair enough question.

The show resumed, but I was slumped in my chair, my new award—a piece of red plastic in the shape of a B—on the sticky floor beneath me. I heard my girlfriend's name being read out through the PA for the benefit of me and all the other people here who loved her too. She'd been nominated for the Female Fox, one of those jokey bNet categories that tonight had lost any humour. I'd been nominated for the Male Fox award too, not that it mattered now.

'And the winner is Kirsten Morrell from Goldenhorse,' the compère said, to my relief.

I'd been so wrapped up in this that I barely noticed when, a few moments later, I was announced as the Male Fox. The *New Zealand Herald* criticised the win, blaming it on the public vote and the sally of middle-aged women who'd been roused from some sexless torpor to give it to Shayne P one last time—or something like that. I snatched the award anyway, thanking my parents and genetics. I hoped news of this was winging its way to America.

The victory was brief. Afterwards I sat in my seat, stoned and bereft, torturing myself with the activities at an unknown address in New York.

Mercifully, the ceremony ended. I needed to be home now and preferably unconscious. I was standing outside in the drizzle, trying to hail a cab, when a woman of dark, fine beauty came down the path towards me. She was married, she said, by way of introduction, but she'd like to have an affair with me, probably now, and what did I think of that?

I thought it was the sanest thing I'd heard all day.

I gave her my address, and she was waiting by my gate when my cab pulled up, and then we kissed. Her lips were like the rain, soft and otherworldly, but the hold of them couldn't last.

Doubt crept in. I pulled back, made another excuse, but the woman didn't seem flustered—maybe she had her own doubts too.

'That's okay,' was all she said, and she seemed to evaporate as quickly as she'd arrived, leaving me with her number, a trace of musk, and the soft crimson bruise of her lipstick.

I never saw her again.

I did see Helen Clark again, at another reception a matter of days later.

'Hi Helen,' I said as I shook her hand. 'The last time I saw you we were having a hug at the town hall.'

'Oh yes, yes, yes,' she said, but too quickly, not knowing who I was.

The security guy with her remembered though, and he gave me the same lift of the eyebrow he'd given me at the bNet Awards.

'Tied one on, eh matey?' his eyebrow seemed to say.

I sank back into the throng, feeling miffed and a bit embarrassed. The PM moved on, into another sea of faces she'd be hard pressed to recall.

*

I won my first award when I was five. I didn't have to do much— just be five. The category was Youngest Person at Dance and the reward was a block of chocolate. As I stepped onto the stage to accept my prize, I sensed for the first time the appraisal of an audience, that feeling of having my existence pondered by a room full of strangers.

'Hasn't he done well?' they might have been saying, poking their neighbour's arm.

My mother was the singer in the band. Her group had come up to Alexandra from Dunedin for a holiday gig, and they played every second night in a hall that, during the Great War, had been the cafeteria of a rabbit-canning factory. Back then, rabbits were scooped up from the huge swarms on the hills and shipped off for the frontline troops.

It was 1970 and a monumental summer. The seasons still came cleanly demarcated and they always ran to time. The temperature hit about 32 degrees every day, and the tar on the roads around the Alexandra Motor Camp melted and set again at night. A large clock with white hands sat redundantly on the slopes above the lodge.

It was the only holiday I remember sharing with Mum, Dad and my younger brother Marcel. Marcel was a baby. Our teenage neighbour Kath Starling was there too so she could watch us kids while Mum sang nights in the hall.

We were excited the day Suzanne came to play. We knew Suzanne from *Happen Inn* and it was unreal to have her among us. I was already a big music fan, dancing to 'Twist and Shout' back home, or wriggling my tiny bum to *The Monkees* TV theme tune. I was a big fan of Cilla Black, especially 'Step Inside Love', her greatest song. Suzanne glittered in the same pantheon of stars.

Watching her perform, it seemed impossible that Suzanne shared the same dull life as the rest of us. Not for her the mundanity of running to the shop, doing errands for her mum, or cleaning between the spokes on her bike. Suzanne lived in a bubble and her only job was to shake her hair and sing what it was to be free. She did 'Sunshine Through a Prism', which was just as good as 'Step Inside Love', and, because Suzanne's voice didn't strangle on the high notes like Cilla's sometimes did, it may have been even better.

On one of the last days of our holiday, Mum, Kath and I went for a swim in the river. A teenage boy came with us, carrying our drinks and towels. Him and Kath had been getting around for a few days now, and they may even have been an item.

We walked down the slope of the motor camp, past the levels of single units, standing in white, wooden, identikit lines. The pebbles on the path burned, and I hopped around now and then to soothe my flaming feet. The Manuherikia River lay at the end of the bottom field, past the sound shell where Suzanne had played.

The river carved a quiet groove between dark rocks, on its way to the Clutha.

Just before the river, in the shade of two tall poplars, there was a small pool. Without any warning, the boy pulled off his top and ran at it. There was a boom when he hit the surface and lumps of water rolled outwards from the shock.

The rest of us ambled up to the hole as the boy floated to the surface, his arms still held out in front of him, like a diver.

'Silly bugger,' said Mum, as the boy stayed prone, face down, bobbing, like he was searching the bottom of the pool.

Five seconds . . . ten . . . fifteen. Too long now.

Mum burst into the water. Waves kicked up as she went. Shockingly, the level hardly got up to her knees. When she reached the boy, she turned him over so his face rolled to the surface. There were red webs on his cheeks, but the rest of his face was pale. Rivulets of water ran down, so it looked like he was crying.

Mum floated the boy to the side of the pool and moved him so he was lying flat on the bank, with his legs still half in the water. He stared up at the poplars, and after a minute he said, 'I can't feel my hands or legs.'

'Thank God you got me, Ricci,' he said to Mum. 'I thought I was going to drown.'

Mum dashed off to find help. Kath and I stayed behind. I didn't want to get too close to the boy, because I was scared some of his bad luck might rub off on me, so I kept my distance, breaking twigs off one of the dry bushes, drawing doodles with them in the soft, wet mud.

I don't know how long it took for the two uniformed men to arrive, but when they did, they had bags, and a stretcher with fold-up wheels. They bent down by the boy to administer their medicine. I hoped he wouldn't need an injection.

I was led away from the scene, and told later that the boy had hurt himself, but he was in hospital now, and the people there would look after him.

Neither Mum nor Kath spoke of that day again.

Many years later, I saw a picture in the paper of a middle-aged man in a wheelchair. He was surrounded by a handful of supporters offering soft looks of encouragement. The man was demonstrating a new wheelchair that could be operated by a tube in the mouth, and he sat impassively, as if suspicious of all the fuss. The article explained that the man was in this position because he'd broken his neck in a swimming accident in Central Otago two decades ago, and only then did I realise that this was the boy from our holiday.

He'd dived into a trough that was dredged up every summer for small children to paddle in.

How far away that boy was now, left in a short pool of water back in the 1970s. I couldn't remember that boy physically, and the man in the paper was a stranger. I scanned the man's face anyway, searching for a clue about the intervening years, hoping to discover comfort, or solace, or a logic for a senseless event. But there was none of that. Just him there in his chair.

After that accident I became aware of life's shitty breaks, of frights around the corner. Until then, I'd been caught up in the child's reciprocal logic, that *this* would happen when I did *this*, and *that* would when I didn't. I wasn't prepared for any of this to be turned on its head. Maybe an anxiety floated in, one that never went away.

It grew darker after our holiday, when Dad told us he was leaving.

There'd been no warning, except for late in our stay in Alexandra when I woke up on another blue day, and Dad was in his bed staring. His look was fixed and heavy, as if there was something on the wall, as if he almost had to see through me to catch it. Marcel lay between us, a baby with thin black hair, safe in his bassinet.

It was an odd look my father gave me, far from his joker face. I smiled over at him to cheer him up, but his expression didn't change.

I think I saw my real father then, or a part he normally hid— it was as if, for a moment, I'd caught him out, and seen into his thinking.

Mum and Dad met at a party. Mum, seventeen; Dad, just turned twenty. Kids. There'd been a fight in the lounge, and, as the lamps got bowled, Dad turned up near Mum. Of course he'd kept his eye on her. She was blond, petite and attractive, with blue eyes, high cheekbones, and a sensual curl to her mouth that hinted she knew more than she really did.

She'd noticed him as well, a handsome young man with Māori features you didn't see that often around here. When they talked as they left the party, she liked him straight away, how he was softly spoken with manners. He had a good sense of humour.

Dad was the first man Mum slept with, and the end result was me. The pregnancy was a crisis, because Mum lived at a girls' home, her latest posting in a dozen years in the welfare system. Mum and her sisters had been separated when she was five and farmed out to various foster placements around Otago and Southland. The people at the home weren't going to be impressed by her new predicament.

A year earlier, the same thing had happened with another girlfriend of Dad's. She was fifteen, the daughter of upper-class parents, and she'd been sent off to Christchurch to have the baby. After that she was packed off overseas to a posh school, to avoid a small-town scandal. The baby was adopted.

Dad was adopted too. He was born in 1943 in a house for unwed mums in Auckland, and his mother left him there and returned to her home near Taupō. She was Māori and from a small town called Waitahanui, which was a dot with a few brown people at the southern end of the lake.

At the time of Dad's birth, his mother's husband was overseas as a private with the Māori Battalion, so it was easy to take a guess. Census records suggest a family friend had been around.

Dad was taken south by the Pākehā Carters, and he went with the Carters as the father followed railway jobs, first at the workshops at Addington and then at the works in Hillside, in South Dunedin, which was then the city's largest employer.

I don't know what Dad and Mum said when they talked about me, but I do know they made a run. Mum snuck out of the home one last time and Dad pawned his watch for the trip. They took the evening train to Christchurch—it left at midnight and wound its way around the Otago Peninsula and then past the swamps at Waitati.

The pair kept low in Christchurch, renting a bedsit in a large Victorian house that had been divided into separate units. A curtain separated their sleeping space from the rest of the room. They made tentative friends with another young couple down the hall, Tom and June, who were also Māori and Pākehā. June was sixteen, even younger than Mum.

June got groceries for her neighbours, because Mum didn't like going out, and June couldn't help noticing that Mum always had her door locked. The new pair seemed furtive and jumpy. Dad was protective of Mum.

Tom found Dad a job on a work site, and although they could bond as young Māori men with their teenage Pākehā girlfriends, and Dad was perfectly friendly, Dad never gave too much away— about him, Mum, their past, their reasons. Mum had to have the baby.

June remembers seeing the couple in the communal bathroom

one night, where there was a coin meter for the hot water. Mum was in the bath and her belly made an island in the water, and she was singing in a grainy, bluesy voice much older than her years. Dad was sitting beside her up on the ceramic ledge, harmonising and strumming an old acoustic. Maybe they were doing 'Donna', which was always their favourite song.

I had a girl, Donna was her name
Since she left me, I've never been the same
How I miss my Donna
Donna, Donna, where could you be?

I was never happy about being born in Christchurch. All that violence. The bleeding Polynesian kid in the Square at midnight, the prostitutes raped, murdered, and thrown in the Avon River. The taxi driver saying, 'This is Avonhead, but we call it Asianhead', like I'm supposed to laugh. Ten-year-old, five-foot-tall Bic Runga abused by passing Nazis.

There's a story about the Dalai Lama landing there and not wanting to get off the plane, and even if it's not true, it fits the ill-tempered atmosphere of bootboys, junkies, claustrophobia, and the uneasy wind off the Alps.

I contributed my own violence to Christchurch by arriving overdue and weighing eleven pounds. Later, when she got drunk, Mum would sometimes say how I'd nearly killed her, but she'd forget that I'd been there too, an unwilling participant, stuck in the birth canal and close to death before I was dragged out with forceps. Whenever I got fever as a child, usually from a sting from a bee or wasp, I'd have the same nightmare—a montage of sensations involving caves, physical pressure, and the iron tang of blood. I've always been claustrophobic.

But I was born on the seventh of July.

When I turned unlucky thirteen on the seventh of the seventh, seventy-seven, my numbers lined up to protect me.

My parents were visited by Social Welfare shortly before I was born. It had only been a matter of time. When Mum opened the door, seventeen and pregnant, the authorities would have realised there was little they could do. Soon after I was born they came to the door again, but Mum wouldn't let them in, and the line went dead after that. Granted their unofficial amnesty, Mum and Dad had their first real taste of freedom.

Dad got a postie run, and the couple found a new flat in Papanui, which was where I spent the first six months of my life. Apparently Mum kept the place tidy, although the chaos inside her shining cupboard doors might have reflected something else.

The couple played folk nights together, at a popular coffee house in town, and adopted new identities. Erica called herself Ricci, and Peter became Jimmi, groovy new names of symmetry and solidarity.

There was another Jimi, a dusky man who could pass for Māori, pictured on a record sleeve with the words 'Are You Experienced' above his head. The record covered a hole in our kitchen wall. He had two Pākehā bandmates below him, his assistants, and he'd spread his giant poncho behind them like a dark exotic eagle. The musician looked apart, yet defiant and utterly at one with his contrariness. I didn't have to hear this Jimi's sound to know what he was about.

My parents returned to Dunedin and rented a house in Brockville, a housing estate in the west of Dunedin that looked down on Kaikorai Valley. Red and cream houses lay like scrabble tiles across a vast and towering hill.

Brockville was one of Dunedin's highest points and the first to get the snow. There was near silence in those flurries. The flakes danced regretfully out of the mist like fairies and melted in soft, wet patches on my face.

Brockville was no-nonsense, and no one poked up their head. It was home to workers from the wool mills and freezing works in the valley, as well as immigrants, the elderly, solo mums and crims. A handful of Māori and Islander families formed a huddle against the overwhelming whiteness around them.

There wasn't a lot to do in Brockville. Its park offered a set of swings, a slide that didn't slide, and a creaking roundabout. There were two large grassy fields at the school, which, out of hours, were usually empty. Young men with half-moustaches fixed cars that sat like broken shells on front lawns. The girls might go to the park, or to the school, and smoke. They had teenage pregnancy to look forward to, or the latest David Essex.

Snotty-nosed urchins gathered on street corners and yelled at passing cars.

Brockville smelt like stew. At five o'clock, dinner time, parents stood on porches, and through cupped hands called out the names of their children.

I have no coherent memory of my early days. Bits go by and splinter. I like to think it was idyllic, that I was cocooned in warmth and generosity. There are pleasant, fuzzy memories. Mum stroking the hair on my forehead as I sit on her lap, sleepy, happy, like a cat. Dad with his funny voices, and his magic tricks that keep me and all of my friends transfixed. 'Abracadabra,' he goes, his hand reaching out behind our ears, and when it comes back he carries treasure. Matchboxes, coins, cigarettes. It's amazing what lives back there.

I'm on the drums at my mum's rehearsal room in South Dunedin, as the sun lies in strips through the window, and I'm flailing away at the tom-toms with a childish, floppy beat.

Someone's put some sunglasses on my head.

Woody Woodpecker calls out in a staccato cry from the stereo, and Charlie Mouse goes *mee mee mee* on the children's radio show that never read out my letter.

A community trolley race rushes down the tracks between sections in our street, and there's the worsening wobble of my new bike before it runs into the bushes, because I can't work out the brakes.

Sometimes an older child calls Dial a Prayer. The telephone makes a tinkle as its dialler rolls around, and we listen to a disembodied psalm read by a priest.

On snow days we use baking trays as sleds, zipping down the track into Turnbull Street, pushing through each of the turns with our childish arses. The thrill of the run is worth the long trudge back.

The lobsters nip in the mossy creeks in the bushes, where they flitter beneath rocks or are lifted into buckets and taken home to die in a backyard paddling pool, or in an outside sink, or in a boiling pot.

But it was never as simple as that. There were parties at 42 Caldwell Street with lots of noise and banging. People coming and going, and Dad left a few times too—to prison, once, where him and a friend did a stint for breaking into a barber shop. 'Those cigarettes didn't just turn up behind their ears, Your Honour.' I'm not sure where else he went.

When I was two, Mum ran off to Wellington with another man. She called in my Aunt Nat to look after me while she wondered what to do about it. The sisters were spending time with each other then. That was something they'd hardly got to do as children, when they'd have an hour's play every few years before the authorities took them back to their separate homes, often in different provinces.

*

I remember a polaroid, the first photo I know of me, and I'm standing in the kitchen before the front door in Caldwell Street with a look of minor bewilderment. I'm dressed in a white top with pale blue tights and I'm flanked on either side by my mum and her sister Natalie. Maybe I'm about eighteen months old. The two girls are radiant, their teeth gleaming beneath dramatic stacks of hair. Mum is a shade of blond and Aunt Nat is brunette, but they have the same top lip and jawline. They crouch down while I totter between them, wobbly but secure in the brace of the two pretty Miller sisters. They have one of my hands each, and with that very gesture they seem to be saying, 'We're here now, we'll hold you up.'

Aunt Nat was always my favourite. I called her Aunt Nat, but I could never be sure because she would change her name back and forth without telling anyone. She usually called herself Natalie Wood, after the star-crossed actress, but whenever I called her that she'd say her name was Vanessa and we'd have to start again. For a while I didn't call her anything, because I was worried I'd get it wrong and she'd come down on me like a wall of bricks. She could be hard work, especially as her mental illness worsened and she lost her sense of decorum and of other people's personal space.

As an adult I often avoided her, ducking into stores if I saw her on the Dunedin streets. Once, when she popped in unannounced, I hid in a small gap between my bed and the wall, lying there suffocating beneath my woollen blankets while she bossed about my girlfriend and ordered up a coffee.

Aunt Nat was never diplomatic, or a soft-shoer, or devious or two-faced, and that's why I liked her. She had an excellent sense of the absurd, possibly because her thinking ran along the borders, and we usually had a good laugh, which in her case often descended into a gross chunky coughing because of all the Rothmans she smoked.

25

When she visited our family home and slept in the spare bed across from me, the stench of cigarettes and granulated Nescafé spread all through my room.

People could be condescending when they saw Aunt Nat, with her unkempt hair and shuffling her dentures. She had a habit of rapid blinking as if she couldn't quite believe what she was seeing— or thinking—or like she was processing a series of cards in her head.

That habit reminded me of a bird hovering, beating its wings, trying to settle on just one thought.

Nobody believed her when I gave her a piece of the Berlin Wall I'd brought back from Germany in 1989. They all thought crazy Nat had lifted a rock from her garden and made the story up.

But she was a smart woman who not only had a genuine piece of the Berlin Wall but who read and wrote—she self-published a biography of an early Otago Presbyterian minister—and played the piano, like her mum. Her favourite composer was Felix Mendelssohn.

I don't think Aunt Nat really cared what outsiders thought, but with her troubles I'd only be guessing. I think that other people just blocked her way.

She became so disabled towards the end that she dragged herself around on her arse at the psychiatric hospital she later died in, because she couldn't be bothered using a wheelchair. I suspect this was also a ploy to offend the staff, who I'm sure she found annoying. Poor old Aunt Nat scuffing across the floor.

There was only me and her two children at her funeral service, and a handful of hospital staff and patients. She looked so little in her coffin.

As I stood by her box addressing the room, with Aunt Nat so small beside me, I did my best to honour her, and convey who she was.

When Dad left home, he moved in with another family just around the corner. Margaret Dickison knew my parents from parties, and she was newly separated too. Margaret had three children, two boys and a girl, all around my age. I'd see Dad going by with the Dickisons in his green Vauxhall, but by the time I got out to wave they'd already have driven past.

Occasionally I'd stay overnight at Dad's new home, but I never felt comfortable there. It was Margaret's place, and she already had her own children.

I'd started school at this point, but I wasn't an enthusiastic student.

There was a teacher we called Boogyman Watson because he had a habit of picking his nose when he thought no one was looking. Pick it, lick it, roll it, flick it.

Maybe we called him Boogyman because that was the name for men who preyed on little girls and boys.

The playground echoed with the idiotic sing-song of small boys, stomping about in protective clumps, chanting, 'Who wants a game of Cowboys and Indians? BUT *NO GIRLS!*'

'BUT *NO GIRLS!*' was shouted in capital letters so the girls knew where they stood, and the boys felt safe—for one more playtime, at least.

The girls didn't care, spinning around on the gym bars with their pigtails flying out.

There were the cast-offs, too—the picked-on kids who hunched sadly over their non-negotiable lunches. You didn't swap sandwiches with anyone who might have fleas. What a terrible way to start your life, as the object of children's derision. The cruelty of tiny hands. Some of those kids made it, and there would have been character in that, one beyond the stone-biffers in the mob, but some of those children didn't make it, and later died violent, early deaths in fires, or after being hit by cars while lying drunk and comatose by the road.

There were those who curried favour. Michael Stokes was the son of a detective, and he stole five dollars every week from right under his cop dad's nose. He'd buy half the school buns and pies, because five dollars was a considerable amount of money. He should have been put in jail.

Eddie Perkins was a ratty little boy who probably became a ratty little man. He'd have lolly scrambles where he would throw out hardboiled lollies in plastic wrappers, and when everyone picked them up he would call them Jews. That's what you called people scroungy enough to pick up small coins or hard lollies. Jews. Perkins cackled rattily as we grovelled on our knees.

There was an old man I often saw walking up Brockville Road. He was always alone on these walks, off in thought, beside the traffic. I could never guess the purpose of his mission, where he came from or where he might be going, but he'd always be out on the hill.

One day I saw two youths on the bus punching the man. He'd spoken up about the language they'd used to the driver. I was six, and it was the first act of adult violence I'd seen. When the bus pulled to a stop, the youths swore some more, threw the finger, and then they ran away.

'I'm all right,' the old man said, as he dabbed at the blood on his nose.

A short time after the bus incident, my mother and I drove by the old man on the lonely road that ran along the top of Brockville, across to Halfway Bush. He was off his normal route this day, walking by gorse and bracken, and he seemed grateful when Mum pulled up and offered him a lift. He showed no sign of recognising me from the bus.

I was excited to have this man in our car, because in my mind he was a local celebrity. I'd admired the bravery and goodness he'd shown that day standing up to those youths, and I'd thought about him a lot since then, about the life he might lead, about whether he had family, and the possible point to his wanderings. I also felt a bit sorry for him, because the assault that had happened on the bus wasn't fair. He looked so alone on his walks.

I hoped we might add some brightness to his day, in our short ride together.

The man was a gentleman as he sat in the front with my mum, as I knew he would be, and he thanked Mum profusely when we dropped him off.

'Goodbye,' he said, turning to me with a smile, unaware of the enigma he'd become.

I'd still see him out at least once a week, in his reverie on the hill, and I waved as we drove past but his eyes never left the footpath.

The walking man was an intrigue in my life until my third year of school, which was when he disappeared.

Apart from Aunt Nat, I had little to do with my relatives. My maternal grandmother died when I was six and I can't remember anything she said. Maybe she fed me Arrowroot biscuits. Mary Fraser was as vague as a small grey cloud, like the wind might blow her away. She came from a Catholic family, one with capable people who became accountants and teachers and Catholic brothers, and her dad was a ship's captain who ran boats on the West Coast. Mary played piano and had been a gymnast when she was younger. For a time she worked with children at the local kindergarten. She married Bob Miller at the age of thirty-two—until then she'd lived with her mother. Maybe she only married Bob Miller because she was worried about being seen as a spinster.

Bob was a remote man from rough South Otago stock, made even harder by years of labouring and existing in the harsh, frosty shades of Balclutha and North East Valley.

Bob was so hard he'd survived being run over by a truck—twice—when he was in his mid-sixties. One day at work a truck backed over him, and then ran forward over him again, because the driver thought he was stuck on a log. That wasn't a log, mate, it was Bob Miller.

Bob was violent and he beat his wife and children. My mum's oldest sister, Helen, remembers Bob's horse whip, and the boots he was wearing when he kicked her, the heavy, worn, thick leather ones with metal on the front. Some evenings, Bob would gather his girls around for fireside chats, and he would tell them about his own floggings from his father, where his father tied him upside down by his ankles and flailed him with a whip.

These tales were related like ordinary family events, like a picnic, or a school ceremony, or a day out at the races. Bob was from a series of redeemers who had earned the right to put his own mark on his children's backs.

Eventually Bob's children were taken away. Mary went into psychiatric hospitals, ones with implausibly serene names like Seacliff and Cherry Farm that disguised their various horrors. Mary had postnatal depression after my mother was born, and when she lost her children her condition worsened and she couldn't get out of bed. I think of her, a silent, meek lady shuffling around her stove.

Bob made token Granddad visits after Mary died. He'd call me 'Chain', presumably because Shayne was too exotic to remember, and that was all he said. He'd pull out a harmonica and start up some shonky twenties honky-tonk, working-man tunes that maybe he'd learned around the fire when he helped build the Balclutha Bridge, but there was no joy in his playing, just a look of fixed determination, like he was filling in time or covering for the little he really had to say.

I'd listen politely to his harmonica but, really, I'd be more fascinated by the nicotine stains across his fingers—black, yellow and brown, dancing up like flames.

Bob lived stubbornly into his mid-eighties, then succumbed to emphysema.

I was helping my cousin Terry sort through Aunt Nat's belongings on the day of her cremation. Her room at the psychiatric hospital was full of papers and obscure journals and sadly little else. There was a thick manila folder full of documents, and when I flicked through the pages, it became apparent that these were my aunt's welfare files. Sadness in bland typewriter script, secrets made official. As if by serendipity, I stopped on a particular sheet and written there were the words, 'Sexually abused by father along with older sister.'

Dirty Bob Miller having his way with the kids. Luckily, Mum was five when she was taken away. She'd just got out in time.

I said nothing to my cousin and put the folder back on the stack. The words were so heavy, maybe their weight would become ours too if they were ever said aloud.

It took over a decade before I mentioned those files to Terry. By then I was beginning to wonder whether I'd seen the words at all—that maybe they were some slander I'd imagined to put a frame around my distant grandfather.

Had I read what I thought I read, I asked Terry one day, when I'd begun to research this book.

Terry paused, caught off guard. 'I'm not sure,' he said, and trailed off.

But it was as if, then, Terry came to a conclusion, and decided, like I had decided too, that the shame of Bob Miller was neither ours nor our mothers'.

Yes, Terry said, his voice now firm, he'd seen the file too.

*

I'm sitting in my Aunt Helen's lounge across from the tip in Green Island, Dunedin. Uncle Stan, a former stock car driver and mechanic, is out in the driveway fiddling with a car, but he's getting older now and moves stiffly, and I have to help him open the boot.

The curtains in my aunty's lounge are drawn, and the windows stay closed, despite the sun outside and the fug of the five dogs sniffing around my seat. Aunt Helen is nearly eighty now, and the last of the Miller daughters alive. She carries around a history that could soon turn to dust.

She talks about Bob's violence, about her mother's illness, and about her grandmother, who briefly looked after the girls before Social Welfare took them away. Her breath catches on some of the details. 'Those weren't good days, no,' she tells me more than once.

All the time, I sit on what I know about Bob, and for the whole two hours I'm on the verge of blurting it out. I feel a silent outrage, like a muted white hat crusader.

But I'm held back by my uncertainty over the facts. My aunt must have dealt with her pain in her own private way, and who am I to burst into her home, demanding a retrial?

At the same time, I'm conflicted by feelings of accountability.

I see an opening towards the end of our talk, so I tumble into it before I lose my nerve.

'This is kind of awkward,' I say, 'but when I was going through Aunt Nat's papers, I read in her files that Bob had actually interfered with her . . .'

I'm not ready to drag my aunt all the way into this yet, and she cuts me off.

'Yes, that happened to me too,' she says quickly, maybe with relief.

We are quiet. One of the dogs laps at the coffee that has gone cold at my feet, and both my aunt and I stare at it but neither one of us cares.

Bob is buried now, his epitaph complete. We move away with our talk and leave him in the dark hole of his making.

*

It was shortly after Dad left home that I developed a habit of crying about one thing when I really meant to cry about another. I could cry for real over the usual childhood mishaps, like the time Paul Swinton smacked me in the face with a bat in a softball game, or when the hailstorm assaulted me with balls the size of marbles, but I'd sometimes cry for private reasons.

I would cry at birthday parties when people sang 'Happy Birthday'. There was something in the labour of doleful, reluctant voices that upset me, and 'Happy Birthday' became a requiem riddled with doom. The worst instance was at a party for Margaret Dickison's oldest son. As soon as the song flared up, I ran outside, crying and in a panic. Other times I'd hide under the table. I felt like an odd boy after these displays, and I got worried that my birthday invites would dry up. Oh, here comes that weird little Carter to make it all about himself again and ruin my child's party.

When my other grandfather died a few years later, I grabbed my grandmother at the funeral and I couldn't stop the tears. I made wet patches on the shoulder of her long black coat. I have no idea where it had come from, because even though I'd quite liked Granddad—well, more accurately, had never been given a reason to dislike him—we'd never been that close. The Carters held me at arm's length, so I'd visit their nice house in South Dunedin and wander about the nice garden with the nice hedges, and sit in the sunlit lounge and make perfectly polite conversation. We once had a small party, because Granddad and Mum shared the same birthday, two days before mine, and the singing of 'Happy Birthday' for all three of us passed with no great drama. But I think I cried less for my adoptive grandfather when he died, than for some other reason.

'You're not very good at funerals, are you?' Dad said once, like I had to deal better with loss.

Once, I was play-fighting with Dad at the Dickisons, and he accidentally hurt me. I got angry and called him a fat bastard—he'd put on weight—and I fled crying and ran, without stopping, around the corner back to my house. Dad misheard what I said, and he told Mum later that I'd called him a black bastard, but I would never have called him that. Nearly all my heroes were black or brown—Pelé, Bryan Williams, Muhammad Ali, Dad.

It was a big day when Dad introduced me to his friends, the big-time professional wrestlers. The pro wrestling circuit was huge in New Zealand, and men like King Curtis Iaukea, Mark Lewin and Rick Martel were gods. Thousands streamed to their fights in town halls and stadiums around the country, and *Big Time Wrestling* was the highlight of Friday night television.

Dad managed the Wains Hotel in Princes Street, where the fighters stayed in Dunedin. The Wains was a bit fancy then, like the Savoy that Dad had also managed, where he'd waited on people like the All Blacks and the Queen. The Queen was all right. She once waved to me from her car in the grounds of Wakari Hospital.

But it was at the Wains that I met wrestling's most notorious villain, the legendary Abdullah the Butcher.

Abdullah seemed to be insane, biting, bleeding, and nearly killing opponents with his favourite move, the Axe, where he'd jump from the top rope and smash his elbow into his victim's throat. Outside the ring, Abdullah was led on a chain by his minder, Big Bad John, and he'd stand beside Big Bad John in the post-fight rants, incapable of speech. The Arabic headdress he wore only increased his air of the Other.

Abdullah's real name was Lawrence, and he came from Canada, not the Sudan. In between fights, he liked to cook.

I was allowed in his hotel room as he prepared for his fight, and I was thrilled to witness the moment where he folded his famous fighting slacks and put them into his pack. They were white, but the bag he had was black. He fielded my nine-year-old questions with tolerance and kindness, and I sensed he took time with me because he knew I was the son of a brown man. The black men on the wrestling circuit were generally cannon fodder, easy meat for all-Americans like Lewin and Martel, or Spiros Arion from Greece, or our own pale hombre Steve Rickard.

Eventually it was time for me to leave, but Abdullah said he'd see me back at the hotel after the fight. Maybe I should join him and Big Bad John for dinner?

I floated out of the room, went back to Dad, and repeated the whole conversation.

*

There is bedlam in the Dunedin Town Hall. Abdullah the Butcher is in the ring stabbing his opponent, 'Gentleman' John da Silva, in the face with a fork. Maybe Abdullah stole the fork from the Wains. The crowd is outraged, and a howl the volume of a plane crash is sweeping the room. Da Silva is known for the decency and classicism of his style, but decency and classicism are no defence against a fork being shoved in your face. Big Bad John stands beside the ring, slapping his hand on the canvas in time with the Butcher's stabs.

I'm caught up in the script and I'm yelling too, forgetting about the good Abdullah. Ross Ricketts, a family friend who takes me to the fights, is beside me shouting abuse, a thirty-year-old going on ten.

35

'Awww, ya fargin' baaaarstard!' he bellows.

Whenever I doubt that a fight is real, Ross will see me right.

The crowd is making another sound now, a high, keening noise, different from their earlier roar. The emergency services have arrived to clean up the mess of the smash. Mark Lewin jogs down the aisles, looking buff and furious in his small black briefs, and he picks up a conveniently placed deck chair and ducks in through the ropes. The Butcher doesn't see him coming, and when the deck chair crashes on his back, I can hear the crack from where I sit. Abdullah crumples into a heap, and Lewin stands above him, delivering lordly blows. Blood is seeping from Abdullah's head, and after a dozen and a half punches he seems to go unconscious. Lewin turns to the crowd and throws a captain's salute.

Don't worry everybody, it's going to be all right.

Again.

His passion spent, Lewin slips through the ropes and jogs back down the aisle. His face is a study in humility.

Back in the ring, John da Silva recovers from whatever coma he was in and flops himself over the Butcher. The skinny wee ref lies down beside them and slaps the mat, counting to three. Da Silva has his arm lifted, even though he can barely stand.

Big Bad John goes into the ring and shoves Abdullah awake. He puts his arm around his friend and helps him out through the ropes. I try to catch Abdullah's eye as he staggers past, but he is dazed, all messed up, leaking sweat and blood, his big stomach ballooning on every breath.

Big Bad John has his German army biker's helmet on, and he's swearing and pushing away hands. They leave to boos and hisses.

I look up at Ross, and his dark eyes are burning.

'Great fight!' he says, 'great fight!' and he throws out a left hook.

I sit quietly at the restaurant table, humbled into silence. Abdullah and Big Bad John are the most famous people I've met. None of the kids at school are going to believe this, and I don't believe it either. That I'm here. With them.

Abdullah has made a miraculous recovery, a thin strip on his forehead the only evidence of his earlier beating. Another man, maybe a promoter, is at the table too, and him and Big Bad John are having a beer with their dinner.

Big Bad John looks younger and softer closer up. When I google him years later I find out he would only have been in his mid-twenties, and I also discover that a decade after this fight he died from alcohol-related liver disease, but that time is far off, and tonight at the Wains Hotel he is serene and funny. As with Abdullah, the wrestler is the opposite of his image. When I ask if I should call him Big Bad John or John, he suggests Bad John as a compromise, and he smiles when I call him that. Later he gives me an autograph which reads, *Shayne. You are a man for nine years of age. Big Bad John.*

Curiously, Mark Lewin sits a few tables away, sharing dinner with his tag team partner Spiros Arion. John da Silva is nowhere to be seen. He must be in his room, keeping gentlemen's hours.

Halfway through our dinner, Abdullah suggests I go over and say hi to Mark and Spiros, and maybe get their autographs. I walk over to them self-consciously, a boy before Mount Rushmore. When I reach their table I say, 'Hi Mark. Nice fight tonight.' But my voice is high and childish. Lewin barely looks at me, and shoos me away with his fingers.

I can still see his fairy-dust flick, and the purse of his lips.

I return to my table, my face flushed red.

'What did Mark say?' Bad John asks.

'He told me to go away.'

John and Abdullah say nothing, and go back to eating their steaks.

I learned some early lessons that night—the good guy isn't always the one in white, and you shouldn't always believe the hype.

*

Tony turned up on our doorstep when I was seven. He knocked at the door and asked for Mum, then he stayed for twenty-five years. With his dusty good looks he could have been from the Mediterranean, or perhaps from up north, but really he was from Ravensbourne, a maudlin suburb on the sunless side of the Otago Harbour.

Tony had a moustache, sideburns, combed-back hair, and messy tattoos that said exactly what he meant them to say, which was, 'Fuck you, your opinion and whatever you plan to do about it.' There was the dot by his eye and the mandatory 'Love' and 'Hate' across his knuckles. Self-made scrawls littered his arms and chest. He even had words on his penis, but I never asked about them.

Initially I didn't like Tony being in our house, so I wrote *Tony is a bum* on a steamed-up kitchen window one night, because 'bum' was the worst word I knew. But Mum saw it first and gave me a kicking, and that's where any discussion about Tony's arrival ended.

Tony was a fit, powerful man with biceps the size of globes, and he'd make a joke of flexing them while pretending to scratch his nose. Across his chest was a large brown burn mark that looked like peanut butter, and one nipple lay melted and flat, pulled out of place. A pot of hot water had fallen on him when he was a child, one of several knocks he'd got. Him and Mum had briefly gone out when they were both sixteen.

I grew to accept Tony, and then to love him, because he was the man who raised me. I experimented with calling him Dad a few months into his stay, but that didn't feel right, so I went back to calling him Tony.

Him and my father were civil enough, but Tony got pissed off when Dad skimped on his five-dollar-a-week maintenance payment. Tony could hold a grudge, and he could dig at the grudge, like a needle going over a sore spot.

He was a superior gatherer of evidence. 'No you didn't,' he'd say to me when I'd insist I had, and then he'd lay out his proof in dry methodical steps, accentuating each fact with a jab of the finger. Tony was canny. He liked puns and wordplay. On Sunday nights he'd tape *The Goon Show* off the radio so I could listen to it later.

We did impressions of Mum's two handicapped adult cousins, who were always on my bus. They never recognised me there, probably because they were related to Bob Miller.

On the bus, the cousins would call out the colour of passing cars in their boxy, man-boy voices. Red car, blue car, orange car.

'Orange car' became funny to us, and we'd stutter when we said it, then crack up.

Sometimes, when him and Mum were back from a night out, Tony would grab his guitar, which he hardly ever played, and bounce up and down on our beds, singing a song in his terrible voice. His renditions were so horrible you just had to laugh. Sometimes he'd secretly fart in a cup and get you to take a sniff.

Tony had a racist streak, although he'd never admit it, and he sometimes talked in a 'dumb Hori' voice for a joke. I can remember Peter Watts trying the same trick with Kenton Hiku in the toilets at intermediate, and getting a smack in the face for his troubles. Tony had been done over once after being smart to a group of Samoans.

I was taught the value of work and the importance of being on time. Tony was always a worker, biffing big bags of barley about at Wilson Distillers, the makers of a local whisky, where he turned up at seven on the dot each morning. Eventually he qualified as a malter, and ran the factory floor.

We were all concerned when, during the eighties, Tony gave up working and put on weight. He got resentful and went on the dole, because 'that was what every other bastard did'.

At the same time, he became weirdly philosophical. He'd spout slogans that these days you see on Facebook and Instagram. Maybe he had a breakdown.

'Isn't it a wonderful world we live in?' his message on our answerphone said.

None of us were comfortable with this new positivity.

But for the most part he was motivated and always on time, and he never shirked his duties. He stayed our provider.

Tony was a proud man, with a strong sense of right and wrong. He had the easy sentimentality common with violent men, and his eyes would fill for small, unobvious reasons.

I can remember explaining to him once, with all the pomposity of the teenager who thinks he's the first person to discover everything, that *Animal Farm* was an allegory for communism, and he laughed at me.

'Do you think I'm thick or something?' he said.

He treated me as his son. Once, he drove me miles to the cinema in Mosgiel so I could see a Bruce Lee movie, even though there was a snowstorm blazing outside. He took me to soccer, and then band practice, and taught me how to trim vegetables and how to sew a bag of barley, and he always made sure I did my homework. Even after him and Mum split up, he'd still come to my gigs, often without telling me, and watch sneakily from behind a pillar.

After I left home, he'd visit me with Mum, and then, after they'd broken up, by himself.

I played him and Mum a Derek and Clive tape once—the obscene, drunken rants by Peter Cook and Dudley Moore—and Mum was horrified, especially with the skit that began, 'My mum came into my room and sucked my tiny knob.' But Tony burst out laughing.

There were hours when he and I would sit together, wondering what we could do about Mum.

Then Mum would talk to me about Tony, and my loyalties were torn.

But my reflex memory of Tony is his violence. I was scared of him. I still have nightmares where he's angry and running amok, and I remember the way he'd go blank when he clipped me in the ear, like he'd signed off and absolved himself of responsibility.

Him and Mum were the same. All their good work was ruined by drinks on Friday night.

*

A strange man is standing in the doorway of our bedroom addressing Marcel and me. Through the murk, I can see he has a uniform and that he's wearing a cap.

'Your dad's beaten up your mum and we're taking him away,' the cop announces, like a train conductor announcing the name of a station.

Mum sometimes ended up in hospital. Ruptured kidneys, broken bones. Once she had a cigarette put out on her face.

I don't know if Marcel and I ever said anything to each other when these incidents occurred. Mostly, we just stared. We were separate, mute witnesses. We came to dread Friday night drinks, and after our sister Natasha was born she grew to dread them too.

Tash was four years younger than Marcel, and her big thing, when she was little, was the Wombles. She gave everyone in our family Womble names—I was Orinoco, the one with the red scarf and hat, and Tash was Madame Cholet, the mother and protector of the clan. Her brothers would have thought this cuter if they hadn't been so caught up looking the other way. We all had our roles at home, the ones children assume in every family, especially a damaged family. The roles become a shield. I was oldest, the achiever; Marcel was the dark sheep who'd often disappear. Tash was the helper, the family organiser, as if her worth relied on how useful she was to the pack. When our youngest brother Kris was growing up, the other children had left home. He was the member who officially coped alone.

Friday night drinks had a pattern. Music and laughter at seven o'clock, Janis Joplin and Lulu on the stereo. Mum singing 'Oh yeah!' at the end of a Joplin song, and starting it over again. By eight o'clock, her voice would be slurred around the edges. She'd get belligerent. She'd start up speeches about the injustices she'd fought and how well she had done in these battles. You'd hear Tony muttering back.

Around nine, there might be a crash that announced that trouble had arrived, and us children would run into the kitchen. Sometimes Mum was sitting there crying, mascara over her face. Tony would be at the kitchen sink with his arms folded, clenching his fists, or he would still be at the kitchen table picking tensely at the cork in a bottle cap. Sometimes we weren't allowed through to the kitchen after a smash, like the time Mum threw her arms back and fell off her chair and the chair fell too, and broke our cat Snoopy's neck.

Once, Mum was standing there holding a knife to Tony's jugular, and he was going, 'Come on, come on.'

Mum gave up singing after she had her kidney split. She'd been doing cabaret out at La Scala restaurant for two years, starting each show with 'Day by Day' from *Godspell*. She grew to be terrified of Tony, and he became scared of her too, of what she might say or do, even though he still poured her drinks the same way he'd got drinks for his alcoholic father, who'd accused Tony of fucking his mum.

Then the next day everyone dusted themselves off and started again. There'd be no mention of the previous night, but you'd still feel stuck in your personal pocket of shame. We all carried guilt over our own role in these events, and the loss of credibility we'd suffered, as parents, as children, as a family. I'd feel embarrassed by my hysteria or crying the night before, thinking it was counterfeit or an overreaction, because whatever had happened had been silently swept away.

It was dirty and discarded, like the butts at the bottom of the empty bottles of Speight's.

Mum always sang around the house. Tony couldn't sing and had an amazing ability to miss every note. His voice was tuned to an unknown planet.

Dad was into music too. The first thing him and Mum had done, when they returned to Dunedin from Christchurch, was to put themselves in a band. They sang up front for a group called the Tempters who, before the pair arrived, had specialised in the tough instrumentals brought into port by the American sailors going back and forth from the Antarctic. The sailors were regulars around Dunedin then, in the clubs, and for the girls, and they were a bridge to the modern world.

With Mum and Dad onboard, the Tempters went commercial and played the hits by Tom Jones, Lulu, Gene Pitney and Sandie Shaw. The singers rotated around each other with their own half-hour sets.

One of the band's regular gigs was at an upstairs club called Sunset Strip, on Rattray Street. Most of the street was owned by the local impresario Eddie Chin, and in the sixties it was Dunedin's most popular night-time area. Around the corner lay MacLaggan Street with its secret dens and brothels.

Eddie Chin was the king of the entertainment dollar. Sometimes, if he didn't like the conversation he was having, he'd pretend to forget he knew English. It was Eddie who Dad approached when Dad hatched his first big plan for the Tempters—a national tour, with each gig paying for the next. All they needed was a kick-start. Eddie agreed to provide one, as long as he had some collateral. Dad put up our car, and, after a disastrous gig in Balclutha where no one came and Dad almost had a fight at the door with a bevy of gatecrashers who walked in and then walked straight back out, we lost our family wheels.

Dad disappeared. Maybe he went to prison. When he re-emerged several months later, he'd taken on a straight guise, selling vacuum cleaners door-to-door. I'm sure he was good at it. He could always sell a pitch.

Meantime, Mum joined a jazzier band, which started a two-year residency at Sunset Strip.

Dad was a rocker. His favourite song of mine was 'Crystalator', an obnoxious instrumental that sounds like the scraping noise that space debris might make along the side of a spacecraft.

'I can hear Māori music! I can hear Scottish music!' Dad cried out when I first played him the recording.

I would put on Hendrix's space blues when Dad came around, and he'd say, 'Now this is my music.'

I ran Sly Stone's 'Everybody Is a Star' past him once, but he wasn't so impressed.

'Do you really think that's one of the best songs ever written?' he asked.

I have a photo of Dad that was taken in Christchurch in the mid-seventies. He's dressed like a member of the MC5—a rebel, half hippy rocker, with round sunglasses, beads and a dark army jacket. He's holding a classic sixties guitar like it's a softball bat, with its whammy bar pointing down. He looks about ready to knock it out of the park.

Dad was still moving in the normal world then, though. During the week, he'd dress more square. After he left home, he got his hotel management licence, and for several years he wore a suit and ran several of Dunedin's poshest joints. For a time, he was in Christchurch, managing the restaurant and bar at the new town hall.

In the late seventies, he and a friend embarked on a new venture, a fast-food chain based on the big American models. Big John's Takeaways they called it, an echo of an earlier era.

Dad poured himself into the scheme. A building had been purchased in North Dunedin and done up in a Western theme, and menus were printed with photos of gleaming, plastic-looking food. On the day Big John's was going to open, Dad and his friend staged a procession in the main street. Although the equipment they needed to make the food hadn't arrived from America yet, and the opening was delayed, they went ahead with their parade anyway because they'd been granted a permit for this specific date. Dad had asked me to put together a posse of skateboarders so we could ride down Dunedin's main street, but we were denied permission to skate, so instead we were herded onto a back of a truck, clutching our boards. When the truck changed gears, Stephen Paterson fell over.

Below us there was a random crew. A clown threw sweets from a unicycle, most of which just hit the footpath. Another man walked along in a hamburger suit with his face peering out between two leaves of lettuce. A woman I recognised as a waitress from the Savoy sat up on the back seat of a sports car, wearing a tiara, waving. The theme tune for Big John's ran through a portable speaker on a muffled fifteen-second loop: 'Get your lips around a Big John's burger, everything's bigger in Texas.'

But the project didn't happen. It was nipped in the bud by a shifty machine importer who never delivered the equipment.

It must have been a major setback for Dad. The failure of Big John's probably ended his financial ambitions.

He shifted to Brighton, a quiet beachside community south of Dunedin, and started growing pot. Maybe he'd had an epiphany. In the early eighties, he swung hard left and started up a disco and a new career as a pyrotechnic DJ. His gigs were booked by an agent called Warren Budge, a disabled guy who worked out of an office in Moray Place, and Dad always had a gig. His name became a fixture in the listings.

When he turned up for his gigs in his purple station wagon with the orange plastic windows, with its confusion of secondhand records and props in the back, you'd never believe Dad was a quiet man.

He put on a show at his disco, letting off smoke bombs, blasting strobes, and miming along on a broken electric guitar. His default expression behind the decks was pouting lips and hammy wide eyes. 'Aaaah,' he'd go as he let off a disc, like he was leading a major discovery. Then he'd do a volcano noise and push out his hands, like he just couldn't take it anymore.

He dressed up for his gigs—shirtless under his waistcoat, with striped trousers, chains, crucifixes, and sometimes a hippy headband. Glitter got thrown around. I can't remember whether he had a microphone, but knowing Dad I'm sure he did, because he gave everything the big build-up.

In between gigs he worked at the slaughterhouse, which he didn't like.

Soon after I was born, my parents went to see a big show where Sandie Shaw was supported by the Pretty Things. The Pretty Things had caused an outrage on their New Zealand tour by drinking, setting fires onstage and forgetting to wash behind their ears.

'These Believe It Or Not Are Men!' the *Taranaki Daily News* had wailed, alongside pictures of the Pretty Things and their filthy fringes.

When Sandie Shaw came out on stage, the pop princess in bare feet, she'd practically be holding her nose.

Dad thought the Pretty Things were great. Mum, like the rest of New Zealand, thought they were revolting.

But Mum was no delicate flower. She didn't tolerate lameness. There was one popular New Zealand singer who she found particularly annoying, and whenever she heard his music on the radio, or on the phone when she'd been put on hold, she'd screw up her nose and say, 'Ew, I can't stand that.'

My mother was once hit on by Howard Morrison, who asked her back to his room for a cup of tea.

Mum was a good singer. For a white girl, barely five feet tall, she had a lot of soul. Like many of her bandmates, I thought she sounded better sitting off the beat. She was on the radio once, in a live transmission of a talent competition from the European Hotel, but I think she'd drunk too much. She was doing a Janis Joplin song but pushing it too hard, so it sounded more grating than the original, which was very rough indeed.

Her performance on a lunchtime show on television was better. I rushed home from school to see that, and she looked pretty and telegenic, and her performance of 'Summertime' was supple and delicious.

It's a shame Mum didn't go further. Later she'd sometimes say that having kids hindered her, but it could have been other reasons too. Singing middle-of-the-road stuff when she had the chops to do jazz; the television show in Wellington that wanted her but she was too afraid to fly; giving music away—you have to fight to stay a musician. It can get discouraging, and there's plenty of bad news.

Maybe it had something to do with confidence and self-

47

assertion. I don't know, because she's not around to say.

But Mum never lost her love of music.

When she made her first record as a sixty-four-year-old, it was a big piece in the puzzle.

My next big musical crush, after Cilla Black and Suzanne, was Donny Osmond. I think it was because he looked like a girl. 'Puppy Love' was full of pathos and desperation, and described perfectly my thoughts about Vicky Murray, who lived one street down in Turnbull Street.

I had posters of Donny on my wall, and fantasised about helping him with the electronic sets that the fan mags said he fiddled with in his spare time. When I was older, I bought a loop pedal made by a company called DOD from Salt Lake City, and I hoped it might stand for Donny Osmond Developments, but alas, only in the acronyms of my dreams.

My first attempt at songwriting was a Donny Osmond tribute, a simpering exercise in balladry called 'Brown-Eyed Girl'. I wrote it when I was nine. The song was inspired by Vicky Murray, and also Virginia Carroll, another pretty Māori girl who also lived in Turnbull Street.

'When I saw her walking down the street,' my song began, as many had before, and then, 'I thought she's a girl I'd like to meet.'

I was moving on from 'BUT *NO GIRLS!*' now.

I can't remember the rest of the verse, but I'm sure it involved Donny rhymes like 'miss' and 'kiss', 'love' and 'above'.

The chorus was the kicker, anyway.

'She's a brown, brown, brown-eyed girl,' it went, over and over.

I imagined the other Osmond brothers, handsome Jay, chipmunk Merrill, doofus Alan, all doing call-and-response backing vocals with Donny. I didn't want little Jimmy in my band, or Wayne Osmond, who looked old enough to be an uncle.

48

'She's a brown (brown), brown (brown), brown-eyed girl,' my hit went in my mind.

I never got to play my song to either of its subjects. A nascent romance with Vicky was blocked by Tony Fellows, who got jealous when he saw me with Vicky at the shops and beat me up. He only stopped booting me in the face when Vicky started shouting. It was never the same between me and her after that.

There was a happier ending with Virginia when I was thirteen. She and her friend Joanne invited me and Paul Guest around one Saturday night to pash them up. Ginny's mother was out for the evening, and the girls wore matching nighties.

I was stumbling on the outskirts of sexuality. Innocent stuff, like hearing moaning from the parents' room and hoping they were all right.

I have memories of a Santa Claus skit, where a group of boys took turns sitting on each other's knees with their pants around their ankles.

There were games of rudies in the bushes, the Brockville version of Doctors and Nurses, where we studied different parts.

Paul Swinton said to us that he was spunking now, but we didn't know what that meant, so he told us to come and have a look. A group of us stood around Swinton, near the small bushes at Brockville School, as he battered away at his cock.

After five minutes we were none the wiser, and growing restless with all the monotony. Eventually we got bored and left Swinton to it, and wandered back to the shops.

I was more interested in harness racing. Nobody else I knew was. I can trace it to seeing a series of ones beside a certain horse's name in the paper and realising that that meant the horse always won. The symmetry of form appealed to an obsessive part of me—the

49

part that still makes me pick out the cracks in the footpath so I can walk in lots of five. There wasn't really a name for these kinds of conditions when I was younger, although I'm sure my obsession with shape and numbers is partly why I write songs.

I preferred trotting to galloping, because trotting was less anarchic and it played out in orderly lines, similar to chess, which I also liked.

I filled several scrapbooks with black-and-white photos of pacers and trotters, with indexes at the back. I could recognise the font and typesetting of every major New Zealand paper.

I read Dick Francis's books solely for the stable action, not for the detective plots.

At first I wanted to be a jockey, and then, when I started developing puppy fat, a trotting driver, because these were usually burly old men from Wyndham. After that I thought I might become a racing journalist, because if I couldn't be involved in trotting I could at least talk to someone who was. My next-door neighbour, who later had his assets repossessed because of a gambling problem, would sometimes take me to the races at Forbury Park and I'd ask at the end of a night how he'd done with his punts.

'Nah, no good,' he'd always say.

Eventually I found another boy who shared my adoration. Trevor Irving was in the same year as me at school, and his parents ran the middle dairy in Brockville. When we discovered that we both loved harness racing, we clung to each other like mussels. Weekends, I'd stay at Trevor's and we'd lie in our beds and discuss barrier draws, and sires, and this horse, and that horse, until his older brother told us to shut the fuck up. We developed a system of racing glass marbles, and named all of our marbles after real horses. The chipped, bigger marbles ran fastest on the carpet, so we decided they were the pacers from America who set all the world records.

Trevor had horse-racing credibility, because his father part-owned a trotter and was friends with a trainer in Southland called Henry Skinner.

The Irvings had a biscuit tin where they kept the shop's spare cash, and Trevor would nick bills from it to finance our visits to the amusement arcades.

Years later, I read that Trevor had been done for theft as a servant by the supermarket he'd helped run.

I remembered the races we had where we pretended our small dogs were trotters. Trevor had an asthmatic, rheumy thing called George, while my charge was a nippy little Sheltie called Jacinta. She nearly always won, timing her run like Young Quinn did in the 1975 Inter Dominion.

When I became a well-known singer, I'd conceptualise the artwork for my albums, and the videos for my songs.

The cover of the first Dimmer album was an image of a lonely racer dwarfed by the floodlights at a trotting track. The album was called *I Believe You Are a Star*, and its cover depicted the fame game. C'mon Sonny, show us what you've got, the big tall lights unblinking.

The booklet for the CD featured photos of my favourite pacers and trotters from the seventies and eighties. But most magnificent of all was the horse in the middle, number seven, named Dimmer— with driver Shayne P. Carter.

I'd arranged a race at Alexandra Park, purportedly to film a video for the title song of the record, but mostly to fulfil an ambition I'd had since I was ten, when I would tie two bits of wool to my bunk and pretend they were reins, while using a knitting needle as a whip. Then I'd mime to my favourite record, *20 Years Of New Zealand Trotting Cups*.

I approached one of New Zealand's leading horse trainers, Barry Purdon, to help with the shoot. Barry was a member of a famous harness-racing family and had stables in the lush pastures of Clevedon. He may have been suspicious of me at first, but he relaxed once he knew I was earnest. I think he was impressed with the trotting facts I pulled out in his office.

'You can't argue with back-to-back Miracle Miles, can you, Barry?' I said, referring to his stable star Holmes DG.

'No you can't, Shayne,' said Barry, in the same voice he said everything. But I sensed that I'd won him over. Barry agreed to give me driving lessons and to help organise the horses for our race.

He showed me around the stables, and Holmes DG was in there, having a shit.

'He won't kick,' said Barry, as I shied away from the erupting rear end of his champion.

In a paddock out the back stood a nondescript bay, who wandered up to the fence when he saw us.

'That's Lyell Creek,' said Barry in the same voice he'd said, 'No you can't, Shayne.'

Lyell Creek was the rock star of trotting and the best square gaiter in New Zealand trotting history.

'Phwoar,' I said, and Barry laughed, the same way he laughed when I drove onto his training track in my too-small helmet.

The race at Alexandra Park, held between Sunday trials, was not only a fulfilment of my dreams, but also the prelude to those dreams. Where other people had counted sheep to sleep, I had driven trotters. Looping the field three wide down the back straight was more than a passing fancy—I'd seen it most nights from my mattress.

We'd prearranged the race, and Dimmer was to be beaten on the line by Barry and his drive Night Mare. The video would continue my clunky metaphor.

Deep in the straight, Dimmer was still out in front and I

genuinely wanted to win. I'd forgotten I only led because we'd put that in the script.

Driving a trotter was different from miming it using pieces of wool tied to your bunk. In a real race you were being dragged by a snorting, muscle-bound animal at 35 kilometres an hour while being pelted in the face by bits of shell kicked up by the other runners. Still, I was excited at the end and slapped the reins on Dimmer's back.

Later, I explained to a friend that the only reason Night Mare beat me was that Barry was a better driver.

'Do you reckon?' my friend said, as if there was ever a doubt about that.

When I was ten we had a next-door neighbour who kept Weimaraner dogs. He was a gangly, dark-haired man who lived with his wife and two girls. His dogs were grey-blue creatures with empty expressions and scrubbing brush fur. Their vacant eyes with the slitty pupils made them look like goats, or sharks, or sympathisers of the devil.

The neighbour showed these dogs professionally, and both the bitch and the male were champions, so his stable had a name. To keep up that reputation, he'd have puppies in his bitch's litters euthanised if they didn't look right, so these floppy, wretched creatures were given a couple of months and then, if they became displeasing, or if there was an error in the shape of their head, they were taken to the vet to be put down.

I always felt sorry for the doomed dog playing with its sisters and brothers.

The senior Weimaraners were cat killers. They would leap fences and tear other people's pets to shreds. The neighbour would apologise and sometimes he would lie and say the cat had come onto his property.

Those dogs killed my kitten Tokorangi, who I'd named after a favourite racehorse.

One Saturday morning, there was a commotion outside my bedroom window, and when I pulled back the curtain I saw my neighbour with my kitten in his palm, and she was a chewed-up bundle, making a tiny mewl. The neighbour drowned her in his washhouse.

Perhaps out of guilt, the neighbour started taking me to dog shows, and he sometimes let me show his dogs when he needed an extra handler. He taught me which pace suited the gait of the dog best, and how to lift their jaw with one hand, and the stubby tail with the finger of the other, when displaying them for the judge.

Different breeds had different poses: back legs back for the gun dogs, straight legs for the toys. German shepherds had their own special stance, with one rear leg bent, like they were ready to attack a civil rights protestor. You lifted the dog by its chest with your hands between the front legs, so the legs were straight when you put them back down.

I enjoyed the dog shows. The animals were always well-behaved, because they weren't defending their properties. There was also the dependable comedy of people looking like their dogs. The fat man with the pug, the redhead with the Irish setter, the blondes and their flouncing Afghans. The ladies with expensive perms, blowing hairspray over vain and precious poodles. A giant with a Great Dane.

I won second prize at the Waikouaiti Dog Show for Best Junior Handler. I put the ribbon on my wall, and it was yellow, white and purple.

The neighbour invited me over once to play me some of his records. As well as being a dog handler, he ran the music section of a big department store in town. One of the records was called

Transformer, and it was by an American man called Lou Reed. I liked the chunky guitars, but I wasn't so sure about the singer's talky, droning voice. Lou Reed sounded bored, and because he was bored, I found it difficult to care much either. His songs weren't as exciting to me as 'Get It On' or 'Ballroom Blitz'.

A song called 'Walk on the Wild Side' started up, and it felt jazzy and illicit. The lyrics hinted at sex, but sex more foreign and strange than sex already was. The song also seemed to go on much longer than songs were supposed to—forever, like a novel with dozens of chapters, longer than even 'Hey Jude'. When the backing singers came in, my neighbour leaned over and showed me *Transformer*'s back cover.

It had a photo of a man who looked like a sailor in a tight white T-shirt, tipping a leather cap. Beside it was a picture of a showgirl with her hands resting on long, stockinged legs.

The neighbour said it was Lou Reed dressed up as a man and a woman.

He pointed to the photo of Lou Reed as a man, and at the lump in the singer's clinging pants.

'Do you know what that is?' the neighbour asked.

'No,' I replied, not quite sure what he meant.

'It's a banana,' he said with a secret smile, putting the sleeve down on the table so the image stayed staring up.

I left soon after that, as the neighbour watched, gauging my reaction.

I started buying records from the neighbour's music section at the department store. I flicked past *Transformer* when I saw it. The first records I bought off my neighbour, who gave me a discount, were Donny Osmond and an album of trotting commentaries by Reon Murtha and Dave Clarkson. I had money because I'd started a paper run delivering the *Evening Star*, and I'd spend this on records, but my picks were hit and miss.

I was a big fan of Gary Glitter, but the live album I bought was terrible. *Remember Me This Way* was full of the screams of thousands of girls, who in retrospect sound like they're fleeing from the pervert that Glitter actually was. Stripped of his studio sheen, Glitter sounded flat and unglamorous on the album, and he got lapped every song by his band. He'd take big gulps halfway through a chorus and struggle to finish his lines. Then he'd just grunt. There was a studio recording at the end of the record, where he was back to sounding like Presley.

I remember a live video of Glitter, with his sleazy saxophone players eyeing up the adolescent girls who danced in huddles at their feet. The horn players were elderly chancers who, like the leader of their pack, could barely believe their luck.

A David Bowie record I bought, *Aladdin Sane*, was equally hard to like. I couldn't get my head around its arty, obscure ramblings. It had none of the appeal of his big hit 'Space Oddity', an alien lament sung in a Rovers Return accent. I was tickled by the song 'Time', though, because it had a line about 'falling wanking to the floor'. I didn't know you could sing about that.

There was a thirteen-year-old girl named Marilyn Kenton who lived in the house below us, and she had school exercise books where she'd written out the words to the hits of the day. Lyrics to songs by the Sweet, T. Rex, Gary Glitter, Alvin Stardust and Suzi Quatro.

Marilyn wrote the song titles in big capital letters, with drawings of flowers and smiley faces beside them. Sometimes she'd surround a title with urgent small dashes like she was conveying its kinetic energy.

I borrowed Marilyn's books and pored over every word. Usually it was the singer going on about how tough and cool they were, and how they'd like to get around with a particular girl. Suzi Quatro just sang about how tough and cool she was.

The only band with lyrics that didn't make sense were T. Rex, who sang about fairy goblins, and unicorns, and touching bumblebees on the nose. That sounded like a foolish occupation to me.

*

I'm being pushed around a playground in Brockville by a series of headbutts to my face. We're in a flat concrete area beside the community hall where children go to ride skateboards, and I'm being attacked by a boy called Smith who has a hole in his jersey and a sort of eczema on his face. He just rammed his skateboard into my ankle and started butting me with his hard, malnourished forehead. I don't fight back. I hardly ever do. I accept this assault instead, and wait for its shower to pass.

My little brother Marcel wades in, six years old and crying, swinging his skateboard at the boy, but Smith pushes him away and gets back to whatever it is he's doing. Eventually he and I have had enough, and Smith steps back to accept the congratulations of his mates.

Marcel and I leave the concrete enclosure as pariahs, both of us crying, as the taunts about the girly Carters dig into our backs.

We can't look after ourselves so well out there, or at home, and an inadequacy is pooling to muddy our name.

I wish now I could protect my little brother the way I couldn't then.

I see us standing outside our house, with our shoulder-length hair and our identical Starsky and Hutch cardies my mother knitted, our dog Jacinta at our feet—unmistakeably blood, but not quite being together.

There was an unofficial heavyweight division in Brockville. Children were ranked not by how good or well-behaved they were or by how many books they'd read, but by their ability to fight. I was somewhere near the bottom. My heart wasn't in it. The feeling of my knuckles on someone else's flesh was revolting.

I tried fighting a couple of times, in the hope I could earn some respect—but it was futile, and I was useless. The fat kid Perkins lay on me and elbowed me in the face, while the flurries of Cry Baby Creighton eventually overwhelmed me. Tony sent me out to fight Creighton. He said I should defend my honour. He seemed embarrassed when I walked away from the scrap, and he announced to the crowd of kids who were watching, leaning on the handles of their bikes, that I'd only stopped fighting because the quality of the bout was beneath me.

I always thought that was an odd thing to say to a bunch of small boys.

'Ahhh, this fight is fucking stupid,' he reported I'd said, a total fabrication.

My fighting set was a disastrous combination of not hitting back and being too proud to run, which made me a simple, stationary target for the neighbourhood bullies, who beat me up for years. The worst culprit lived in my street, and a large part of my childhood was spent listening out for the dull thud of his footsteps and watching the dull look in his face as he whacked me. He only had one expression—a vacant squint that pinched his piggy eyes.

Years later, a group of skinheads pulled up in a van outside a gig I'd just played in Dunedin. The bully was in the back, head shaved, radiating menace. I wasn't surprised to see him. It seemed right that he'd be there. His fight club—they had their name stencilled on the side of their van—later killed a man in a bungled initiation ceremony on the banks of the Leith River.

I think Tony was disappointed in my fighting skills, because him and Mum were proud of his, at least in the scrapes he had away from home. Mum told a story about Tony beating up a group of men at her gig as if he'd won a cup in a competition. The men had been acting the goat, flicking the PA system on and off from the side of the stage, so Tony flew across the room and across their table, and sorted the lot of them out. There were four of them, but Tony was hard to stop.

I hit another boy when I was eleven, an effeminate kid who everybody picked on. He'd been sitting on a desk, and he kicked his legs out when I hit him. It was a cheap shot, because I knew he wouldn't punch me back. I found no satisfaction in my act, or any proof that I was better than he was. There was just an ache in my hand and a rising red splotch on the boy's cheek, and some water in his eye.

I had a game where I'd stare into the mirror until I started spinning out. Looking into my eyes, I'd see a picture of a picture of a picture, and I'd drift outside myself and become a stranger staring back. If I stared too long I'd feel dread, like I was tempting fate, playing with existential matches. By keeping this up, I might never get back into my body. I felt the same dark lift when I stared at the night sky and got scared about the apocalypse. We grew up in the shadow of the bomb, and it had gotten big enough to end the Earth. I'd freak out on that, and grow dizzy, imagining my existence disintegrating like it sometimes did in the mirror.

Mum would hear me whimpering out on the porch, and she'd come out from the kitchen, and even if I couldn't explain myself, she'd put her arm around me, under the night sky, and say, 'Shish, it'll be all right.'

My memories of the seventies are of fondue sets and Ouija boards, and the new roughcast ceiling on the extension Tony built, and the splotchy orange paint patterns on the bathroom wall the parents applied by sponge.

The seventies was fighting in the kitchen, the Commonwealth Games in Christchurch, the All Blacks with Bryan Williams and his gigantic side-step, and Smith, Fellows or Hancock bopping me in the head.

Mum had breakdowns, and she went to Ward Ten on a hill over the Brockville bushes. They tried out various cures, like shock treatment or a deep sleep that didn't seem to work. I'd visit her sometimes in hospital, but I never stayed for long.

Mum quoted her psychiatrist all the time, but it felt like she was only picking the bits that suited her. She liked to repeat her regular doctor's comments too, as if these opinions were as irrefutable as those of the Catholic nuns and priests she'd grown up with.

I always knew Mum was miserable when she played Leonard Cohen. The descending sad arpeggios and dead, gloomy voice. I grew afraid of Cohen's *Greatest Hits*, and 'Suzanne' and 'So Long Marianne' became even more ominous as they crackled around the player.

Much later, I covered 'So Long Marianne', put it on an album even, and I sang those lines with all the blood I had.

My own depression hit hard during my first year of high school—all the issues of the previous years piling up in an awful, churning bucket. I'd struggle to make it to the bus stop. The theme to *A Dog's Show* on television on Sunday nights became as portentous and threatening as Cohen's 'Who By Fire', because it meant the next day I had to go to school.

I hated school. Kaikorai Valley High School was one of the biggest schools in Otago, with a roll of around twelve hundred, and because I'd been put a year ahead at Brockville I was one of the youngest there. Tubby, short and insignificant, I was invisible, lost in a forest of much bigger kids. The school grounds were hit by biting winds and often slick with frost.

KVHS drew on the surrounding working-class suburbs—

Brockville, Green Island, Concord, Mornington and Abbotsford. Abbotsford became famous in 1979 when, after a heavy storm, half of it slid down a hill.

The parents of the students worked at the mill, or the freezing works, or the oil refinery, or the other light industry polluting the Kaikorai Stream.

KVHS was often rough and tumble, but it was co-ed and it seemed sensible to me, even then, that boys and girls got to mix. The weird rituals and violent hazing at the single-sex schools in Dunedin were proof of that, as were the boys' and girls' Catholic schools, with their curriculums of shame and fear.

On my first day at high school, my form teacher, a superior Welsh man with an unconvincing comb-over, asked me where I was from.

I said I was from Brockville.

'A lower socio-economic area,' he announced, pompously, to the rest of the class.

He was looking so far down his nose when he said that, I was sure he could see up his arse.

My third-form year was terrible, because I couldn't concentrate and I was convinced I needed to be home looking after Mum. That worry would overwhelm me. The guidance counsellor called me in, but the sessions didn't do any good, because we didn't discuss any of my actual problems. Maybe I hoped he'd guess.

To talk about my troubles seemed to be a betrayal of the people I had to protect.

I asked the counsellor once if I could be home-schooled, but he said that wasn't possible.

Another time, he asked if my mother drank, because she'd rung him up at lunchtime and abused him for singling me out.

When our family doctor asked me why I was unhappy, I said it was because I didn't like maths.

I'd heard rumours of a new musical movement where bands vomited over their audience or bonked each other onstage. Apparently the songs were full of swearing and abuse. Someone told me about a punk rock band who killed themselves because they were about to turn twenty-one.

The stories might not have been true, but they interested me nevertheless.

I found the answer one Sunday night, when *Radio With Pictures* played a clip of the Sex Pistols. It was the most powerful music I'd ever heard. Primal, thundering, objectionable, convinced of its own might. The Sex Pistols and 'Pretty Vacant' made a joke of Casey Kasem's *American Top 40*, which the music teacher played to us while he sat back and read a book.

A friend brought a tape of the Sex Pistol's album to school, a white cassette with thin gold stripes, and when I listened to that tape it set off a revolution in my head. A cataclysm, an avalanche, a world-adjusting event.

The Sex Pistols became my saviour. They were where weaklings got to swagger. Vicious and Rotten led the charge, with the plainer Cook and Jones.

The Pistols' lyrics throbbed with malevolence and expressed everything I felt. Resentment, alienation, frustration. Yes, things were totally screwed up, in Brockville, in Dunedin, in Otago and wherever it was that Rotten and Vicious lived. Society, royalty, snooty form teachers and sneering rugger buggers—who wants to be part of that? I loved that the Pistols were scrawny and pimply— in their deliberate ugliness they were the exact opposite of what heroes were meant to be. Screw that, their music said.

Punk rock gave me a setting and a purpose. It made being rejected, outside and alone the proper place to be. I dug in and sent up my flag, because I'd finally found my tribe.

We were too young to go to the punk rock dances at the Beneficiary Hall, which we only heard about through rumour. Two of the older kids at school went to those dances, and one of them, to me, was a bit of a hero. He had spiky blond hair and wore a razorblade earring, and he'd walk around the playground with his hands in his pockets looking surly. Roger Grey. We never talked.

I'd heard that the dances in town could be wild, but that they usually passed without real violence because the punks and surfies had a pact. A surfy shat on the floor at a Beneficiary Hall gig once, but it was unclear if it was in protest or as an expression of support.

My social life was more measured than that. I'd made friends with some kids in my class and we went to each other's houses on Saturdays to carefully work our way through less than half a dozen beers. We'd play new wave records on the stereo in the lounge, and slowly sup our glasses. One of the albums was actually called *New Wave*, and the cover was a picture of a punk spraying a can of lager.

Jeff Harford and I went to see Split Enz at the Regent Theatre once, because he thought they were on the cusp of the new movement. It was my first big show. I enjoyed the louder Split Enz songs, like 'I See Red', which they played twice, and 'Give It a Whirl'. Noel Crombie looked like a mental tapping away at his spoons, and I wondered whether he was the member they only let out for gigs.

The Boomtown Rats were the first British group with a punk connection to come to our town. When they played the Dunedin Town Hall, I stood at the front with my elbows on the stage, trying to look like Roger Grey, so the band were aware that punks lived here too.

When Bob Geldof saw me, he swaggered up and stomped on one of my elbows. I stared up to challenge him, but he just smiled down at me like we were sharing a private joke. He looked like a Dickensian version of Mick Jagger.

Inspired by the Sex Pistols, I started writing punk rock lyrics, spiteful ones about the most punk subjects I could imagine—society, workshops for the mentally disabled, and how Jillian Humphries, the classmate I'd been in love with from the first day of high school, hardly seemed to see me.

I wrote 'Rich Bitch' about the Queen, because the Sex Pistols didn't like Elizabeth, and she was beginning to bug me too. The wave I'd shared with her at Wakari was now consigned to history.

I showed the lyrics about Jillian to Tony, but I think he was a bit embarrassed by their rawness.

'Ah hah,' was all he said, as he handed me my folder back.

We finally got a taste of the Beneficiary Hall at the end of our fourth-form year, when the band the London SS were hired to play at our school hop. Usually our socials were discos, where feathery-haired teenagers would line up and do the Brooklyn Hustle, pointing their finger in the air like Travolta in *Saturday Night Fever*. The Bee Gees or KC and the Sunshine Band were usually blaring out.

The girls gave lunchtime disco lessons so the boys wouldn't ruin their dances, and I'd occasionally take a lesson, but I'd feel resentful, because it wasn't very punk.

The appearance by the London SS was my chance to break away from that and to announce my new conversion. I bought a six-dollar razorblade earring, like Roger Grey's, that would later lead to a pus-filled infection.

The London SS were fronted by the oddest man I'd seen, and, coming from Brockville, I'd seen some. Someone said he was the vocalist from the Enemy, and that he was the guest singer for the night.

Chris Knox wore a mohawk shaved artlessly at the sides, which clashed deliberately badly with his old-man polyester flares. There were long, criss-crossed scars on his arms, visible because he'd torn off the sleeves of his shirt. When Knox stood at the mic, silently accusing the crowd, I shrivelled before his gaze. Then he crouched on the lip of the stage and bunched his big nose in disdain. Only he knew what crime we were guilty of and what penance we would pay. Beside him stood a diminutive youth in sunglasses with long Ramones hair and a leather jacket, strumming blockbuster chords on a black Ibanez that had fingerprints smeared all over its body. He seemed just as empowered as Knox and just as unimpressed. Their songs were like bubblegum hits sped up and bludgeoned into oblivion. I didn't know the names of the songs but it didn't matter, because I was consumed by a storm that didn't need a name. All I heard was gigantic guitar and Knox singing like no one I'd heard before.

His manner confirmed everything I'd suspected—that you didn't need to be part of the big bland wave, that you could reject that and make your own way with courage, self-assertion and, somewhere in the middle of all that, a strange sort of humour.

This news was too much for our school principal, David Rathbone. He appeared suddenly at the side of the stage, waving an arm in protest and shouting, 'No, no, no!'

He began pulling across the giant stage curtain. The London SS set was over.

The music disassembled like roadworks. Knox stood smirking, his mic by his side, as he vanished behind the drapes. The gig had lasted less than fifteen minutes but his work here tonight was done.

Beside me, a fifth-former with a pimpled face that looked like the last of the coleslaw hooted some abuse.

Soon after, 'Boogie Nights' by Heatwave came on, soft and safe as a cushion, to calm the fracas down.

One mufti day I raided my parents' closet and picked a pink shirt and a black corduroy jacket with buckles that Mum hadn't worn for years. I wore tight white pants that she'd had taken in at the bottom. I looked punk. Other children stared at me like they were ashamed on my behalf.

At the end of mufti day, as I was waiting in the bus queue, a boy from Green Island, dressed in standard issue sweatshirt and jeans, came up to me and said, 'You know you made a fool of yourself today, don't you?'

*

I'm chanting one of my songs and throwing sausages at the audience. Three classmates chant in unison, standing there beside me.

We're performing at the talent quest at the Tautuku Lodge in the Catlins, on our fourth-form end-of-year camp. We're doing a song called 'Mentally Deranged', which I've written about the community.

Today's public are a bore
Thinking it's like the Second World War
But we're the good guys
They're the Kraut
Forever trying to kick us out
Well, in my influenced mind there is no doubt
That they're
Men-ta-lly de-ranged
Men-ta-lly de-ranged
They make me sick!
Men-ta-lly de-ranged
Men-ta-lly de-ranged
Want us to quit!

We accentuate the 'Make me sick' line with vomiting sounds and we chew up Weetbix so we can spew it out like chunder. In verse two I foam toothpaste from my mouth like a frothing, rabid dog. I also have half a dozen forks poked into my shirt, which go with the sausages we're chucking at our classmates.

Joining me in this a cappella effort are Jeff Harford and two other boys from our class, Darryl and Barry. They are our Saturday night drinking friends, and they've agreed to join Jeff and me in this, our debut gig. We have settled on the band name Bored Games because it's better than our original name, NZ Commies.

We're spitting foam, vomiting cereal, and throwing processed meat, because this is our concept of punk.

Our performance at the school camp causes a few ripples, strong enough to get us in the end-of-year magazine.

'Punk at KVHS' the headline says above a photo of us posing in front of a blackboard, where 'Bored Games' is written in chalk.

Jeff and I have the most committed punk poses. I'm wearing sunglasses, a Sid Vicious wrist band and a tie around my neck that doesn't match my T-shirt. I appear to be illegally chewing gum, although I don't have any gum. To my right, Jeff strikes a Man-Machine pose that is extremely new wave.

Darryl and Barry are less convincing, because Darryl has a ski jacket that could belong to a disco bunny and Barry is in his rugby jersey. Barry tries to compensate for this by staring vacantly at the floor.

For the article we have given ourselves punk rock names. I am Peter Putrid, Jeff is Jeff Nasty and Barry is Basil Spazz. Darryl has called himself Charles Prod, after the country and western singer Charley Pride.

Over Christmas, before my fifth-form year, I became convinced that we needed to play these songs for real. Because my parents both played in bands—went to practices, headed out for gigs—I knew it was possible. Jeff owned a drum kit, an orange perspex number he'd set up in his parents' lounge. Jeff's dad played jazz piano in bars downtown, and Jeff could already hold a beat. With my lyrics and my innate need for revenge, I thought I could be the singer. I also had no other equipment, apart from the mic that Mum kept at home at the back of a drawer in her duchesse.

When we went back to school, we advertised our plan for our band. This was the cue for Wayne Elsey to make his move.

Wayne was our classmate in third and fourth form. He was small and slim with fine blond hair, and his nickname was Mouse. He had been adopted. He had scar tissue between his fingers and toes because he'd been born with webs, and his digits had been surgically separated, which left scars that looked like burns.

When I got to know Wayne, I'd do cartoon drawings of him, because with his turned-up nose and protrusive top lip he was easy to lampoon. I'd pass these doodles to him in class, or, when I was feeling more malevolent, show them to the other kids to tease him.

Wayne was an excellent racquet sports player with an almost feminine way to his walk. His wrist could be floppy when he was thinking of other things. When we became friends, I'd meet him at his house in Glenross, a suburb off the bottom of Brockville, and he'd thrash me at tennis and squash at the clubs along the road.

Although Glenross sat at the bottom of Brockville Road, people who lived there were quick to stress the difference. 'Oh, no, we're from Glenross,' they'd say, to stay above the slum.

Wayne was one of two kids in my class who were called into the counsellor's office. The other one was Lesley Paris, a girl from Bradford with Lauren Bacall hair and moon-pale skin. Lesley's mum had died, and Lesley seemed to spend a lot of time looking after her dad, who was elderly and played golf and maybe drank too much. Lesley became a part of our punk rock cartel too. It was her neighbour Robin Siataga who owned the white and gold cassette of *Never Mind the Bollocks*.

When Wayne heard that Jeff and I wanted to form a band, he said he might be interested. His brother had taught him twenty-four guitar chords and he was currently in negotiations for a bass amp that would cost him ten to fifteen dollars.

He also said we could jam in his parents' basement if we wanted, down there with the tins of paint and stripper.

A jam. The word wobbled with the weight of legitimacy.

Unbelievably, we were in the Elseys' garage two weeks later. Wayne had set up his new bass rig, which was a ten-watt box with the guts of a transistor. But the amp had double channels where I could also plug in my mic.

Jeff's full drum kit sat regally in a corner, in front of the Elseys' car.

Charles Prod was at our first practice, to help however he could.

We started with an abstract noise. My voice sounded like it was coming from inside a box in a cupboard through the buzz of the ten-buck amp.

Wayne didn't know twenty-four chords. He didn't know one. But he still stared ahead, defiant as Sid Vicious, deaf to the uselessness of his thud.

He already seemed comfortable that it was everyone else who was badly out of time.

I was riffing on a song I'd called 'Here in the Workshop', which was about remedial classes for the mentally impaired. 'I eat minted flies / And stick pins in my eyes' it announced, predicting a lobotomy.

Charles Prod joined me in the chorus, which we chanted while pacing about the garage, two teen drongos stinking up the space.

Here in the workshop
We're in the workshop
There in the workshop.
They're in the workshop . . .

Charles became inspired at this point, and picked up a wrench and started hitting it on a bench. I fell in with him, like a baby, or a monkey, and began bashing a hammer too. The sound of workshop noises went on for fifteen minutes, while we tried to find a shape to the song. We failed, and got disillusioned, and tried 'Rich Bitch' instead, but we failed at that one too. So we went back to 'Workshop' and hitting the bench, because that was our only plan.

We were holding talks with another boy at school who, like Wayne, advertised himself as a proficient and capable guitarist. Gavin was a heavy metal kid with lank carboy hair and a harelip, and he had a habit of doing a small cough in front of everything he said.

(Eh-heh.) Sure, he'd come and have a play with us. (Eh-heh.) It was no skin off his nose.

Gavin knew fewer notes than Wayne did—approximately minus one. He threw out a terrible noise full of unknown chords and unrelated lead that he insisted was legitimate. 'It's a seventh,' he'd say, all frustrated, coughing slightly, and we'd look at him like he was nuts.

On our second play together, Gavin fluked a chord, and our practice crashed to a standstill.

We rushed over to the portable tape recorder and played that note back over and over, stunned.

Gavin never found that chord again. It was like it floated out of the Elseys' garage and off down the Kaikorai Stream.

He usurped us by leaving the band before we kicked him out, ahem-ing and muttering something about musical differences—he was more into Zeppelin—and I think he thought our lyrics were a bit stupid. That was all right. I hated Led Zeppelin. I'd barely heard them, but I loathed the pictures of the singer who tossed his hair like a proud and cocksure lion.

Charles Prod drifted away from Bored Games, having found no

resource beyond a wrench. We'd still go to his house on Saturday night to experimentally drink our beer.

If only we could find a guitarist who could play the same song as us, in tune and in time. That person wasn't at Kaikorai Valley, and if they were, it was doubtful they'd be into punk. The answer, we decided, was to spread the net, so we put an ad in the paper.

'Wanted', it said in the *Otago Daily Times*, '15–16-year-old guitarist for original new wave band.'

After we placed the ad, Jeff got a call from a boy who lived in Opoho. He was a fourth-former who'd been playing guitar for two years, and his brother was the singer in another high-school band, the Same. From Logan Park? Perhaps Jeff had heard of them?

No, Jeff said professionally, writing this résumé down.

We went to Opoho on a Saturday to audition the guitarist. Opoho was a more ostentatious suburb on another high hill in Dunedin, above the Botanical Gardens in the north. Janet Frame had lived there once. The boy's house was a bit flasher than ours, spread over two storeys with plenty of space. I was wearing my jeans with a patch that said 'Disco' sewn on one knee. Mum put that on. It was important that whoever was waiting here knew that we were serious.

We were greeted at the door by an open-faced boy with light freckles on his nose. His name was Fraser Batts, and there was another boy behind him, peeping over his shoulder. This was Fraser's older brother, also called Jeff, and he had bushy eyebrows and dark straight hair, and he did most of the talking. When he spoke, it sounded like an inquisition or a complaint, which, we grew to learn, it usually was. Later, we discovered that Fraser's brother had snuck downstairs after we'd arrived and called up his mates.

'Come look,' he'd said, 'they've got safety pins in their trousers.'

Fraser showed us through to the lounge where the gear was already set up. When he lifted his guitar, he did so with an assuredness we'd never seen with Gavin. Gavin was wrestling a fish. But when Fraser strummed a chord, it came back true, and when he struck another, it sounded just as sure. I walked up to the microphone and shuffled my pages of words.

My formative singing style was based on Johnny Rotten's. It was a nursery rhyme *nyah nyah nyah* that went up in pitch at the end of each line. An extra syllable was added to the closing consonant. *Deranged—AH! Workshop—PAH! Frustration—NAH!* It rammed home whatever point.

My first-ever performance through a microphone had been in form two at Intermediate, when I'd bored an entire assembly brainless with a racing commentary that I'd slaved over for a week. I'd feigned looking through binoculars while reading my seven-page script, with four friends beside me playing punters. The tepid applause at the end made it clear what everyone thought.

I'd become an expert at doing a Reon Murtha voice, which was the same as an auctioneer's voice and, come to think of it, Johnny Rotten's.

The secret to singing, and commentating, is that you just have to open your mouth and go. It's like jumping out of an airplane and hoping your parachute opens. You can't concentrate on the listener, only on what you're trying to describe, whether that's the 1981 Trotting Cup, the sheep in the coming lot, or your crush on Jillian Humphries. It's a leap of faith, and once you've committed to it there's no turning back. You can only wonder afterwards if anyone thought it was good, and by then it's too late.

I liked the power of being on the mic and that I could impose myself over the other noises in the room. Sometimes I'd try heavy breathing on it so I'd sound like an unwell Dalek. I usually sang in tune.

Fraser suggested a song he already knew, an easy one called 'Mongoloid' by the American band Devo. The tune was unfamiliar, but we respected its theme of simpletons and morons. These were our punk rock brethren—outsiders that people sneered at. Many punk songs celebrated the grotesque or misshapen, as an 'Up yours' to convention, but also, we were young, and just as bad as the others, poking fun and grossing ourselves out with the sickest concepts we could imagine. Jeff Batts showed me the Same's songbook and they had a song called 'Thalidomide Baby'.

'Mongoloid' was three chords. Wayne kept up the entire way. He had his pride. He was probably imagining he was Sid, spitting on his fans at Winterland.

Jeff sounded strong. Fraser was giving us a new court to play on. There was nothing flashy in his style, just the relentless drive of his barre chord, the home base E-shape used by bluesmen, sixties garage bands, the Ramones, the Buzzcocks, and everyone related to Chuck Berry.

I wrote many Bored Games songs on one guitar string, and we'd turn that into a barre chord, and that was the music done. Apart from the shapes D and A, which we may have used once, E was the only chord we used.

'Mongoloid' was basically a chant, so it was no great vocal challenge. With my commentating, I'd been chanting for years. But anyone walking past the house might have thought we were a real band, maybe rehearsing for a gig at the pub. If that had been me going by, I would never have guessed it was us. 'Mongoloid' was the first full song we performed.

I suggested having a go at one of our originals. 'Frustration' was only two notes, but back in the Elseys' garage it had been swamped by our ineptitude and Gavin's free-form expression. We'd only got as far as the first chorus, where Jeff brought in a beat a bit like 'New Rose' by the Damned.

But now there was the glue to link us and power us all the way. When we crashed over the line, two and a half minutes later, there was a short, disbelieving silence and I could feel my knee trembling behind its sarcastic 'Disco' patch. A song I'd written had just been played to the finish, and what's more, it hadn't sounded weak, or delusional—it had, in fact, kicked.

I backed down from the mic. Here was a new world of sound. Its sky was borderless, and its horizon curled off a previously flat earth. I'd been given a virtual super power and a flame to shoot from my fingers.

There was a ding. The doorbell. A stranger from the street, eager to meet us? But no, two members of the Same, with another friend tagging along. They'd come around minutes after Fraser's brother Jeff had called.

Big Paul played drums in the Same, and he bounced around like an overgrown puppy. The guitarist, Craig, played it cooler, with his hands pushed deep in his blazer pockets, straight-faced beneath Johnny Thunders hair. When he spoke, it was in a mid-Atlantic drawl that maybe he'd picked up from the international section of the Botanical Gardens.

Their friend was a boy called Chris, and Chris had short curls, glasses and a laugh from the middle of a pipe. He wore a black bomber jacket and the requisite Bata Bullets.

We looked at one another with a small amazement, dismayed to find that here was a whole other pocket of kids on a parallel punk-rock trip.

We were like Bedouins, stumbling over ourselves in the barren Dunedin desert.

The next time we went to Opoho, Fraser brought along his friend Jonathon.

Jonathon was quieter than Fraser, sensible like his clean pressed shirt, but he was also another guitarist. When the pair of them played together, the glass table in the Batts' lounge rattled.

We tried the Stooges song 'I Wanna Be Your Dog', with its inevitable drop to E. The tempo was too slow, but that just made it heavier.

The guitars sounded thick, like Steve Jones on *Never Mind the Bollocks*, where he'd stacked up all his tracks. The Pistols were my favourite because they had the fattest sound.

It was obvious that Jonathon should play with us too, so after that we practised every weekend to build our first set.

The Wiki page for Kaikorai Valley High School lists myself, ex-police commissioner Howard Broad, film director Robert Sarkies and loathsome murderer Clayton Weatherston as alumni. It's a fair representation of the people on the roll: ghetto dwellers, squares, an occasional psychopath, an occasional able person.

There were prolific outbursts of violence at KVHS, and the girls were as tough as the boys. Tracey Mills once dragged Yvonne Steel around by the ponytail and smashed her face on the metal bowl of the drinking fountain more than a dozen times.

'She called you a slut, Tracey!' squawked one of Tracey's minions.

A girl called Fulatau smacked me with a George Foreman hook once that nearly took off my head. You didn't hit girls, or at least that was my excuse, because if I'd actually engaged Fulatau she would have blended me into a pulp. Later that year she impaled Paul McGilvrey on a coat hook in the lockers, by the eye.

The tactics in the brawls were filthy and direct. None of that namby pamby Gentleman John da Silva rolling around. You got your victim on the ground and then you hit them with your fists, your feet, your head, or a fork, right in their fucking face.

Kaikorai Valley was mid-table in more legitimate sports, dawdling at interschool athletics and fielding an average First XV. Its debating team was usually outwitted.

75

There were the standard cult figures among the staff. Ian Sime, a.k.a. Enzyme, was a bald man with glasses and perennial walk shorts who operated in a robotic, efficient manner. He was the deputy principal, and was often fairer than the principal ever was.

The attractive English teacher entertained the whole school at swim day when her bikini top slipped when she got out of the pool, and she walked the length of Moana Pool with her left breast hanging out. She was only made aware by the rising in the stands.

But, mostly, for five uneasy years, high school was a chore.

I liked English, because I enjoyed writing, reading and making things up. History appealed to me too, because it had an air of melancholy and nostalgia—all those past lives and their mistakes, hopes and secrets. The specifics of geography could be dull, but it also suggested romantic, far-off places.

The more practical subjects—science, maths, tech drawing, economics, metalwork—were puzzles that seemed to offer little that I could use.

I wasn't very good at tests. Writing essays for exams seemed to be about providing uniform answers and anything beyond that lost you marks.

In my school cert English exam, I wrote a free-form essay about a simple man who was happy about being led to the guillotine, because he thought he was getting a prize. In his mind, the people cheering and the ladies knitting were his fans. To make my story more potent, I wrote from the point of view of the man himself, employing simple, childish language—but the marker obviously thought that the only simple person was the one who wrote the essay, and my English mark was poor.

I clashed with some teachers, and spacked out on one or two. Mr Perkins, a young teacher whose casualness I quite liked, once made the mistake of hitting me across the head with a sheaf of papers. I really let him have it. Even I was shocked by the vileness from my mouth. But I was sick of people biffing me in the head—as though someone had given them the right.

One day my form teacher, a chain-smoking alcoholic, needed to cane me, but I refused to go to his office. There was no way he was having a go too. My form teacher crashed into my next lesson, demanding I be handed over, but my teacher there, Mr Thom, protected me.

Stu Thom was a fair man with a quiet humour, and despite himself he'd laugh sometimes when Jeff Harford and I spoke in our secret code. We thought Mr Thom wouldn't understand, but he was cleverer than that and he'd sometimes decipher our message.

Mr Thom stood up to the form teacher and told him not to interrupt his lesson, and he suggested the form teacher leave. It was a crucial vote of confidence from an authority figure.

At the end of the year, when he was leaving the school, Mr Thom took Jeff aside and told him to look out for me because I 'wasn't another sausage'. He probably said that to Jeff because he recognised that Jeff was more stable and sensible than me, and that I was more rebellious.

I wrote to Stu Thom many years later to thank him for that. He was teaching in Central Otago then, and I sent him my email twice. I thought the first one had got lost so I wrote and sent the message again and he ended up with two different versions. I hoped that didn't undermine the sincerity of the message.

I was in the school gym late on a Saturday night when the Same came on TV. They had a spot on *Telethon*, a twenty-four-hour television event where the whole country stopped and became involved in car washes, Lions raffles and odd acts of endurance.

People came up with the most extraordinary, and super ordinary, ways of raising money for *Telethon*: holding your breath until you turned blue for twenty dollars, pushing your cat in a wheelbarrow, pulling off your sister's toenails and shoving them between your teeth. Children gave up their piggy banks to crowing presenters. Rural men handed over plastic buckets filled with cash and said it was nothing. Both New Zealand islands were fully engaged. The charities were interchangeable; they all focused their efforts on disability and disease.

The new national total was flashed every hour on an electronic scoreboard to a din of car horns, bells and yelling. Whoever was in the television studio—D-list celebrities, telephone operators, the random public—formed a human chain and lumbered about to the *Telethon* theme tune, merrily shaking their hips.

Thank you very much for your kind donation
Thank you very much, thank you very very very much
Thank you very much for your kind donation
Thank you very very very much.

It was as if another 'very' was added for every thousand dollars.

There was a procession of amateur acts to keep us awake—the usual talent quest flotsam. Dancers, ventriloquists old enough to know better, magicians, singers, clowns. Celebrity presenters pashed up for money or sat on balloons until they popped. Everybody laughed.

The Same came on around one o'clock in the morning, where they were safely tucked out of the way. Fraser's brother Jeff had mussed up his hair and when he sang he rolled his eyes impertinently, like he'd already seen enough. Jeff was a star. The only person who could derail Jeff was Jeff. Craig stood to his left, chopping at his instrument like he was trying to start a motor. The other guitarist, Martin, was wearing a dressing gown that looked a bit like a trench coat. The bassist was a girl with a haircut like Tina Weymouth-Gaynor who worked the record bar at Terry's

Bookstore, which we'd sometimes visit on our Friday night struts downtown.

At the back, Paul bashed away at the drums, the big boy who loved hitting things and didn't mind if they hit him back.

I was proud of my new friends, and to have them sucked into the vortex and beamed back out again was both surreal and uplifting.

Suddenly this was possible.

The Same played one of their best tunes, 'Protest Song', with its tight opening lyric:

I've suffered for my music
Now it's your turn
I've suffered for my music
Now it's your turn

And *Telethon* did suffer, for three and bit minutes, taking a major strike for our force. It made me more excited for when my own band played.

I met another singer in the gym that night. His name was Carey Hibbert, and he fronted a band I'd heard about from Otago Boys' High School called Static. I was unimpressed by the stories of their expensive equipment, and their cover versions of sixties songs and punk standards, because that seemed too commercial. I'd heard no actual evidence of them having any songs of their own. Bored Games may have initially written our own songs because we couldn't play anyone else's, but our failure was a form of success. Your songs were about who you were and what you felt. It wasn't right singing all night about how someone else felt.

Hibbert had been brought along to KVHS by Lindsey Hudson, a blond girl who lived in Turnbull Street, close to Vicky Murray and Virginia Carroll. Turnbull Street had become a factory for heartbreaking girls. Lindsey was the daughter of my boyhood soccer coach and the sister of my teammate Darryl, and she'd put green streaks in her hair, because, even though she was younger, she wanted to be in with us.

I was up for it when she introduced me to Hibbert, because I was sure he was a fake.

'What do you think about the Sex Pistols?' I asked him straight off, certain he'd be wrong.

'I think that *Never Mind the Bollocks* is one of the most important records of the last twenty years,' he said in an authoritative voice. He couldn't have really known that, but he said it like he did.

Hibbert had cut me off at the pass. I was impressed too when Lindsey told me he made his nose bleed at his gigs. Reluctantly, I decided Hibbert was okay, even if I couldn't stand his band, who I'd never actually heard. Hibbert said goodbye when the Same finished, and that he'd probably see me around.

Eventually Carey Hibbert became my friend. It was him who, much later, suggested I should take the marker out of the book Wayne had been reading just before he died—a torn piece of paper in the middle of *Under the Volcano*.

Carey was smart. He was a real music fan, and he'd play Hüsker Dü records at an indecent volume while staring at me with a squirm on his lips, like he was daring me to object. When Carey told me I rocked, it was a compliment, because Carey was someone who knew.

His boozy antics were legendary and did a lot to distract from my own. He did crazy stuff like stepping out of speeding cars and doing handstands on the ledges of six-storey buildings. A lot of his stunts involved nudity, and it was nothing for him to be at a party, urbanely cradling a cocktail and discussing his point in the buff.

Him and his good pal Jan, who became a doctor and was later

killed when a truck knocked him off his bike, were once found naked and unconscious with hoses sticking out of their arses. They'd been doing cactus juice by enema, when they were mutually overcome.

It was normal to visit a flat and hear that Carey was in the backyard tripping, naked and rolling around in the grass.

Carey wasn't a buffoon. He was always very polite. When I quit drinking in my twenties and became full of evangelism, I sent Carey a book of affirmations, a limp attempt at an intervention, which Carey never criticised. No defensiveness. No sarcastic jibe. He was far too considerate for that.

I never knew what really bothered Carey, and I never asked him.

Carey drank so heavily it was a miracle he held together, like he'd been preserved in a jar of formaldehyde, or uncommon luck. Even with his drinking, he held down a big-time law job in Wellington for years. That is, until the last time I saw him, and the whole facade had gone. I was playing a show and I didn't even recognise the old man standing too close at the front. I just thought it was some crazy old coot, so I threw a lead break right into his face. It turned out to be Carey, looking like the Old Man from the Sea. Of course, he loved the lead break.

Carey developed serious liver disease, and one morning, unable to see a way out, he went out into his backyard and killed himself.

It was shocking the way he did it. It was also very Carey. I believe he would have seen an honour in that act.

*

I didn't like having my photo taken when I was young and I still don't, which, considering my profession, is a drawback. But from the age of nine I disappeared from the family photo albums. Every time a camera came out, I scuttled off, almost afraid. I felt self-conscious and perhaps a little unworthy. Our household seemed to revolve around bigger, more adult concerns that were more deserving of recognition. Maybe my absence in the photo albums was a protest about that.

One photo made it into the album—a terrible studio portrait of myself and Tina, Tony's daughter from his first marriage. We've both got fat faces. Tina had had the mumps and I'd been eating tomato sauce sandwiches. Tina and I both hated that photo, and we'd always biff it out, but it kept reappearing at birthdays and Christmases. It was as if a factory had been set up in China to make more prints. Tony thought it was a great laugh.

But I was fifteen now, taller, and growing into my size nine-and-a-half shoes.

I was ready to reappear.

*

I usually forget that I'm a rock star.

It's not an honour I pull out and examine as I plod through the everyday.

I'm more likely to be measuring how much milk there is for my tea and coffee, or being annoyed by the condescension of the radio presenter who acts like he knows, and is interested in, everything. I'm more likely to be examining a new blemish that's popped up overnight.

It's hard to believe you're a rock star when the milk's run out, and the radio drones, and there's a fresh mark on your neck.

But I am a rock star. Not the big, obvious sort projected onto the Sky Tower, or pounding my chest while swinging off its spire. I don't sell millions. I've sold barely anything.

But people who've seen me, know.

When I do what I can do, anyone with half a brain gets it.

I don't collect groupies or speedboats, or snort cocaine, and people who do impressions of rock stars are pitiful. One of my favourite TV shows is *Rock of Love*, where the singer from Poison finds a new soulmate every season, and he and all the LA rock chicks who try to get to him are as desperate and oily as each other. He plays 'Every Rose Has Its Thorn' in a dimly lit restaurant, where there's only him and the woman, and then they have a tongue pash. It's excellent TV.

Some rock stars appear in dingy bars or warehouses to an audience of two dozen, because they're too extreme for the malls.

What makes them great is the exact same reason they'll never be fit for popular consumption, but they have that thing you can't quite name that draws you in. It makes them, and whatever they say, compelling.

You can't pretend to be a rock star, although plenty out there have tried. It's probably why the term 'tryhard' was invented. Those two blunt syllables. Tryhard.

Rock stars are born, not made. They are, in the way most people aren't. You can't fake X factor, the same way you can't plant charisma or borrow a cup of soul. You see the pretenders on those Simon Cowell TV talent shows confusing hysteria with passion, thinking that whoever shouts the loudest will be heard.

Real stars do that on the tip of a pin.

The world shifts with a lift of their pinky finger. Their softest breath is compelling. 'That is all,' their smallest motion says, bringing a minimalist classic to a close.

It leaves people wanting, and imagining, more.

There has never been a better way for showing off to the opposite sex than rocking particularly hard.

It makes you seem mysterious, and women wonder what you're like to talk to or fuck. When you play, they'll often look at your trousers, which is base but true, like the purest rock 'n' roll.

Meantime, their partners squirm a bit in their seats.

People watch and think, 'I wish I could do that.'

It's an excellent head start.

It took a while to shake itself out, but this is what I was born to do—fly the flag of rockdom and bang the fucking drum.

I could fill libraries with areas I'm useless at, like relationships, science, and every mechanical activity in the world. Being a rock star is one of my few areas of expertise, a topic I swotted obsessively, sorting through the chaff, discovering what it was to be moved by music.

I learned from good music and terrible music. Knowing what not to do was half of it.

I'm sure many of the melodies I've written are subconscious inversions of the shitty AM radio songs I grew up with and only half heard but that snuck into my head by osmosis, like the advertising jingles you know all the words to without knowing what they're selling.

Get the gas where you can. Preferably from places no one else will guess.

Being a rock star was never difficult like much of my life was. It was like opening my veins and watching the blood course through.

It was an essence that was always in me, so I woke up one day, and there it was.

*

We're standing on the same school stage that the London SS played on, behind the same green felt curtain. We can hear the crowd on the other side, bubbling and humming. I'm ready, standing at the mic, one hand on the clamp, the other holding the adjustment thread halfway up the stand. I'm wearing a black blazer and a pink shirt and my hair is messed up with Johnson's baby oil. The rest of the band have plugged in their guitars with trembling hands. Jeff does a test rattle on his snare. Jonathon looks moderately worried, but then again he always does. Fraser has his first chord in place, his finger a bar over fret three. Wayne is constructing his bubble of pride. Tonight, our band debuts.

The school hall is packed with hundreds of parents parked on the benches that their children use daily, the benches that, at least once a year, someone farts on to liven up an assembly.

Tonight, however, the crowd are here for more noble purposes. It is this year's Kaikorai Valley Talent Fest—Fest, not Quest, note, for tonight there'll be no prizes for first, second or third. The children will be performing without pressure or judgement, purely for our and their own pleasure.

There have already been several delightful items.

Margaret Teller's excerpts from *Oklahoma!* were beautifully sung.

Bruce Carver's magic show was actually rather good, although one or two fathers said they could explain how it was done.

There was appreciative applause when the First XV formed a scrum and sang their bonding song in unnaturally manly voices.

Victoria Roberts came out and tap-danced, smiling the whole time above her supple clattering feet.

Now there is to be a rock band, although the name appears to be misspelt in the programme. Bored Games? Board Games, surely! Not that it matters. These boys will do very well to equal those already done.

We plan to stick it to them from the top.

Fraser smacks down on the opening chord of 'I Wanna Be Your Dog' before the curtain even moves, and by the time it's shovelled over he's already down to E. The rest of the band trundles in, the trailer behind his truck.

Ted, my little sister's teddy bear, is tucked beneath my arm. I'd planned to use Ted as an ironic prop, but from the opening note his days are numbered. Within the first minute he's been torn limb from limb and scattered across the stage. My seven-year-old sister looks on from her seat, horrified.

The audience now realises there will be no pleasant musical build-up as there is in 'Stairway to Heaven'.

I have my performing philosophy intact before I sing even a word, one I'll use from this moment on. I'm here. What am I going to do—break down and cry? I'm certainly not going to beg.

1—2—3—4.

I have Iggy Pop to thank for the first line I ever deliver onstage: 'I'm so messed up, I want you here . . .'

It's hardly what the crowd expects. It gets worse in the so-called chorus, where one line is repeated until it becomes clear that what you think is being said is actually being said.

'Now I wanna be your dog! Now I wanna be your dog!'

The parents must find it disconcerting to hear a young boy asking to be degraded while he stands below the school motto 'Seek and Ye Shall Find'.

There's a shifting on the benches.

When Fraser gets to his lead break, I boot Ted's dismembered torso around the stage. Then I go back to my mic stand and hang off it like Johnny Rotten. Wayne stumbles around like Sid Vicious, when Sid took all his drugs.

The hall hasn't heard this sort of abject noise before. The only other acts in the space this year have been Rob Guest, who led a rousing singalong of 'Any Dream Will Do', and the smiling Christian band Certain Sounds.

I glare out at the audience, as if to say, 'So what?'

When our first song ends, the clapping is the same as that that is given to the other acts. The adults want to appear generous. It's like they're miming to canned applause. We don't acknowledge them. I'm mentally blowing at the hot spots on my fingers.

Jeff does his Ramones count in—'WUN—DO—DAY—DAH!'—and the twin chords of 'Frustration' crash in.

Jillian Humphries is in the audience, sitting with Nicola Leyden, several rows down.

Tonight she finally sees me. Hers was the first face I saw.

I take special pleasure in the 'Why the fuck torment me?' line, and the fact that I am actually singing this at full volume to five hundred people in my school hall.

I put a special snap of emphasis on the 'fuck', savouring the 'c' and 'k'.

There is no hiding the other offensive line either, because we've signposted it, as large as the 'Mind That Child' sign on the back of a Mr Whippy truck.

'You know you've got me . . .'

Jeff does a tom build, as if he's swinging off a stripper.

'. . . crawling up your arse!'

Ker-bissh.

That's an arse too far for our principal Dave Rathbone, who makes a great show of getting up and trudging towards the exit. The only thing missing is a crown, a cross, and seven dozen lashes. Several parents nod towards him, like supportive parishioners, their lips pursed in common protest. The rear door bounces behind Rathbone as 'Frustration' comes to a close.

The identical robo-clapping from the audience slaps in again, like seals performing for food.

Despite this ovation, it's clear that the people have had enough. But we're not finished yet. We'd like to do one more song.

'I.H. 4 Me' is a new variation on our favourite theme, this time from a more compassionate angle.

People put me down, people always look around
I know I may look funny but don't treat me as a clown
I'm retarded so I'm told and Mummy being bold
Says Daddy threw me down some stairs when I was two years old
Ooooh–ooooh–ooooh

No one apart from a few friends and my family is here to hear this, and the general air is one of shock or resignation.

I'm crouched down like Chris Knox now, drawing little mental circles around my temple with a finger.

The dutiful applause comes in again anyway, the same amount of rice grains rustling through the same-sized can.

We leave the stage as a helper brushes up Ted with a broom and shovel.

Well, that went all right. Wayne's lead had tangled around his legs during 'Frustration' and my mic stand had started slipping, but all that aside, we'd remembered our parts, and 'I.H. 4 Me', our newest song, held together. It had been a blur of heads in silhouette, and the giddy empowerment of being the one voice in the room. It was a thrilling but also vaguely empty feeling, like you've really risked a lot.

No one around us backstage says anything, and the way they look down or busy themselves seems to indicate if not quite disapproval then certainly some confusion over what we have unleashed.

No one is sure yet, but the temple may have been desecrated.

Our supporters are having none of that afterwards in the foyer.

'That sounded good,' says Jeff Batts from the Same. He's genuine, but he still sounds sarcastic.

Chris Hughes agrees and gives a small thumbs up.

Robin Siataga is standing a couple of groups over, but he delivers a secret smile as if to say well done.

The crowd parts, and my five-and-a-bit-foot mother pushes through, leading the family tribe. Behind her, my sister Tash looks bereaved. Ted lies dead in a bin parked out the back.

Mum's blue eyes are sparkling.

'That was absolutely brilliant!' she says, grabbing my cheek and giving it a tug. 'As soon as you came out.' She keeps on tugging, and then she gives my cheek a tap. 'Whatever it is, I'll tell ya, you've got it, kid.'

She looks around the room to see if she can get an 'Oh yeah' or a 'Hallelujah', but there are none forthcoming. So she gives my arm a stroke and stares contentedly into the middle distance.

It's the proudest and maybe the happiest I've ever seen my mother.

There were letters to the student newspaper *Mercury*, three or four of them, each one a complaint.

One parent threatened to boycott future talent fests, but considering the entry fee was fifty cents it was hardly a killer blow.

'Punk Basher' weighed in and reminded everyone that a good kick in the balls would send the average punk reeling.

Sixth-former Murray Brass wrote an insightful letter pointing out that punk was 'used mainly by paranoid, unstable people to feel as though they are anybody, rather than the nobodies their style hides'. Punk was dead in England, he assured us, and it would soon die here.

I wrote a reply in the next issue of *Mercury*, doing my best to be diplomatic, but I spoiled it at the end with a Tourette's-like rush. 'We were only there to provoke a response,' I explained initially, which was rubbish and something I'd made up. I didn't really care what the audience thought and I'd taken it as a given they'd hate us. But it sounded like something Johnny Rotten would say.

'Finally—I'm sick of brainless morons putting us down,' I wrote at the end, 'when they don't have half a brain cell to share between them.'

That was more like it.

I noticed a new respect around the playground. Boys who last week had said 'Punk rock's dead' now didn't bother. Little third-formers scuttled past and threw half-fearful, half-impressed looks from the corners of their eyes. The girls who'd been too good for us, the ones picked up by their much older surfy boyfriends after the final bell, asked after us now, and wondered where we were going to play next.

Lesley Paris consolidated her position as Bored Games' best supporter by making a set of earrings based on our new logo—a safety pin stuck through a dice. She'd come along to our practices, and in the breaks she'd play her own beats on the drums.

Things were smoother at home, although it still flared up at times. We stayed ready for any action, listening from behind corners, hoping the coast was clear.

Mum and Tony ran a fruit and vege store in North East Valley, and the long hours and focus brought them together. Spending all that time in public probably shrouded them in everydayness, a normality where people were friendly and polite, despite the occasional issue around overripe goods.

I remember the dust on the potatoes I bagged, the crunch of decent apples, the optimistic scent of citrus.

Arthur, our big German shepherd, a gentle-natured dog, loped about out the back, as if keeping his guard's eye on our work.

Tony had been inspired by the success of his older brother, who ran a fruit shop in town and made his profit by being a scrooge.

Tony's brother employed me as slave labour once, as part of a school work day. He had me dig through boxes of rotting oranges for eight hours because there might be three or four sellable pieces per box. Peeling off soggy cardboard, slime through my nails, it was nauseating work, and I only got five dollars. That was the minimum work-day wage.

Waste not, want not.

Two or three times a week, I took two buses after school to work at our shop. But I had another stop on the way.

Records Records was a secondhand record store on Lower Stuart Street, just off the Octagon. I'd heard that the man who ran the shop wrote music reviews in the *Star* and *Rip It Up*.

I wasn't impressed with the sign outside his store, which was written in hippy letters. I hated hippies because the punk manifesto told me to do so. Sex Pistols slogans like 'Never trust a hippy' and 'Cash from chaos' rattled emptily in my head. My interaction with real-life hippies was limited, although I may have seen some at parties. American Bob out at Brighton could have been one, because he wore an ethnic-looking headband and had long grey hair, but despite the pong of patchouli he never posed a threat.

At first glance, the man who ran Records Records looked as iffy as his sign. He was a small man in glasses tapping away on a typewriter behind the row of new arrivals. His beard was a mistake. Records Records was a converted living room with him at one end, and he talked quietly to customers, which made him seem shy or hesitant, but I grew to learn that that was just a ruse. He was always watching, although diabetes had left him half blind. The man behind the pillar, as he once referred to himself.

When a schoolboy in short trousers tried shoving a record under his jumper, he would say, 'Are you going to put that back?'

Roy Colbert was an observer and a great raconteur. He liked people with talent, but he also enjoyed the eccentrics who visited his shop, like the teenager he'd christened Heavy. Heavy came in most days. He was Heavy for the records he brought, the bands he saw, and probably the way the bus driver clicked his ticket.

When I first visited Records Records, it was ostensibly to trade an LP. The second album by the Damned was nowhere as good as their first, so I swapped it for Gary Glitter. I pushed through the exchange, hoping Roy wouldn't notice that I had the better deal. But Roy was happy to do that, because he thought the same thing too.

The real purpose for my visit, though, was that I knew Roy was an influential figure on the scene, and he needed to know about me.

But Roy already seemed to know. He said 'Aw, yeah' when I told him I sang for Bored Games a minute after I'd first met him.

I became a regular visitor to Records Records, and although I was fifteen, I tried to match wits with Roy. He probably found that amusing. This shy, cocky boy.

Roy had an inexhaustible supply of stories. He told me about interviewing Lou Reed, Brian Wilson and the Ramones, about all sorts of local politics, and, most surprisingly, about sport.

I found solace in sport. It was a dependable, consistent companion on the weekends when I was dreading going back to school. The cosy rituals, and how there was always a second half. Great sports players were creative to me, masters of free expression. In their spontaneous invention, they were a lot like musicians.

I'd sit inside and watch *Sport on One* until I got a headache.

None of my friends were interested in sports, in who had or hadn't won. Roy was though, and his tales of cricketers, rugby players and golfers were just as entertaining as the ones he told about rock bands. Always the gossip from the back room that the paper didn't report. He was the only person in my sphere who knew that Robalan had won the 1974 New Zealand Trotting

Cup, and he had a picture of the finish in his study.

Sometimes I stole the lollies he kept in a drawer under the till to stave off his diabetic comas.

It was Roy who gave me live cassettes of the Enemy, and the demos of the band that the Enemy would become. When they left Dunedin they changed their name to Toy Love and added a new bassist and keyboards. Knox remained blasphemous, but he'd grown out his ugly mohawk.

You could see live clips of the Enemy on *Radio with Pictures* then, recorded in a practice room. That was down in Dowling Street, and later some of us practised there too. In those clips the Enemy were strident, curt, bathed in a putrid green.

The camera got too close to Knox, so his big beak looked even bigger, but he didn't care. He was too busy spitting and being disdainful. 'Really don't believe I'm gonna die,' he sang in 'Green Walls'. Then he commanded everyone to bury him and read his will. 'Goodbye.'

And then they charged into 'Pull Down the Shades', which was a put-down of the car boys that we hated too.

They wouldn't like the Enemy at our Talent Fest either.

I played those tapes until they wore out. One of them got twisted and the middle section played backwards, but in some ways that sounded better. I pilfered bits for my own songs, and I recognise threads of them in Bored Games numbers like 'Bridesmaid' and 'I Don't Get It'. No one would have guessed it was the Enemy, but the Enemy in reverse.

It was probably Roy who passed on our name to Toy Love, because we were asked to support them at the Concert Chamber. They wanted to give an opportunity to the city's newest bands.

It was like Malcolm McLaren ringing up to offer a support slot with the Pistols.

Years later, I opened for Johnny Rotten. But by that point he was a thirty-five-year-old being spat on by nostalgic fans. His band were hired musos who couldn't play the song 'Public Image' properly, so one afternoon at our soundcheck my band played it the way it should go. We were approached by the road crew and told to never do that again.

*

It's 2017, and I'm beside a hospital bed in a room in Lees Street, Dunedin. Roy is unconscious, lying under a crisp white sheet. His cancer has returned after a two-year respite and manifested in his head. For a small man, he has taken an amazing battering. Cancer, diabetes, cataracts, half-blindness, even a kidney transplant. There was a one percent chance that the medication for the transplant could spark off cancer, and Roy has drawn the short straw.

I'm singing him a song. If he was awake, he'd enjoy the joke. Him and I have a band called Rim Shot Frenzy, and 'Nobody Saw It Coming (Rim Did)' is the last song in a trilogy we've written and recorded over twenty-three years. Roy was Rim, and I was Shot, and together we were Rim Shot Frenzy. Rim would usually record a guitar part, and Shot would do the vocals.

'Nobody Saw It Coming (Rim Did)' is about how Rim could be a blowhard when it came to American professional basketball. He'd annoyed me with his predictions for the 2014 NBA playoffs because his picks were always right. I'd gone back to Auckland and written a song about it, virtually a solo effort, because when Roy heard my recording he said there was nothing more to add. Today, perhaps as a final act of big-brotherly disdain, he snores through my rendition.

Ten days before he died, we wheeled Roy from the hospital and took him down to the theatre playhouse, where his grandchildren were in a play. The show was directed by Roy's wife, Christine, a schoolteacher who every school holidays put on productions that she sometimes wrote with friends. Christine is officially known as the Lovely Christine, and she's a skilled conversationalist who was always holding the Colberts' dinner parties together while Roy went on with his quiet man ruse. He was probably mentally composing the savage, hilarious reports he'd send to friends.

We put Roy at the front of the stage in a wheelchair, with a blanket on his lap, and he smiled most of the time, as his grandsons, his son-in-law and his friends' children acted out their fable. Sometimes he'd go into a seizure, trembling in his chair, but then he'd come around again and go back to smiling. He was savouring the last sweet drop.

He said to me, 'Finally, front-row seats for Rim Shot Frenzy,' and I had to go out and cry.

When I was a teenager, I'd visit the Colberts' home, a rambling house at the end of a leafy path, in upper Cargill Street. Roy had a tremendous record and video collection. The table-tennis room in the basement was lined with thousands of singles. I'd ask him to play my favourite video from the Monterey Pop Festival, the one with Jimi Hendrix and Otis Redding.

I found Redding's version of 'I've Been Loving You Too Long' moving. When he sang the line 'You were tied', he drew out the word 'tied' with a knowing, ancient heartache. Later, I'd sing the word 'speeds' in exactly the same way.

Hendrix was a master of voodoo. Before the start of 'Wild Thing', he checked his tuning, and the G-string was flat but he battered on anyway. When he smashed his guitar, there were shots of the crowd and distressed hippies looking like they'd been violated.

Roy also had the film of Woodstock, and the best part by far was Hendrix decimating the national anthem—the panic and bombs set off by his long black fingers. That became the blueprint for my own guitar-playing, and when I finally got an amp I practised feedback for weeks before I bothered with any chords.

At the end of sixth form, while working at the shop, I had a really bad stomach ache. I was taken to Wakari Hospital, where they diagnosed appendicitis, and I was wheeled away to the theatre.

Roy was in hospital then too, recovering from a gall bladder procedure. I was happy to see my friend and his equal amount of suffering.

We were sitting in the TV room in a ginger state when the news came through that John Lennon had been shot in New York. It was tragic, because out of all the Beatles, we agreed, Lennon was the best. We sat in the room that smelt of meat and disinfectant and glumly reviewed his discography.

Later, I had a girlfriend who used John and Yoko as an example of perfect communion. She'd wield this like a small knife whenever she confronted me about the little I had to offer.

When Lennon died, the radio played songs from a new album they'd made called *Double Fantasy*. The album cover was John and Yoko kissing with their eyes closed, wrapped in endless bliss.

Decades later, another version of *Double Fantasy* was released, but it was stripped of its eighties effects. They'd taken out the snare cracks, the flanges, and the *boing* on the bass. This new issue sounded warm, dry and intimate.

The liner notes by Yoko Ono were even more revealing. She wrote about how her and John had ruined their marriage with the smack, the drinking, the time when Lennon and Harry Nilsson got thrown out of the Troubadour, the infamous lost weekend with May Pang that Yoko had convened.

I hoped my old girlfriend saw this too—*Double Fantasy* in reality, shorn of its pretence.

*

We met Toy Love before our show at the Concert Chamber and they were friendly, like older siblings meeting their junior versions.

When we took the stage, the complex of the PA and monitors felt like the dock of a spacecraft. A group of our friends bopped at the front, skiting a bit to the older people in the crowd, who were intrigued but also suspicious of our youth.

One of our new songs was called 'Nerds', and it was about Mormon missionaries, our school mates, and anyone stupid enough to watch *The Ray Woolf Show*. It had a fake disco introduction that sank into a punk rock sludge.

They criticise everything that I say
Nasty nerds!
'Hey buddy, have a good day'
Mormons are nerds!

We played our version of 'Pull Down the Shades', too, but not how Toy Love did it, truncated, sped up, tossed off like a song they'd played too often. We played it more like the Enemy, who went at a slower pace and had an extra verse and less thought-out words. When I introduced the song I said, 'This is a song I wrote yesterday.'

Later, Chris Knox would say, 'This is a song Shayne Carter showed me.'

When I was given a tape of the show, I heard him say that at least a hundred times.

Dad didn't get to see those gigs, because he was in prison, busted for selling pot. He'd been in town one morning, fossicking in the back of his purple station wagon, when a cop walked up and asked if he could have a look too. A big bag of tinnies sat shining between the boxes of records and lights.

Dad never said much about the time he was away, although he wrote letters to Tash from prison. He'd draw small cartoons and make a joke. It was the start of a tough time for Dad, but he didn't talk about that much either.

After his prison lag, he would have manic episodes where he stayed up for days, going dizzy on one thought. He'd invent new languages and wander off to places where no one could find him.

The first time he spun out, he went to the university campus and on the lawn he gave a lecture about ones and zeroes. I don't know what the lunching students made of that. I'm sure they were watching more than listening, but ones and zeroes were Dad's landing points. They were immoveable and resolute, like the Easter Island rocks.

Dad was given lithium for his condition, but he often didn't take it. He told me once he'd rather be half crazy than fully without a brain.

In some ways, he said, he kind of preferred it up there.

There might have been an occasion when Dad and Mum were in the mental ward at the same time. It's impossible to confirm this now. The idea of it appealed to me—I can't say why—maybe it made me a martyr, and defined me from the straights.

People sometimes wondered whether Dad was Lebanese or Māori—maybe even part Indian. Identity was an issue. Dad was a classic example of a generation of Māori who were cut off from their roots. The effect of that upheaval on him, and his people, was profound.

He'd make up false whakapapa, and he once threatened to set

up his own marae, somewhere out on the Taieri. There was a hastily convened meeting by local Māori after the word got out, and my father was confronted.

'Where was it you were from?' one man asked, just to be a cunt.

When Dad was a teenager, the Carters sent him to a college up north, where the only language spoken was Māori. His adoptive mother said he needed to be with his own people, and I don't know what kind of message that sent to Dad. The trip was a disaster, because Māori was the only language spoken at the college, and Dad had grown up around the Carters' plummy accents. Soon he was back in Dunedin, hemmed in again by its pervasive whiteness.

Dad made up a lot of stories about who we were and what our lineage was. I'd sometimes recognise names from other places he'd put in his tale. Then I'd clam up in despair. It was hard to know what was and wasn't true. Dad wrote out a lot of his theories, in folders, books and pads, and after he died, my sister and I acted on some of his information. Our quest to find his real parents took us to Rotorua once, and we stood in the house of strangers, essentially accusing their own dead father of having an affair. We couldn't back up our facts. It became an embarrassment.

Dad drank too much for a while. I went to a couple of his discos where he was on his hands and knees. Once, he took me to Milton to do a punk rock set—which caused no offence, because no one there understood it—and afterwards, at the place we were staying, Dad was rude to the motel manager.

She listened to him, and then she kicked us out.

She said, 'I've met you before and you were nothing like this.'

We spent the night freezing, lying on wooden benches in a shed beside the tracks at the Milton railway station.

As a drinker, Dad was generally quieter than Mum. He was also more into drugs. He experimented with Datura and smoked a lot of weed, and concocted things like cake, fudge and even a marijuana wine that still had bits of stalk in it.

When I went flatting he once gave me a couple of bags of pot to sell, and he said that Tony would kill him if he ever found out. He may have been half right.

Dad was an odd mix of shy and loud. He liked kids, because they were innocent, and he got in on all of their jokes.

I inherited Dad's racial confusion, because even though I grew up white, I can feel the brown part in my veins, in my attitude, in my rhythm and, even if it's a cliché, in my trickery at sport. Like my father, I've often aspired to be a peaceful warrior despite my failings.

I shied away from things Māori, because I wasn't confident with rituals I didn't understand and words that I couldn't pronounce. They taught none of that at school. According to our teachers, Cook had found New Zealand. We learned about Napoleon, not Tītokowaru.

'You're not Māori,' other kids said, talking about my light skin and my dirt-blond hair. I found their words deflating, and often I was scared they were right.

Dad came to Auckland a year before he died, because I wanted him to be in one of my music videos. When he arrived at the airport, his belongings were in an orange post office carry bag and he had on tracksuit pants and his hair was held in by a headband. He'd grown a long white beard that he often stroked thoughtfully.

He got excited going into town, seeing all the brown faces spilling out of the schools. 'Would you look at that,' he said.

He couldn't believe that Aucklanders paid three dollars for a coffee and he laughed at every round. In the city, he paced up and down K Road, saying 'Kia ora' to anyone who caught his eye.

When Dad got back to Dunedin, my sister Maria, who shared his house in Dunedin, said he was quiet for a week because he'd enjoyed his break so much.

Dad appeared in the video for a Dimmer song called 'Evolution'. It was a song about how life leads to the current moment, the grind to where you are. Dad had said something like that when I'd complained to him when I was younger about the events at Caldwell Street. He'd said something about how events shape you, and how, just by surviving them, you're still ahead. I'm sure he meant it philosophically—maybe it was his way of comforting me—but at the time it seemed a bit dismissive.

Later, Dad said if he'd known the situation at home was as rough as it was, he would have stepped in to do something about it. I hope that was true.

The video for 'Evolution' is based on a clip from Elvis's 1968 TV special, where Elvis stood in front of five tall letters spelling out his name. Elvis never looked better than he did in that show, grown up, tanned and handsome in a fly white suit. In the jam part with his band, he goes back to black leather. His performance of 'If I Can Dream' is an all-timer—he takes what would be a piece of schlock in most people's mitts and turns it into his testament. You can see the moment happen after the middle eight.

'Deep in my heart there's a trembling question,' he sings, and his voice quavers on that line because he knows it to be true. I get shivers when I see it, because he's making his discovery, and turning inwards, beyond the cameras, beyond the lights and pressure, to his feeling. Despite the cartoons and the slander, Elvis was usually an artist.

We used plywood and two hundred red lightbulbs to build our own six letters for the Dimmer clip. My drummer Gary had made them at art school with the help of some of his art school friends. We found two boys for the clip who resembled younger versions of myself. One was nine, the other fourteen, and they sang the opening section. I came in near the chorus and, in the spirit of evolution, Dad comes in at the end.

When he stayed with me in Auckland, Dad often refused our offers of outings and stayed at home instead to learn the words to the song, but the day we filmed the clip, most of them were gone. You could tell he felt put on the spot, and there were sweat beads wobbling away in his beard. He got the part we needed anyway— him going, 'It's all evolution, yeah, yeah, yeah!' and pointing his finger, like he had in his days of disco. His cameo was affecting and it carried a lot of mana. Every character in the video pointed their finger.

At the end of Dad's stay, we had a picnic on the grass bank in front of the Auckland museum. Dad told me and my girlfriend we should buy a house instead of wasting all our money on rent, but, like many sons, I didn't listen.

On our drive back to our flat, I shared some news I thought Dad would probably appreciate.

'Hey Dad,' I said. 'You know how you had that thing about one and zeroes?'

'Yeah,' he said from the back seat, trying not to sound too interested.

'Well, you know with computers and stuff . . . do you realise that all that digital information, all the information in the world, is now transmitted in ones and zeroes?'

There was a short, significant pause.

'And they said I was crazy!' Dad said, mock-shaking his fist, and the three of us laughed. But he was only half joking.

*

Bored Games played twenty-four times in two and a half years. People took advantage of us and we were paid at less than half of those gigs. We never had many options for where to play, either.

Fraser's dad said Fraser couldn't play in pubs, although we were granted a special dispensation to enter a heat of Battle of the Bands, where we beat a much older band that did the bluesy stuff that put you to sleep. After the result, their guitarist wanted to hit me but he was held back by his girlfriend. He was a professional, he said, and he'd played, more than once, at gigs in the North Island. Despite winning our heat, we weren't invited back.

We gunned for the older bands, because it's a rock 'n' roll tradition to pull down the icons in your way. These bands were generally the same—older, proficient musicians who now dealt in space themes and chukka-chukka guitar. They posed in their photos with their cheeks sucked in, trying to look all surprised. Usually, they wore drainpipe suits and shirts of pink or yellow, and according to us these bands needed to die.

The Knobz played at our school once. They'd been Rockylox, one of Dunedin's slickest and most popular pub bands, but like many groups of the day, they'd had a major new wave makeover.

At KVHS they dedicated the Members song 'Solitary Confinement' to Bored Games, presumably in reference to our ghettoisation as an underage band that couldn't find gigs. We stood down the back with our arms grimly folded.

The Knobz had a hit with a song called 'Culture?', which was a rebuke of the then prime minister. Rob Muldoon had placed a sales tax on records, because pop music wasn't culture. The Knobz even brought in a Muldoon imitator on the record, and the novelty of this appealed to middle New Zealand, especially in the small towns where the names of the hairdressing salons and discount shops always end with z.

Don't give me Culture
I'm not hearing you Rob
I could buzz around like a Beehive boy

But I'd like to see you do my job.
Upfront with the Knobz!

'Upfront with the Knobz' had the clout of a dish cloth, and we'd laugh about it at practice.

After the Knobz played at Kaikorai Valley, another student stuck up posters around town. He'd cut up a publicity shot of the Knobz and added images of puppies, and across the top he'd written 'KNOBZ WANK DOGZ'.

Bored Games were invited to support another new wave band at the Gardens Tavern, up the North End. Dad and a girlfriend had run in there once waving around toy guns, because they were drunk, for a bit of fun. Then they ran off laughing.

Lip Service were down from Auckland, and they looked surprised on their poster too—the singer was caressing a mannequin, with his cheeks sucked in to China. They had to be in their mid to late twenties, which to us was as old as the pyramids. The bar ban from Mr Batts meant that we couldn't do the gig, but because we were suspicious of Lip Service, we didn't bother telling them we weren't coming.

There was another Battle of the Bands but we couldn't play at this one, because Fraser was away with his family. It was held in the town hall and it pulled in a crowd of thousands. The entry was free after Dunedin's big festival procession, the annual parade where skirling pipe bands punctuated floats that were usually advertising light industry. There'd always be a beauty queen in the march, with two others who hadn't done as well, the runners-up, sitting on a slightly lower section of the float, smiling bravely, waving to the town. The festival procession was a big event, as was this Battle of the Bands.

I reviewed the show for my school newspaper and, probably out of envy, smashed the entire card.

I saved a special serving for Static, who I'd seen for the first time. Carey Hibbert had left the band and been replaced as singer by a boy called Tex.

David 'Tex' Houston later became an engineer for many Flying Nun acts. Frills or pretence didn't wash with Tex. Once, I handed him my headphones because I was shocked that 'Kashmir' by Led Zeppelin was actually okay, but Tex gave it less than a minute.

'That is the most pompous pile of shit I've ever heard!' he said, throwing the headphones back at me. The Earth went back on its axis.

Back at the town hall, though, Tex was a pimply dick fronting some dodgy covers band.

Alistair Penrose, the Static guitarist, seemed to be an exhibitionist, and I was afraid he might be a star, so in my review I gave him an extra shafting. 'If Penrose wants to satisfy his ego at the expense of his band, he may as well go solo and pretend he's Peter Frampton,' I sniffed.

I also rubbished the evening's compère, a local radio DJ called Jim Mora, for fronting such a shitty event.

'Here comes Jim Mora,' I wrote, 'prancing, posing, practising, posturing.'

The review devastated Mora; well, it upset him enough to write a response that was printed in the following issue of *Mercury*.

If he walked oddly, he wrote, with a wet teabag martyrdom worthy of Dave Rathbone, then it was cruel to 'malign him for a congenital defect'. Shayne Carter, he continued, was 'like his review . . . risible, egotistical and pretentious.'

I wore Mora's letter like a badge of honour. It tickled me to be attacked by someone famous who I heard most days on the radio. It was like being picked on by Woody Woodpecker or Charlie Mouse.

Bored Games had a set of about twenty songs. I wrote a lot of them on one string on an old acoustic at home that I'd plod along on, up and down. I'd show these notes to the guitarists and then they'd turn them into barre chords.

My songs were self-righteous because I was finally getting my say. It was a magical new power. I'd realised that lyrics were worth working on, because it was like giving yourself a speech, and the better your speech, the better it was to sing it. You could grab on to lines then, look forward to them, and really get your teeth in.

I found that songs were about balance and having the right amount. It was amazing how taking out one small bit could make a whole tune come alive. Songs lined up then into an ideal shape, like a row of ones beside the name of a trotter.

We were a good band, full of teen fury and ire. Fraser and Jonathon were a machine, and Jeff became one of the tightest young drummers around. Wayne had as much cool as anyone as he stared the audience down.

Decades later, I heard the recording from our second show with Toy Love at the Concert Chamber. I'd lost my own cassette of the gig, or maybe they'd stopped making cassette players then, but I was impressed by how strong the band was—tight, emphatic and forceful, with a singer who delivered.

Our material was getting better. Our song '15' satisfied the unwritten rule that every punk band should have a song title with numbers in it.

I might not be a kid and I might not be a man
But I'm not the little fool that you think that I am
I'm 15
I'm not a punching bag to give your ego a boost
I know when someone's lying—when they're telling the truth
I'm 15

I'm only 15
I'm just as good as you and I'm proud
I'm only 15
I don't care and I'll sing it out loud!

There was a boy in the year behind us at school, with a side part and glasses, who we thought looked like Joe 90, a TV puppet character. Every week Joe 90's dad put him in a capsule like a giant half-peeled orange and poured data into his brain. Then he'd be sent on a mission. We'd walk past our own Joe at school, and say, 'Gidday Joe' or 'Yes Dad', but Joe just laughed.

With its puppetry puns and catchy chorus, 'Joe 90' became the most popular Bored Games song. But when we were singing 'Woaaah, Joe 90' at the end, we were really celebrating the nerdy kid from school. It was fun having him in our song. I liked singing about him.

We'd started rehearsing in the basement of a flat in London Street where some older kids lived, and it became a punk HQ. One of the tenants was Damon Crowe. Damon had cousins in Auckland who were up-and-coming cricketers, and another cousin called Russell who later went to Hollywood, but no one cared about any of that then.

Damon wore the best punk haircut and rightly distressed jeans. When he played guitar, his strap was so low the instrument grazed his knees. He'd later die in a house fire in a village in a remote part of Australia.

The tenants at London Street dreamt about being English. The *New Musical Express* depicted a world annoyingly out of grasp. 'Stranded' by the Saints was a constant fixture on their stereo, because it rocked, and it described our location too. Someone had defaced the picture of Debbie Harry in the practice room and written 'Sad old hag'.

The Gordons came to play at London Street once, but the cops turned up and stopped them.

Bored Games played with the Gordons on the same visit, at the South Dunedin Town Hall, an ageing community centre that the Gordons nearly wasted. They were serious boys with frayed jerseys and wrinkles of concentration between their eyes, yelping slogans like 'Future shock! Adults and children! Quality control!' over sails of jet-engine noise. The audience stood before them, swaying like daisies in a tornado.

Offstage, the Gordons were quiet.

Another band we met at London Street were the Clean. They were slightly older, and had long noses and classical good looks. They'd just returned from Auckland, and Peter Gutteridge wore a cool Stars and Stripes belt that you'd never find in Dunedin.

Two of the Clean were brothers, David and Hamish Kilgour, and they'd been at Otago Boys'. David told me later he had long hair at school and looked like a girl, so he got picked on and kids called him 'Woman'. When he had his hair cut off, one of the bullies got in his face and said, 'You still look like a fuckin' woman.'

Gutteridge left the Clean early on, but his replacement lived above the practice room. A bass player called Bob Scott, known as Norbert then, had come in from Mosgiel to go to art school. One of the Clean's early songs was called 'Art School'.

Just because you go to art school doesn't mean you've got it made
Got it made
You don't have to go around lookin' like that

Norbert's bass lines were as tidy as the alphabetically ordered tapes he kept all lined up in his room.

We started doing gigs with the Clean at the Coronation Hall in Maori Hill, with other bands like the Same and the Drones. The Drones' most popular song was called 'Bugger the Boat People' and their singer had glasses, which was a big rock 'n' roll no-no back then. One of the Drones was rumoured to be Gene Pitney's illegitimate son.

The crowds at the Coronation Hall kept growing, because the kids had cottoned on, and two to three hundred of them would turn out for a dance on a freezing weekend night. But it also meant kids were all in one place now and could be sorted like calves in a freezing works pen. Vultures circled the hall, sinking piss in their cars and probably shining their knuckles. After years of beating up students, Dunedin's bogans and carboys now had a fresh set of targets. They'd called that sport 'scarfie bashing', but now 'punk bashing' was more their style. As victims it taught you commitment, because you would be punished for your art.

It got out of hand. Slit-eyed youths, bigger and older than us, formed gauntlets outside gigs and clocked us coming out. Sometimes they'd come into the hall, and you'd see the dance floor spin into chaos as some fuckwit waded through. At one gig, I stayed on stage for twenty minutes after the gig ended, because a group of bodgies were waiting for me at the door. Weirdly, they didn't just drag me off the stage. I guess that space is sacrosanct.

The violence spread to the streets and into the everyday. Some of us were bashed in broad daylight and we'd seek refuge in shops. A loud car exhaust was the signal of incoming danger. We hid behind lampposts or hedges, dashing block to block or cover to cover, like frightened mice.

I was walking with three female friends by the Regent Theatre once and a car pulled up and a guy just got out and planted me one in the face.

My cousin Terry got hit one day too. He was sitting at a bus stop and a man walked up and broke his nose. Without saying anything, he just booted him in the face. Terry was thirteen, but he had a blond streak in his hair.

The ritual was the same, a car pulling up and the standard inquisitions—'Are you gay?' 'Are you calling me a liar?'—followed by a beating.

It was Dunedin conservatism and a deep-set propensity for violence. Kiwis play rough while keeping it shy and modest. *You're not that good, are you?* is the subtext to many of New Zealand's slurs. If Dunedin didn't have a university, it'd just be another port town populated by sailors, labourers and farmers from the satellite districts. The university gives it vitality, and—when students aren't rioting, burning couches, or involved in warped hazing—something resembling thought.

Toy Love made a second visit to Dunedin on the back of a disastrous campaign in Australia. Australia didn't take well to uppity Kiwis or their weird clattery music.

The failure of what was a flagship band made us all suspicious of Australia, and it took years before any of the Dunedin bands bothered to go there.

Toy Love had also released an album, but none of us liked it because it didn't really capture their sound. They were coming to an end, but they could still do the business live.

We supported them at the State Theatre once, and it was the most violent show I've ever seen. When Toy Love went on after midnight, the crowd was psychotically tanked. Carboys staggered about, obliterated, swinging at whatever was in front of them: boy, girl, it didn't matter, as long as it was dressed weird. Wayne and Lesley were bailed up in an alley outside, and had to run to save their skins.

As Toy Love were playing, a man lurched at the stage and threw a bottle of unopened Speight's at the keyboards. Jane Walker ducked back at the last second and it smashed, in a burst of amber, just behind her head.

The violence briefly became a media matter. The *Otago Daily Times* ran an editorial headlined 'Trouble At Dance': 'It's a shame that efforts by young people to provide entertainment for themselves are being stymied by certain groups of youths looking to create trouble wherever they go.'

A senior sergeant was quoted. His teams were shocked by the number of youths outside our dances, he said, and by all the booze that had been hidden in the bushes. Grog had been running down the gutter. According to the sergeant, the police were slow to respond because it was Saturday night and they were putting out fires elsewhere.

We'd been left to fend for ourselves, with no form of security, and no one went to court or was ever held accountable for the dozens of assaults.

At the end of 1980, we played a Sunday afternoon show at Coronation Hall that was run by the police. Maybe they felt guilty and that they needed to do something for the entertainment-starved and frequently beaten youth. The police were already running Blue Light Discos at the Concert Chamber, and this gig was a part of their new campaign. Bored Games appeared alongside the Clean and a new band called the Chills.

Thickset men with bushy moustaches, dressed in polo shirts and canvas trousers, stood behind a table at the back of the hall, trying hard to relate, while selling fifty-cent cups of fizzy.

Martin Phillipps from the Same had started the Chills with Peter Gutteridge. Jane from the Same was on bass, and Martin's sister Rachel played keyboards without once adjusting the sullen expression on her face. We all liked Rachel. I pashed her a couple of times before she went out, for ages, with Jeff Batts. Rachel's friend Jayne sat in the audience, and everyone turned to look at her when Martin sang the new song with the chorus that went, 'Jayne with a why why why?'

The Chills had another song about the chugging new wave bands that none of us trusted. It was called 'Motels and Cars', and it was catchy too. 'Make lots of money money money money money money' went the chorus, summing those charlatans up.

Martin sang with bewilderment. He sounded like he'd been driven all around Otago Peninsula while recovering from dental drugs, and now he was overwhelmed by this experience and bursting to express it. The songs Martin wrote when he was seventeen or eighteen are notable local efforts, and they spill with colour and sparks.

Martin wore long motorbike boots that went up in a series of straps that almost reached his knees, and with his heavy lidded eyes he was a stoned boy genius, out of it on comics, garage rock and full moons over water. His soft blue eyes were the colour of his guitar.

To his left, Peter Gutteridge was his own enigma, pushing through each chord change with a secret purse of the lips. Gutteridge was another story waiting to be written.

I thought I might need to be careful in the Bored Games set, because I'd just gotten out of hospital and I still had stitches from my operation. I could possibly bust a gut. But when the music started, I got lost in it and slid all over the floor. The police had set us up in front of the stage, maybe so they'd be closer to quell the riot, but the only upset came afterwards when a Kilgour was sorting out our mess.

'Jesus, that Shayne Carter's a vandal,' said Hamish, putting a microphone that the Clean owned back in its clip. He hadn't noticed that I was standing right beside him.

A few weeks later, when we asked the Clean if we could borrow a mic for a recording session, the Clean said that we couldn't.

This sparked off a band war, and we wrote a song called 'Missing Mike' that attacked the Clean for their age, not their music—we couldn't run that down because their music was too good. But Hamish was rumoured to be twenty-four.

The Clean watched us perform the song at an outdoor concert at Broom Valley, and they sat on the bank in front of us with blank, straight faces.

Relations stayed strained after that, and the conflict was still simmering when the Clean had their early success.

Our recording session was a failure, even though we found enough mics.

The engineer was a blind man whose heightened auditory senses we figured could be useful, but when we listened back to the tracks they were struggling. We couldn't connect on the separated tracks. The drums had been put behind a buffer, and the guitars in another room, but the vocals were too loud in my cans and I found that off-putting. I liked to sit in with the music so that I had to sing hard to get across it, but now I could hear every sniff and the spit in my mouth. The blind man didn't seem to have a strong connection to punk. I couldn't recognise our band that usually sizzled live.

The demos we recorded at the Dunedin Folk Club were better. We'd recorded those for Mike Chunn, the former Split Enz bassist who was now an A&R man for Mushroom. He wanted to sign a young band. Those recordings had more crunch, even though they'd been recorded in folk rooms, but when we sent off the demos with a letter, we never received a reply. Chunn signed another young band instead, the Dance Exponents from Christchurch, which was probably a cannier decision for a major label.

I put his snub in my pocket anyway, and left it to stew for a few more years.

Wayne quit Bored Games at the end of 1980. His exact reason was that he wanted a band like the Clean. He left school during sixth form and got a job driving a van for a charity shop, picking up bundles of used clothes from depots and street corners. He also shifted out of his parents' place and went flatting with an older crowd.

The Clean were a band to aspire to, because they were going someplace else—somewhere more explorative than our own punk buzz. Their surf instrumentals and their twanging cover of the James Bond theme became the basis of a new sound. David turned the reverb and treble up and the bass knob down to zero. His guitar went off in shards around the timber of community halls. Behind him, Hamish rattled away like a giant human maraca.

I can't hear the song 'Point That Thing Somewhere Else' without feeling the heat of Coronation Hall and the danger of the bogans waiting by the doors.

The two brothers sang in unison and swapped vocals like they were finishing each other's sentences, and Bob made sense of it by powering up the middle. Even though no one ever mentioned it, the Clean also had sex appeal. There's footage from an early gig at Auckland's Rumba Bar and all of the dancers are women.

Wayne formed a band with Jeff Batts, and they were like a baser, brattier version of the Clean—the same driving bottom and echoey guitar, but dirtier, with next-level sarcasm. They called themselves the Stones, and their first record cover was a pastiche of *Exile on Main St*. Wayne rediscovered the flow of his squash game in the Stones, pushing and pulling at his guitar like he was daring it to stay. With his pudding-bowl haircut, he looked about twelve.

Jeff was one of Dunedin's most entertaining front men, bone dry and sardonic, and he'd do talks between the songs about how cool he was. Other times he'd say his band was terrible and we were stupid for liking them, because Jeff had a gift for talking himself into circles.

The Stones' drummer, Graeme Anderson, had grown up as Wayne's next-door neighbour in Glenross. He was their Charlie Watts, regular and bemused by the pair upfront.

We found Wayne's replacement at London Street—Terry Moore, the bassist for a couple of other bands who were casually using the rooms. Nineteen but already balding, the son of English immigrants, Terry played with a frown that broadcast a serious intention, and his spectral, throbbing basslines later informed the Chills.

Terry could get moody sometimes and go off on dark trains. We were driving in his car one night, along the tall white wall in London Street, and a sudden ominousness filled the vehicle, as though Terry was pondering a drastic action, like driving into the wall. Later he admitted he'd considered that. Everyone in the car had felt it. That moment hung in the air like a dream.

There were happier drives in Terry's car, like the day we egged joggers at Logan Park through the front windows, and the eggs splattered on the runners' calves. Then we drove to South Dunedin and hit a painter up a ladder, a good shot, like a bullseye, or a bouncer, and the shock on his face was priceless. Terry pushed the pedal and our back wheels squealed.

Terry was on bass when Bored Games played its second Talent Fest, where, that year, they had a winner. Dave Rathbone walked out again, but the judges liked us and we were awarded a hundred dollars. It was our second biggest payday.

People complained about Rathbone's attitude afterwards, saying he should have been more respectful, but Rathbone argued it was too loud and that he couldn't handle the volume. It would have been a letdown if he'd even half liked us.

Jeff and I played in another band that night, where we all donned disguises. We called ourselves the Hoods, a good name for a band from Kaikorai Valley, and our two guitarists were David Kilgour and my cousin Terry, who was thirteen. David was still talking to us then. He wore a red handkerchief around his face, sunglasses and maybe even a wig. I was on bass and wore a handkerchief too and a yellow and purple beanie.

Jeff drummed with a large paper bag on his head that had a Mr Four Square face painted on the front, and he'd poked himself a pair of eyes.

Despite our win at the Talent Fest, Bored Games were starting to falter. 'Young Band's Bind', the *Otago Daily Times* said, over an article with a picture of us missing our bassist.

We were playing the same songs to the same teenage set, with no new opportunities. We couldn't play pubs, or get out of town—we could hardly afford our gear. TV and radio were foreign territories. We were given a TV chance once, for a new show called *A Dropa Kulcha*, which consisted entirely of New Zealand bands—it didn't last long—but when we recorded our song at the TV studios, the atmosphere was mirthless. The technicians spoke into headsets, and when they talked to us they were bossy, arranging us like we were cutlets in a butcher's window. Our clip was never shown.

Bored Games fell to bits midway through my seventh-form year, when Terry Moore left to join the Chills, and a few months later Fraser became the Chills' keyboardist. I couldn't blame them. There was a new scene on the brew.

Bored Games made one last stand at a roller-skating rink in South Dunedin. We already knew we were breaking up, but the fee of $250 was too attractive to turn down. It was more than double the amount we'd been paid before.

We ran through our set for the final time and set up our gear in the middle of the rink, as skaters, including Mum, Tony and the family, fell down around us.

My family were back in the bleachers when we did 'I Wanna Be Your Dog', and I went over so my nine-year-old sister could join me in the chorus. Tash was excited to be on the mic, and she sang her backing hard, with a voice as flat and tuneless as her dad's.

When John Key said in 2008 that he couldn't remember his position on the Springbok tour, he was an exception. Anyone else alive in 1981 knew exactly where they stood. This was no time for a fence-sitter. The tour unzipped us, and liberals and conservatives accused each other from either side. A chasm appeared that we hadn't seen before.

I was against the tour. I wagged school to go to protests, and sat on tarmac and joined in chants like 'Amandla! Ngawethu!' Power to the people. But the people were split. Pissed rugby heads staggered out of bars to make their counter-protest. They couldn't understand why the pinkos wanted to stop the two things we were good at, which was rugby and beating the Boks. Robert 'Piggy' Muldoon was happy to agree with them to earn political mileage.

I didn't like Robert Muldoon. There were novelty replicas of his head called Piggy Banks made from brown plastic with a money slot in the top. I had one, and I shoved coins into it as if they were pieces of lead.

Towards the end of his life, Muldoon grew soft and made jokey appearances on game shows, and he even took the stage as the narrator for *The Rocky Horror Picture Show*. Some people felt better about him then, but I could never forget the cynicism and megalomania, the damage he did to keep power. Muldoon stayed my most loathed politician, although John Key would run him close.

When the Springboks played Otago at Carisbrook, we protestors were told that our march would be allowed to go to the Scotsman Grandstand, an area above the ground where those too stingy to pay could watch a game for free. But we were stopped before that, around a blind turn, and the protesters bayed uselessly at the lines of police, impassive behind their visors, tapping black wooden batons behind their clear perspex shields. We felt thwarted. Duped. A happy roar from the stadium travelled down to taunt us.

For the second test, I was in Wellington on a secondary school journalism course for Māori students. A dozen of us had been selected from schools around the country. We ran around the light industry surrounding Athletic Park in a small brown mob, but there was nowhere to actually go. The Blue Squad were on the other side of a corrugated-iron fence, and when they became aware of our presence, they bashed on the metal with their sticks to scare us.

A miserable mist clung all day to the desolate Wellington streets.

Our school newspaper *Mercury* was packed with anti-tour rhetoric. During my final year I was co-editor with Tanya Green, a girl who wore 'Halt All Racist Tours' badges and joined in at the marches. Tanya also reviewed the rock shows my band played at, because my view might be biased. I saved my writing for record reviews, and a hearty slag-off of a school camp where we were rained out in the Routeburn Valley. The highlight of that trip had been a teacher complaining about his sore ear because he'd slept on it folded over.

I had a mystical experience the night before that camp, in Glenorchy. I'd wandered off on my own after dinner, as the sky was colouring and a quarter-moon sat vaguely off the mountains. There was a field of lush grass with several dozen cows in it, most of them black-and-whites.

I sat on a corner post, and, seeing me, perhaps sensing they had the advantage, the animals gathered and carefully shuffled towards me. The lead cow came so close she was nearly against my feet.

We looked at each other in an exquisite quiet, interrupted only by the odd hoof rustle or a random moo that was quickly shushed by the crowd.

I could feel the heat off their two-tone hides, and their silent inquisition.

I thought journalism would be my real-world skill because I liked words. Journalism suited my enthusiasm, if not my disposition. Onstage I was invincible, shielded by my punk-rock persona, but I was shakier than that on the inside. The punk bit came from desperation.

I didn't let on in the playground though, which I now presided over like a king, resplendent in my seventh-form mufti. My blazer had badges on the lapel: the Buzzcocks, the Pistols, the Clash. I'd imported them from England for three dollars.

The dissolution of Bored Games taught me some lessons about loyalty and fair-weather friends. Some people didn't want to know you if you didn't have a band.

I decided to form a new group with my cousin Terry. Terry was living with us at Caldwell Street then and his sister Juanita lived with us later, because Aunt Nat couldn't cope with the stress of having them live with her. Later, Tony's daughter Tina stayed with us for a year as well, because, despite the turmoil, Mum and Tony provided a sort of refuge.

Terry was fourteen now, and left-handed like me, with musical tastes that were sophisticated for his age. He was into the post-punk bands, the angular ones where people tied limited skills to brave new ideas. It was an innovative time in music and many of the best bands still sound relevant now.

Terry liked PiL, Joy Division, Siouxsie and the Banshees, Magazine, and the Cure, and when he played guitar it chimed with a metallic edge, like Keith Levene from PiL, or Magazine's John McGeoch.

I'd bought a sixty-dollar bass that I'd debuted with the Hoods, and being the one-string master, I played it in our group,

Sparkling Whine.

Sparkling Whine was a pun too far and the worst name I've ever conceived, but my bass-playing got better. I liked the physicality of bass and the backbone it provided—its satisfying thunk. I explored gloomier themes in the new songs, as the zeitgeist then demanded. Jeff Harford from Bored Games joined too, adding solemn drums. Sparkling Whine rehearsed in a side room at Pharaoh's Tomb, an underground all-ages venue behind the Exchange, and when we played our sole gig we only had to slide our gear a short way into the venue.

After that show, Terry left to form his own band—Requiem Paradise, who did maudlin songs with depressing Ian Curtis vocals.

There is a tape recording of a Sparkling Whine practice at Pharaoh's Tomb. Partway through, my little brother Marcel— who I'd brought along because the parents were busy—interrupts to announce a discovery. Marcel had found a secret room up the stairs in a dirty attic. There were triangular symbols on the floor that pointed southwards towards an altar. Candles lined the walls and a curious smell stuffed the room, a mix like incense and meat. On the tape, Marcel sounds excited as he tells us about the room.

'Good one, Marcel,' I say, and the tone in my voice is awful. Such dismissal and disdain. I hope I talked like that to everyone else too, but I doubt it. Perhaps it's the usual impatience of a teenager towards a younger sibling, but I doubt that too. Somewhere in my voice, I hear the opposite of empathy, like my brother and I live in separate pods.

Listening to the tape now makes me think about Muldoon's divide and rule. How families become fractured and individuals are left to deal with the mess on their own, in isolation, in roundabout ways that do no one any good. Violent homes are like that. With diversionary tactics, blame gets thrown around and anger misplaced.

If we had ever talked about what was happening at home, or presented a united front, then we would have exposed someone else—the drinker, the hitter. Then they would have to confront their own failings or, even worse, give them up. Better to go in silence, then, with all of us divided.

Marcel was born five years after me. Marcel Tetahi. Marcel the First—which he was, in a suburb of Garys, Brians and Kevs.

Marcel never got much time with Dad, because Dad left soon after he was born, but he still has our father's descriptive sense, where everything is grand and superlative and, if it's not the biggest in the world, then it's certainly from the very top shelf.

I wasn't happy when Marcel arrived. I'd have accidents outside his bedroom, falling over and whining like I'd hurt my leg, so someone would have to come through to check on me. But I eventually tired of this schtick and accepted our new family member.

I inflicted the standard big brother tortures on Marcel, like pulling off his trousers and farting in his face, or hurling his pyjama pants out the window so he'd have to run out and get them, with his little diddle wiggling.

Once I locked him in the hallway cupboard, and as he squealed from out of the sheets I felt every inch of his horror. This hurts me more than it hurts you, I might have said, if I hadn't been struck dumb outside the door, appalled and slightly fascinated by my own behaviour.

When he was asleep on a beanbag I picked a giant scab on his ankle. I always picked my own scabs, but doing this was different. I can only quote the mountaineer who said, after conquering Everest, that the only reason he did it was because it was there.

It was Tony who brought Marcel up, and Tony was the man who called the shots. When Mum and Tony were going through a rough patch, Tony threw blame at Marcel, which seemed, even then, to be another diversionary tactic. I think he was hurt when Marcel said he didn't want to be adopted.

Marcel left Dunedin when he was seventeen, and it was years before he went back. He did a stint in the Territorials at Waiouru after he left, and then he went to Auckland, where he worked as a hairdresser. Eventually he ran his own salon.

Marcel became business partners with a man called Mike, who the rest of us have called Mike the Cool Guy ever since we first saw him and he was wearing cowboy boots. Mike shares Marcel's penchant for scheming and even now, thirty years later, the pair are in constant cahoots. First they went to Australia, then to Asia, basing themselves in Hong Kong and, later, Phuket. They've made patents for temperature indicators on plastic coffee cup lids, aerosol-free spray cans, and recovery drinks for travellers. These days they distribute a boutique version of rum.

None of their schemes have hit pay dirt yet, and our family waits for Marcel to make his fortune the same way they once waited for me when I had my biggest band.

For a long time I thought Mike and Marcel might be lovers, or mercenaries, or drug runners, or human traffickers, but no, they're just enthusiastic. Always about to egg the other on.

Marcel still announces a scheme in a way that reminds me of Dad, and always there's Mike, or the spectre of Mike, nodding his head in agreement.

*

My older sister Maria and I have just picked up Marcel from the airport. He's returned to Dunedin because our mother has just died. It's 2015.

Marcel lives near Kata Beach in Phuket, in a street patrolled by a friendly street dog they call Shelley. Obviously Mike lives right next door, with his Singaporean wife and their two kids.

It's Marcel's third time back in Dunedin in the last fifteen years. The first time was when Dad died, and then he came back seven years later as a surprise when Mum was turning sixty. Mum walked past him then, because she'd never thought he might be there. Then she did a double take, and dropped to her knees and cried.

Driving away from the airport, Maria crosses a railway track with dinging red lights and a goods train bearing down on us only half a paddock away. She's away with the fairies, but we all are.

Maria is Dad's daughter from before I was born. She was adopted into another family, but in the late eighties she tracked my father down. Her marriage had ended so she packed up her kids and left Christchurch for Dunedin to live with Dad.

We've decided to swing past our old family home in Brockville. Maria's never been in that house. I've popped back once before, when I was visiting with my band, to show them where I was from.

Caldwell Street looks the same. It's all scuffed fences and scruffy lawns, the slaps of undercoat on unfinished extensions, the snotty kids and the broken cars. Fallen ornaments on dust-covered ledges that snatch at yellow curtains.

When we arrive at number 42, the property has a new brown fence that stands as high as the fence around a pā. Across the road, a group of neighbours sift around suspiciously on their porch, watching us.

The new tenants of number 42 are home, just like they were the last time, and again they invite us in. I think they were chuffed when I first came by, such was my moderate fame as the local boy who'd done, well, you know, all right. That day, the husband brought out some of my old school exercise books he'd found at the back of the cellar.

The house is the same but it seems smaller now, and fresher and more contained.

'Hey, it's the washhouse!' Marcel says as we wander past, in case I hadn't noticed.

When we move into the kitchen, a cat looks up from its bowl and wonders who we are.

There's the bench that the Māori minister Father Wall put his bible on when he came around to scare me. His lectures always finished with the same conclusion—that I was doomed to burn forever in Satan's fiery oven. Mum and Dad would mill about, busying themselves, too scared to contradict him.

I believed in Santa for longer than I believed in God.

Marcel and I are walking past the old bedroom that Dad had once come into dressed as Santa. It was my fourth Christmas Eve. I'd been too drowsy to recognise the face behind the beard he'd made out of white cotton wool.

'Are you asleep, little boy?' asked Father Christmas.

'Yes, Santa,' I replied, earning a tweak of the nose for my fib.

In the lounge a stranger sits in a chair by the window that Tony and a friend put in sometime in the eighties. It took Tony years to finish that lounge. It became a thing around his neck.

We exchange hellos with the stranger, though we're not sure who's greeting who. Behind her, you can see the whole city, from Mount Cargill in the north all the way around to the South Dunedin beaches. The suburbs of Roslyn and Maori Hill sit lower in the foreground, like the first layer in a pop-up book. These days, real estate agents use the view as a selling point.

'Brockville Heights,' scoff its residents, as if they're toffs.

We move into the hallway and past the closet that once rang with the squeals of terrified children.

'Hey, it's the closet,' goes Marcel, but I shift us right along.

Eventually our tour is over, and Marcel and I stand before

the front door at the end of the hall, the glass one, that when we lived there was used only by strangers. Maria has melted into the background like she often does, but she steps forward to take our photo.

I stand in our house with Marcel, who knows this place as intimately as me. Standing in our haunted hall with the brother I'd needed to protect.

Maria gives us a countdown before she clicks the shutter, and when she gets to two, I lift my arm and put it around my brother's shoulders.

*

For the first few months after high school, I worked at the whisky factory. Tony was the foreman and, to the suspicion of the other workers, he gave me my first job.

I swept barley, poured barley into sacks, and cleaned malt barrels with ammonia while Arthur the German shepherd bounced around and snapped at rats. There were rats everywhere—in the bags, in the silos, lying dead and misshapen in corners, flattened by the poison that sat in innocuous boxes of grain.

I didn't fit in at the whisky factory. The staff at the factory were all smokers, bogans running across three generations. 'Ahhh well,' they'd sigh at the end of every smoko, before heading back out to work. I'd sit quietly in the corner, sipping my tea, trying to think up things to say that might amuse them.

After that I became a journalist at the local private radio station, 'Dunedin's Solid Gold', 'Your Destination Station': Dunedin 4XO.

I felt like a bit of a sell-out working there, because commercial radio was as far away from punk as you could get. But I wasn't there for the music. I was there to write sports reports and call the cop shop and ambulance once an hour to see if there'd been any disasters. I was allowed to read the news sometimes, and I did this with the same fake radio voice that everyone else used. The mics with the fat mufflers added more bass.

A radio station is a perplexing place. It's populated by goblin-looking people with big sonorous voices. It's as if the wind changed when they were talking in a golden tone and they got stuck with a voice that didn't go with their body.

The place could be sleazy, too. The new promotions lady was always bonking the programme director, and there'd be talk about the brothels that the cops and councilmen used.

It was at 'Less Talk More Music' 4XO that I realised how interconnected the powers were, and that not only did they run this town but, it followed, cities and nations as well. The media people and the cops and the politicians sat around having a laugh at Friday night drinks. They were the source of your information; they were the ones who told you what should concern you and which way you should look.

Just before an election the councillors would grovel to the media, hoping to get their toe in and their opinion on the news.

The morning show at the station was run by a J.P. and ex-councillor known around Dunedin as 'the housewife's friend'. He liked younger men too, and I remember him all over me in the broadcast booth once, going, 'Shit, I'm horny. I'd love a blowjob,' as his face grew red and sweaty. He was in his sixties. I was seventeen.

I made some crack about how he could go to the loos and pull himself together—and then I ran away.

Eventually I was given my own slot: Shayne Carter's 4XO Spot On Sport. No one else on the news staff was interested in sport, so I'd do phone interviews on a Revox two-track tape machine and then later re-record my questions in a deeper radio voice. The cricketer Warren Lees got pissed off at me once because when I replaced my normal voice with my deep radio voice I'd rephrased the question. He thought that made him sound stupid. I apologised, because that wasn't my intention, and he was big enough to let it go.

Once, in the middle of an interview, the long plastic casing on a neon light fell down and hit me on the head. My groans of pain mid-question were immortalised on tape.

One of the nicest people I interviewed was the yachtsman Peter Blake, who talked about the freedom at sea and the wonder of passing pods of whales. The cricketer John Wright had a good story about putting sardines in the gloves of the objectionable Aussie wicketkeeper Marsh, so that each of the New Zealand batsmen would ask about the stench when it was their turn to bat.

The rugby coach Laurie Mains was gruff and patronising, because he was involved in rugby, and rugby was holy in a way I couldn't understand. When the All Blacks lost the World Cup final in 1995, my main consolation was that Mains was their coach.

I was studio-bound as a reporter because I couldn't drive. I also avoided going out to see people face to face, because I found that gruelling. I was young and uncertain.

Because I never left the studio, I was encouraged by the editor to steal the progress scores from sports matches from our opposition, 'Dunedin's Sports Leader', 4ZB. The reporters there soon got on to us, though, and two minutes before the hour they'd give out a wrong score and then correct it after the news.

I sometimes covered the District Court. It was noticeable straight away that all the people in the sad, ashtray-smelling waiting room were poor and unprivileged. A butcher's apprentice from Green Island or a Māori kid from Pine Hill caught the eye of a copper quicker than a councilman or a J.P.

Once, at Friday night drinks, I called my boss a wanker. I was loose after a few cans of Steinlager, and it was the wrong thing to say but it was also something Tony might say as a joke or a jibe.

'Aw, ya wank,' was a favourite Tony saying, as was, 'Aw, ya grip.'

It was a josh, but my boss didn't get it and he slapped me in the head. The other news staff threatened to go on strike. On Monday the general manager called me in and warned me about my drinking.

4XO put me off working for other people, and when I left there as a nineteen-year-old I never worked fulltime for anyone again. It convinced me to go my own way. I felt that my boss, the editor, picked on me too. He worked too much and expected everyone else to work that way as well, and he may also have had youth envy—a syndrome I didn't recognise until I got older myself, and realised a future and a good complexion were enviable assets to have.

There were people at 'Hits from the 60s, 70s, and 80s' 4XO who were more suited to commercial radio, people like Mike Hosking who turned up as an eighteen-year-old from Wellington, smoking pungent cigarillos and smelling of cologne. Hosking also had a voice that didn't fit his body.

There were a lot of egos in radio. The DJs and newsreaders thought the public hung off their every word.

I left 4XO in 1984, convinced that the world should hang off mine.

When I'd started working, I'd left home. I couldn't wait to get out, partly to escape the oppression of our domestic troubles, and also to experiment with creative masturbation and develop my fledgling career as a teenage alcoholic. I wanted to be free to run with my friends and get out of it and hoard as many copies of *Penthouse* as I liked.

Dunedin was a tour of hovels in the student end of town, through decaying Arctic villas with useless showers, unusable kitchens, and ovens full of the debris from up to four generations. The only consolation was that these places, uninsulated, parked in the shadows of the Dunedin hills, were far too cold for vermin. It was accommodation for students and people who were too poor, young or stupid to leave those slums. We were a combination of all three.

A group of skinheads invaded my eighteenth birthday at my flat in Cumberland Street, and set fire to the shell of a car that had never left our drive. The party bottled the fire service, and, when the police arrived in full riot gear, with helmets, batons and shields, it was the first time the riot squad had been used in Dunedin since the Springbok tour. My editor at 4XO was angry that I didn't report this event, but there was no way I was going to advertise my ruined birthday or the fact that some of my friends were arrested. But the cops that night were looking for trouble just as much as the skinheads.

The bootboys were a new phenomenon. They were lookalikes with shaved heads and boots and braces who'd appropriated the individualism of punk. We never claimed punk back from the bootboys, because they reduced it to a cartoon. Many of the bootboys seemed to be updates of the carboys who'd cut a swathe through our dances; in fact they may have been the same people, except now they had a new excuse to obliterate themselves and anyone unlucky enough to be in their way.

While middle Dunedin stoked up the fire after a long day shovelling coal, the youth ran amok. Designer drugs were for designer cities, so the Dunedin versions were nasty and improvised. Drugs stolen from gardens—cactus, Datura, opium from poppies, magic mushrooms that grew in the grass—and these were snorted, smoked, shoved in the arse or, among the burgeoning hardcore, pinged up with a needle. Methadone and morphine arrived. Some folk died. Canisters of nitrous oxide were stolen from the university. People scaled the walls of the science department, several stories up, and tried to raid the labs. A friend once drank formaldehyde mixed with soda then lay on a lounge floor foaming from the mouth while we stepped around him. My flatmate at Cumberland Street tried snorting fly spray through a handkerchief.

One night the fly-spray snorter paralysed himself by drinking Datura, so the rest of the party picked him up and carried him ceremoniously around our house, chanting his name like a tribe. He lay on our shoulders, stiff as a plank. We took him to his bedroom, laid him down, and covered him in his intellectual books. It made a most curious shrine.

Peter Gutteridge wrote a song about that flatmate. Peter was living in the flat next door and he often came over the fence. 'Born in the Wrong Time' became one of Gutteridge's best-known tunes, and he recorded it later with the Great Unwashed.

We're sending him, him away
His form of socialising is a bit too strong
We're pushing his bags out the door
We're pushing his bags out the door
There's no room for his head in our minds or our hearts
There's no country that would take him when he falls apart
He's just one of those people born in the wrong time
One of those people born in the wrong time.

Peter was always observant. He had an artist's eye. His lyrics were filled with insights that he'd never say aloud otherwise. He would make those same observations later, when he became an enthusiastic junkie and sank into his own torpor. The things he said were something cutting, but correct, although it was a wonder he could see out of the fog.

I didn't like needles, so I avoided that path because I never saw it working out well. There was no evidence that said to me 'That looks like a good idea', so instead I lost my mind on more common drugs and drank myself into oblivion.

It was obvious from my formative teenage drinking experiences that I wasn't equipped to handle it. Unlike other people, I couldn't stop. There was no gate to the dam coming down, no instinct that said 'Buddy, enough is enough', so I drank until I disappeared into a pit of belligerence, false confidence and blackouts. I had the bad gene.

My only cover was that this was almost standard behaviour in the dazed Dunedin environment. I may have woken up still drunk on a strange couch, or peed in someone's closet, but at least I wasn't that other friend wanking in the hallway at the party because he didn't know where he was—and then there was Carey Hibbert, too, nattering away in the nude. The extremity was normal, at least until you took a step back and realised it wasn't. Everyone was going hard.

When I was in the sixth form, and still in Bored Games, Jillian Humphries had a party at her house. An aching, devastating party, because as the night progressed it became clear how much more she liked Fraser Batts than me. I sat on my beer, growing sourer. Finally, to end the situation, I shoved Fraser in the chest and challenged him to a fight. Fraser put me in a headlock and threw me onto the ground. Then he lay on me like John da Silva.

It was the first time I remember getting aggressive on booze, but it wouldn't be the last.

I once set myself on fire on a plane. I had been drinking a bottle of scotch. It was in the days where you could still smoke on planes, and when I lit my cigarette I also lit up the vinyl jacket I was wearing. I yelled at the stewards as they killed the flame with blankets.

'How dare you put out my fire!'

I could write a book on alcoholic disgrace, but it wouldn't do anyone any good. It would add nothing to the literature of oblivion and wouldn't make any of us feel better. These stories are full of clichés—the self-loathing, the piecing together of events from fragments you hear through the following week, the memory of gin, scotch or Black Russians clouding your sinuses as, all through the next day, you wonder what you've done. It's a joke: a confidence trick that rips up all the confidence, and you drink again to bury the shame.

I never got good at drinking. I've had long periods of sobriety, but booze still plots from an arm's length away, threatening to post its message.

Carey Hibbert once wrote a play called *Trash Hotel* that a group of us performed at the Dunedin Art Gallery to an audience of about 120. The characters were historical and mythical figures—Goebbels, Medusa, Elvis—caught in a place halfway between Earth and Purgatory. That place was Trash Hotel. Carey spent weeks working on his play and his script was tight and witty, but when it was time to perform the play he was badly let down by his cast. There is an excruciating video from the night, and it shows the backstage scene at half time. The actors are staggering about, completely out of their minds. Our pre-show drinks to steady our nerves had become a race to annihilation. Everyone was so far gone that the second half became a reeling, hellish improvisation with actors inventing their own scripts all at the same time. I was Elvis. I'd dyed my hair and dressed in black leather for the night, but my version of 'Heartbreak Hotel' was lost in the melee. A pair called the Siamese Buttfuckers, Siamese twins joined at the butt, simulated aggressive sex. Goebbels lurched around muttering. Medusa threw half-filled paper cups at the audience. Sid and Nancy threw the finger. Other figures behaved in a manner never reported.

The audience sat there quietly appalled.

Helen of Troy went backstage and stole everybody's wallets. Then she went home and slit her wrists. Some friends who were supposed to make an entrance through a skylight fell through the skylight and one of them was left dangling by his dreadlocks. Later, after the play, another associate broke into the gallery and nicked the night's takings.

The director of the art gallery told Carey that the performance 'had a certain panache', but an associate who worked at the gallery and had helped organise the show was nearly fired.

Carey avoided drinking that night, because he cared about his play, and he was so devastated that he left town and went to Central Otago for a week.

We had a friend who wore dresses and kilts and danced like a loon at our gigs. He was an adventurous person, but the review he wrote in the university newspaper was sober and reflective. *Trash Hotel*, he said, was a dismal report on our scene. There were more constructive ways of expressing yourself; there were alternatives to self-destruction and debauchery.

A few years later, this friend committed suicide, leaving a note for his children.

'Please don't smoke,' it said at the end.

Graeme Downes was another of my flatmates at Cumberland Street. He was too busy studying Mahler at university and writing songs to get sucked into all the foolishness. Graeme stood slightly apart: tall, dark, and thin, like a poet, or a yet to be doomed romantic.

He was quickly claimed by an older woman.

Graeme had a band he called the Verlaines, after the poet not the guitarist, but he was inspired by the Clean and the Pistols as much as by the classical records he'd play in the lounge, which was freezing but had excellent acoustics. I couldn't decipher his records. To me, classical music was a pile of notes in some dreary random order.

With his build, Graeme could pass for a pace bowler, and he was in fact a tremendous cricketer. At high school he was one of the region's hottest cricketing prospects. Graeme was also an excellent soccer player—wiry, brave and quick, with all the tools for a striker. Later on, he and I would team up to devastating effect in the annual football matches between Flying Nun and the student radio station in Auckland, and every year we punished them, even if they had played our records.

All in all, Graeme was a golden boy, and it's curious that he came along at the same time as a collection of golden boys from one town. Journalists and sociologists have tried explaining this, but most of their theories seem shaky.

Graeme's cricketing form wasn't so hot the year we flatted together. The only things golden were the golden ducks he scored as his batting and commitment fell away. It was another promising sports career cut off at the base by rock 'n' roll, cigarettes, whisky and sex.

Graeme was always more cerebral and serious than me, but we came from a similar place. He'd grown up in Pine Hill, another working-class suburb on an undesirable hill, just as rough as Brockville. Motorists coming into Dunedin off State Highway 1 were often greeted by the sight of slaughtered horses hanging on scaffolds, bleeding out at the back of Pine Hill.

It was Graeme who taught me my first guitar chords.

Bandless, increasingly friendless, I needed to get my act together, at least in a musical sense. I started writing songs using the basic chords I'd learned from Graeme: D, A, E, G and sometimes, if I was feeling experimental, a C. Really I was more into making feedback noises in my amp. I got good at playing the national anthem like Hendrix, except I played 'God Defend New Zealand'.

I was seventeen when I made my first recording.

The Clean had become successful, and now they were putting out records. These had been released by a young record store manager in Christchurch who'd been blown away by some shows the Clean did at the Gladstone, Christchurch's biggest venue.

Roger Shepherd was so impressed, he formed his own record label.

Shepherd called his label Flying Nun, after the silly Sally Fields TV show, and the Clean's single 'Tally Ho' was its first release. Surreally, 'Tally Ho' crashed the Top 20.

To see the Clean in the countdown with the other acts on the Saturday night chart made little sense. The other acts may as well have been from Saturn. I recall seeing Graeme in town afterwards, and in my memory we high-fived. But I don't know if the high five had been invented in Dunedin yet.

Encouraged by that success, Roger did other releases. Some of the kindred Dunedin bands—the Stones, the Verlaines, the Chills and a new group called Sneaky Feelings—were released on a double EP. Doug Hood, Toy Love's former soundman, recorded them on a TEAC four-track tape machine while Chris Knox dispensed spiritual advice. Disillusioned by the battering Toy Love had taken from the industry, Chris had decided a grassroots, home-recording style was the only way to go, and, because Chris is charismatic and persuasive, he convinced everyone else to think that too. It suited the situation, because no other record company in New Zealand would give these bands a chance. Also, no one could afford a proper studio. Blah blah blah.

*

I get bored relating the Flying Nun story. It's like copying someone else's card. The facts are all there on Wikipedia, and it's a tale that's been told a million times, always bent around the phrase 'Dunedin Sound', which is a term of convenience that some journalist once used and all the others copied. We resented being lumped together, because it never acknowledged the disparate characters we were, each with our own pig-headed vision of what rock 'n' roll should be. You have to have that solitary purpose to make anything worthwhile, because people who copy other people don't last. There's already a better version of you out there, and, like I've said, I'm not into playing covers.

Yes, we were—mostly—friends from the same town, who ran together and shared practice rooms and record collections, and the same limited musical tools, who picked each other up in our cars and stole each other's girlfriends and skited in front of each other at our gigs, trying to get one up, feeling jealous when someone's song or show or tour was better, but being more inspired with our own. Standing in your rehearsal room slagging off every other band in the world is a standard rock 'n' roll practice, even when some of those bands used that same room. It's bravado, and most often bullshit, but when you go back to your own song you play it harder. There were some aspects of the other Dunedin bands I didn't like, and I'm sure they'd pick holes too—but it's all a part of the fabric. Let the other losers make the mistakes. Their mistakes can teach you.

I can't talk on behalf of the other musicians, or Roger Shepherd, or Doug and Chris, and explain what really motivated them, or what they had stirring in their chests. I can't tell you what any of them envisaged, or how they felt when they sat down to write a song, or what they were hoping to achieve, or what song they were half ripping off when they wrote their own.

I can't tell you what any of the other musicians were thinking, but I can tell you what I was thinking: 'Fuck you.'

'Fuck you' when I bawled into a mic. 'Get fucked' when I peeled off some tasty, abrasive guitar. 'Fuck you' as I slaved over a song, over and over until I made myself sick, shaping a lyric that was just out of grasp or a particular chord sequence that I just knew was, or wasn't, triumphant. All through that was my determination to prove you wrong.

I still think 'Fuck you' when I play, but only if it's good. It's a necessary mantra that gives me strength and reinforcement. Its target is the universal 'you', because you're the one I need to show.

I didn't want to jangle like some Dunedin bands. I couldn't stand the thought of being fey or polite, and being friendly was out of order. I still loathe music whose main purpose is to ingratiate itself, like the friendly chap down at the pub. Being likeable is easy, and it's the blandest thing to do. It's easy to go right past the likeable.

I didn't want to play winsome pop or comfy Byrdsian jangle, or have harmonies like the Band or the Doobie Brothers. I wanted to play roaring, defiant rock music that made sense of the mess I was in. Thank Christ I had that outlet. If I hadn't, there's a good chance I'd be dead or locked up in the loony bin like some of my relatives.

My motivation was often revenge—on the kids who beat me up and on a community that seemed determined to keep me and my people down. I was a sensitive, angry boy who'd been given a megaphone to address a hostile world. 'Fuck you,' it said, as the little speaker crackled and started feeding back.

At twenty-one, Roger Shepherd seemed to be one of us. He liked drinking—in fact it seeemed to be his substitute for food. The only condiments in Roger's fridge in his Sumner flat in Christchurch were half-full bottles of flat ginger ale. Red label Johnnie Walker was his spirit of choice. There were drives back out to Sumner late on a Friday night, with Roger outside the car, sprawled across the bonnet. His demented edge was reassuring to us and somehow endearing. He was head of the label but we felt we could trust Roger, and we didn't need a contract to make it official.

In mid-1982, word came through that Roger was interested in a Bored Games record. Bored Games had disbanded, but everyone thought it would be a good idea to have a representation of what had been, for two years at least, an important band on our scene. And truthfully I had also begun to feel left behind by a lot of my musical friends, so, now, even retroactively, I could run on the track too.

We recorded *Who Killed Colonel Mustard* in a studio at 4XO that was usually used for jingles. The programme director at 4XO, a little man with a huge booming voice, was the engineer and producer. His name was Leigh Harrison. Apparently Leigh had walked on the wild side before he found God, and even though he was a committed Christian now he was into the Bored Games sound. We recorded over two nights on a budget of $250, planning to record five tracks, but by the time I got to sing 'Sactab Overdose' the beer was beginning to win.

'You're slurring your vocals,' Terry Moore said through the feed from the booth, heavily unimpressed. The fifth track never made it.

We were allowed three colours for our record cover: black, white and red. Full-colour was too expensive. I designed the cover and glued headshots of the band onto Cluedo cards, each of us a different character. Jonathon Moore was Madam White— literally, because I accidentally spilled some Snopake on his head. Even today, on reprints of the Bored Games cover Jonathon's face is half covered by a big white splotch. It was too expensive and inconvenient to redo the cover.

The back of the cover was a Snakes and Ladders game. Offending a local radio personality took you up a ladder, being beaten up slid you down a snake. A snub by Mike Chunn sent you back seven squares. There was even some reference to Martin Phillipps meddling in band affairs. Martin got his hands on the back cover as well, writing 'Yay the Chills!' on the tail of a long snake.

It was exciting when the record came out, because being on vinyl made your music official. When you played records on your stereo, it was a kick to know that yours was up next.

Even then, however, I knew that Bored Games belonged to

a different era. With punk rock swallowed up by the bootboys, people were turning to other outsider music and the sixties were coming back—not the sixties of the Hollies and Herman's Hermits, but music from the fag end of the era, made by drug casualties, heroin addicts, people on LSD, suburban kids in America defacing the Beatles and Stones. The Velvet Underground and Nico, Syd Barrett, Skip Spence, the sixties garage punk compilations like *Pebbles* and *Nuggets*—these were the records we sought. Embracing the stranger. The more damaged the better; bent, exploratory pop music that went to different places. It was music you'd never hear on the radio but that people would still listen to decades down the track. That ethos is all over early Flying Nun.

The older influences were coloured by contemporary music—shades of Joy Division or the alien, synth-driven music of Suicide. 'Candyskin' by the Fire Engines was a favourite. Australia's musical landscape was as barren as its outback, but there were exceptions—kids as disaffected as us, like the Birthday Party and the Saints and, later, the Go-Betweens and the Laughing Clowns. Kindred spirits have a way of finding each other, helping each other climb out of a lonely hole.

Because rare records were hard to get, when we got them they were valued. There could be a wait of months for an album you'd read about in the *New Musical Express* or that had been hinted at in some obscure rag, so you had to commit to that record. You listened to that record until you knew it. If rock 'n' roll was important to you, it took up all of your time.

These records were exotic to us, and the bands were enigmas. They stayed glamorous, because we didn't get to hear them make boring conversation or see them staggering through the local pub.

The early Christchurch bands on Flying Nun generally sounded like Joy Division and the Velvet Underground, miserabilist twin-chord dirges from people like the Pin Group, the Victor Dimisich

Band, and Bill Direen and the Bilders. But their music made sense to us. 'Girl at Night' by Bill Direen was one of my favourite songs. When the Christchurch and Dunedin scenes started crossing over, when we began making the reciprocal 360-kilometre trip up and down the east coast, we'd party together and enthuse over the same records. Those people made sense to us then too. A community began to prosper—one totally apart from the protectors of music like CBS Records, the New Zealand Broadcasting Corporation, and 'Less Ads More Music' 4XO.

I was getting more proficient at guitar. I had the calluses to prove it. The journey from A to D was no longer so monumental, or a struggle, usually out of time. I liked the surfy twang that David Kilgour got on a single string, so I took that and placed it between 'Fuck you' major chords. I bought a fuzz box, although it broke the first time I stomped on it.

'It's not a bloody trampoline, mate,' said the man at the music shop, who probably sells computers these days. He's the one at the counter who knows more than you about RAM.

I bought a left-hand Maya electric guitar from the same bloke for $130. He obviously thought it was a crappy make, but that was all right, I wanted to play crappy guitar. None of that Jimmy Page stuff or whatever was up with Dire Straits. Eric Clapton was completely despicable. I didn't bother learning scales, because I didn't have the time to sit in my room reducing music to a mechanical task or to play the same shapes that everybody else did. My need was more urgent than that.

I started playing odd string combinations, throwing my hand at the fretboard and trying to make sense of wherever it landed. 'That's actually D-minor seventh,' someone might say, 'or the root notes of that,' and I'd be, 'Yeah, whatever.'

Much later, I would make a record playing piano. I'd never

played the piano before. Each key was a puzzle, and if I lost my way at any point the train fell from the rails. I once hit a chord that I thought sounded amazing. 'That's G,' said a nearby pianist.

But from the beginning, guitar was visceral—a burn that surged up from my stomach and came out through my fingers. I needed to arrive at a heavy conclusion as soon as I could, and I'd push out my lips if I did it. I smacked my strings so hard I always had extra little E's on hand.

Being left-handed was a drawback, because it's a right-handed world. Can openers, scissors, fountain pens, and guitars. My dad was left-handed, and because this was the devil's hand, he had his desk lid slammed over his hand by the Catholic nuns. He learned to use his right hand instead, but his handwriting was always shonky as a result.

My cack-handedness has meant there's usually only one or two guitars to choose from in every music shop, so when one day I found a store in Pasadena, California dealing in exclusively left-hand vintage guitars, it was my personal nirvana. There was even one of those twin-necked things, but it was a bit too Jimmy Page.

I use my right hand for other tasks, like throwing, and I kick with my right foot. But I write and play guitar and racquet sports with my left. Sometimes, if I play tennis, I forget.

I'm a right-handed golfer, although I've never played golf. Like the rest of me, it's a bit of a mess, but I shamble along.

Because Peter Gutteridge and I were neighbours, we started having jams. I liked Peter's music straight away, because his songs were groovy and effortless. His music just felt right. Peter was another rock 'n' roll scholar, but he didn't have time to sweat the details, because he wasn't a trainspotter—his expertise was more general than that. He just knew what sounded good, and he had great taste in sunglasses.

When Peter set off on a mesmeric riff, playing his own invented chords, I'd be surprised and impressed, and I'd hop on, adding my own made-up chords and sometimes singing a harmony.

We'd busk in George Street, although we never made much money. I don't think our songs had mainstream appeal, especially 'Bad News for Jesus', a song Peter wrote for the door-knocking Christians who bothered us on Sundays, looking hopeful and carrying a pamphlet.

Bad news for Jesus today
God got married and had another son
There's zombies at the door
Zombies at the door.

That was all the lyrics he had, but we sang them harder each time, until our voices boomed back off the shop windows across the road. Shoppers shuffled past with their heads bowed down, reluctant to hear our message.

Peter got bossy. He wasn't that good at listening. As soon as we started playing together, we started arguing, because he always thought I was playing too many chords, which, considering I only knew about four chords, was rich.

'Play there,' Peter would say, pointing to a spot up the neck. I'd sigh and do what he said.

We soldiered on and decided to form a band with a left-handed bass player called Kathy Bull, who played in a group called Look Blue Go Purple. Kathy lived next door in Cumberland Street as well, with her husband Martyn Bull. Martyn was the drummer in the Chills. Like Terry Moore, Martyn had a lot to do with classic early Chills songs like 'Pink Frost' and 'Flamethrower'. The Chills had come back from Auckland with those hits in their pockets, but then Martyn had been diagnosed with leukaemia.

My other flatmate, Gordon Perkins, and I went next door once and performed an improvised comedy skit for Martyn. We thought it might cheer him up. He lay in his bed smiling with big black rings under his eyes. Martyn died within a year. He was only twenty-one.

Kathy Bull was Canadian, and stroppy, and she didn't mess about. She'd been arrested at my birthday party when the riot squad turned up, after a copper said some crap to her.

'Nice American accent,' he'd sneered, from beneath his Springbok Tour visor.

'It's Canadian, fuckhead,' Kathy said, and then she was put in the van.

All-female bands like Look Blue Go Purple were a rarity then, so rare that it was the first thing they were asked about whenever they did an interview. Rock had to be different for girls. Surely they couldn't be serious?

Look Blue Go Purple were serious, even if they'd deny it. They built a seminal set—songs embellished with keys, flutes and harmonies, none of which featured a lead break. Lesley Paris, my old schoolmate from Kaikorai Valley, was the Look Blue Go Purple drummer. Lesley had kept fiddling with drums and now she played in a powerful confident manner, like an expansive Moe Tucker with more than a snare and kick. Lesley was another rock scholar with a dress sense as savvy as her classic Citroën car. She was also the manager of the EMI Record store in George Street and her record collection was one of the best in town.

Lesley and Kathy became the rhythm section in our new band.

They were patient at our practices, because Peter and I took forever to tune. Forty minutes of a ninety-minute rehearsal would be filled with the *boing* of our strings.

Dung—dung, dung—dung, dung—dung, we'd go, staring at

each other, frowning, saying, 'Hang on, that's not right.'

Then we'd turn the wrong machine head and have to start again. It never occurred to us to buy a tuner.

Peter may not have been anal about his rock 'n' roll aesthetic, but he was tight with his amps. The vibration had to be right, the treble knob at a precise point between four and five, and Peter would spend forever over his amp, twisting buttons, turning knobs, making adjustments that no one else could hear. Then, when he'd found a good tone, it was back to the torture of tuning.

All this took so long that Lesley started bringing along her knitting to our practices, and a scarf might be a quarter complete by the time we were ready to go.

Peter could be overbearing at rehearsal. He couldn't help himself. One night he was ordering Kathy around, and by then I'd had enough.

'Let her play whatever she fucking wants to play,' I said across my out-of-tune Maya, while Gutteridge huffed and puffed.

We made up the name Cartilage Family, after the TV show family band the Partridge Family. David Cassidy was their star, and he'd been my second favourite after Donny Osmond. We didn't actually realise that 'Cartilage Family' was also an amalgam of Carter and Gutteridge, but, like many good ideas, it just happened.

Peter had the best songs. 'Born in the Wrong Time' and 'Can't Find Water' were later recorded with the Great Unwashed, although I prefer the Cartilage Family's versions, and so does Kathy, but then again, we would.

Because of the tensions in our band, we only played one weekend—two nights at the Empire with Bill Direen's new group, Above Ground. In my memory I see a poster for that show that includes a band from Tīmaru called Say Yes to Apes. Their singer was Kevin Smith, who would later become a famous actor and would die tragically in a fall from a tower on a film set. He was

Dad with his adoptive sister Mary,
South Dunedin, 1952

Marcel, Mum, Dad and me, 1970

Me, Mum, baby Natasha, Tony and Marcel, 1973

Me, Granddad Carter and Mum at our shared birthday
party at Granddad Carter's place, 1974

Jimmi P. Carter about to knock it out of the park,
Christchurch, c. 1974

Terry ('the best-looking man in Dunedin') at the Savoy with Dad and an associate,
Dunedin, 1973

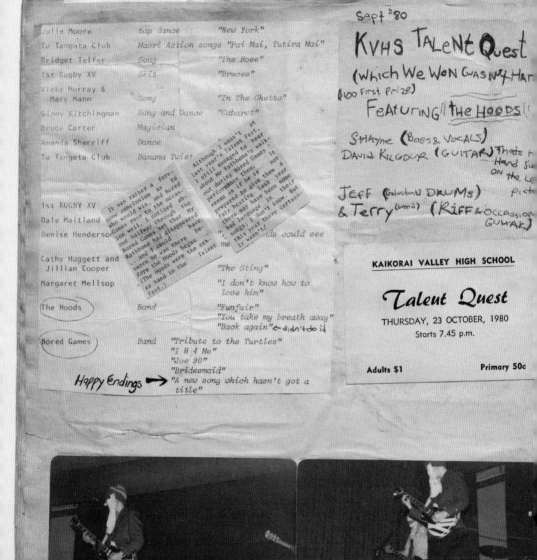

Julie Moore	tap dance	"New York"
Tu Tangata Club	Maori Action songs	"Pai Mai, Tutira Mai"
Bridget Telfer	Song	"The Rose"
1st Rugby XV	Skit	"Bruces"
Vicky Murray & Mary Mann	Song	"In The Ghetto"
Ginny Kitchingman	Song and Dance	"Cabaret"
Bruce Carter	Magician	
Amanda Sherriff	Dance	
Tu Tangata Club	Banana Twist	

1st RUGBY XV

Dale Maitland

Denise Henderson

Cathy Huggett and Jillian Cooper — "The Sting"

Margaret Mellsop — "I don't know how to love him"

(The Hoods) Band — "Funfair"
"You take my breath away"
"Back again" ← didn't do it

(Bored Games) Band — "Tribute to the Turtles"
"I H 4 Me"
"Joe 90"
"Bridesmaid"

Happy Endings → "A new song which hasn't got a title"

Although I wasn't at last year's Talent Fest, I still managed to hear about Mr Rathbone's walk-out during Bored Games performance then it seems as if he is not prepared to give them a fair hearing. Last year there may have been some bad language in their songs, I don't know. But this year there certain ... ly wasn't ...ds could see me in the Talent ...

It was rather a foregone conclusion us to ... who would win, and Bored Games road to the occasion well. I noticed about out halfway through the Bored Games set that Mr Rathbone had disappeared ... and I could have sworn he was there be- fore the Hoods began ... (The Hoods were the oth- er band in the Talent Fest.)

Oct 80 &
Terry's debut **KVHS**

"And it seems to me your LIVING LIKE A TURTLE"

Toy Love

After seven weeks of flat-out touring, the members of Toy Love were in a state of mild collapse when they reached Auckland at the end of their back-home tour. We spoke to them over a glass or two or three of tonic. The most obvious place to start was with the question most returning expatriots have to face, have we changed?

"No," says Chris Knox. "Things have improved with regards to Propeller and Ripper getting things down on record, but I don't think there are any better groups than when we left.

"I thought before we came back, that Sydney audiences were much blander and more conservative. But now we have been forced to realise that New Zealand audiences are every bit as bland and uninspired."

Paul Kean adds, "There are always a small percentage who are into what you're doing.

"Some bands did impress us, though. There were the Playthings in Christchurch, and Bored Games in Dunedin, Shoes This High in Auckland, they are all doing original material."

RiV Sept. 1980

the **Clean**, **Bored Games**, the **Same** (who played four songs) and **Heavenly Bodies** opened for Knox and Co at the Concert Chambers. Craig Scott was seen near the premises.

RiV EXTRA
SEPT 1980

1980

HE"S SO IN

STATE CIRCUS THEATRE WITH AXOLOTL & BORED GAMES
SAT 16TH FEB "LATE NITE SPECTACLE" CATCH IT
11PM

The Sunday gig was excellent value in all respects—5 bands for $2. The Clean, up first, played in Gordons' vein and were consistent if not enthralling. Bored Games, in contrast, were the surest I've seen them in a while and Shae in particular dominated. He seems to exhibit some of the better qualities of the more obvious frontmen (John Lydon and Bob Geldof spring to mind) and Chris Knox was impressed.

The Same were, Heavenly Bodies weren't, for some reason. I'm hoping for sensational gigs from them before they dissolve.

Toy Love, naturally, were the highlights of the day and by then I was able to appreciate them. They'll be back, of course, but when? Maybe when Bored Games have taken over the residency at the Cook? Maybe sooner? Fortunately they have left us an album and 45 to enjoy.

UNIV. CRITIC SEPT 1980

RADIO OTAGO
PRESENT

TOY
LOVE

BACK FROM AUSTRALIA
FOR A 6 WEEK RAGE!!
"SUNDAY - DANCE-JAM"
CONCERT CHAMBER
TOMORROW - SUNDAY
Aug. 24th - 2 p.m. to 6 p.m.
GUESTS' BORED GAMES
HEAVENLY BODIES : Admission $2.

ODT

Fraser and Wayne at Bored Games' second gig, Concert Chamber, 1979
PHOTO: JEFF BATTS

Audience at the KVHS Talent Fest
OTAGO DAILY TIMES

WHO KILLED COLONEL MUSTARD

BORED GAMES

A LARGE audience attended the Kaikorai Valley High School festival of items by magicians, tap dancers, orators and a choir last night.

Soundcheck

Who killed Bored Games?

TIME WAS in this country when a record company would only release a band's record if the band were out there gigging themselves senseless to promote it. But now we have labels like Flying Nun, who show scant respect for such conventional marketing procedures. Flying Nun would think nothing of releasing a record from a band who had broken up a year earlier, who were unknown outside their home town and who were adamant they would never re-form regardless of what happened to, or accrued from, such a record.

Which is exactly what Flying Nun have done with Dunedin's Bored Games and their four-track EP, *Who Killed Colonel Mustard?* It's a bit like the good old days really, when singles (and EPs) were put out simply for what they were, and not as tax-write-off promotional tools for upcoming tours or forthcoming albums. Roger Shepherd at Flying Nun heard the tapes — made one afternoon at the 4XO studios for $110 — and decided there and then they should be 'a record. The fact the band did not exist was furthest from his mind.

So, who were Bored Games? The band came together in early 1979 with Shayne Carter (vocals), Wayne Elsey (bass), Jeff Harford (drums) and a guitarist called Gavin, whom Carter recalls as being awful — "he made up all his own chords".

An ad was soon placed in the local paper for like-minded 15 to 16-year-olds to complete the band. Enter guitarists Fraser Batts and Jonathan Moore, exit Gavin.

There was only one more personnel change before the break-up in mid-1981; Terry Moore (no relation to Jonathan and, at 19, wizened by comparison) coming in on bass for Elsey in August 1980. This freed Elsey to play guitar, which he now does spectacularly for Dunedin's quaintly-named Stones. And it was this final line-up which came back together earlier this year and recorded *Mustard.*

"We were sickened by some of the things that were getting on record from further north," says Carter. "We felt we had much better songs, and we also wanted something to show for over two years' slog." And it was a slog. There was simply nowhere to play for this brash young schoolboy band in 1980-81, and consequently they performed just 25 times in their 27-month career.

"We broke up out of frustration," Carter says. "We were tired of seeing the same old faces when we played, and we usually had to organise the dances ourselves as we couldn't play in pubs. We had no money to get out

Before the demise: from left, Bored Games members Jonathan Moore (guitar), Terry Moore (bass), Fraser Batts (guitar), Shayne Carter (vocals) and Jeff Harford (drums).

of Dunedin, and we were still at school anyway."

Well, you'll be thinking, Bored Games must have been something of a legend while they *were* playing. Surely. Would a record of four of their songs have been released more than a year after their demise if they had been anything less?

Yes and no. Anyone keeping a scrapbook on those 27 months would have found little of the stuff of which legends are made. Real legends, that is.

There was the time they entered the 1981 Battle of the Bands (they pulled out of the 1980 event) and won their heat against a heavy metal band whose singer punched Carter out at the end of the night. "He wanted to know how many weeks I'd been playing for," recalls Carter. "He said he was a professional musician and had been to the North Island." Bored Games weren't chosen for the final.

Then there were some good tapes done at the local folk club which were duly sent off to Mike Chunn. He never replied. And a couple of clips were done for *Dropa Kulcha.* They were never shown.

A pub support gig with Lip Service looked promising, but that was blown at the eleventh hour when Fraser's dad said he couldn't play in a pub. The band then decided to maintain some kind of young soul rebel credibility by not telling Lip Service they weren't coming. Nice.

But then there were the good nights — the *great* nights — when Carter, a precocious amalgam of Chris Knox, Pete Shelley and Johnny Rotten, would lead the band hurtling through their set of (mostly original) songs which, by 1981, had become quite excellent. Knox himself, always studiously careful not to be caught short

of a comment, could only stand and gape when Bored Games supported Toy Love at the Concert Chamber and delivered a version of "Pull Down the Shades" which made a mockery of Toy Love's own.

The *Mustard* EP is a fine representation of the band — four of their best songs, tightly played, and mixed with rock and roll radio firmly in mind. One doubts if there has been a more accessible release for the Joe 90s Carter sings about in the Flying Nun catalogue so far — and that has been achieved without losing one whit of the band's on-stage power.

Ironically, since Bored Games broke up, things have improved immeasurably for Dunedin's young bands. An under-age club, The Pitz, opened in August — every New Zealand city should have one of these — while the Empire Tavern has been laudably committed to young bands for more than a year.

Bored Games played for 20 minutes at the Empire's one-year anniversary party in July, but apart from two *Radio with Pictures* clips done with Peter Janes, that is all anyone is likely to see of them in 1982. Or ever again.

Terry Moore is a vital member of The Chills, a band Batts also spent some time with before leaving to form a new band with Jonathan Moore and Harford.

Carter, possibly too abrasive to be accommodated in the continual cross-pollination that has gone on in the young Dunedin bands these past 18 months, has been fiddling with guitars and talks of having a new band soon. The chief writer in Bored Games and a great singer/performer, Carter will surely re-surface before too long. He is, after all, only 18.

ROY COLBERT

So in the beginning there was The Enemy. Their name culled from the magazine, the band, according to Chris Knox, were too old to be punks. The ex-frontman, now Ponsonby father of two, claims The Enemy were more a natural reaction to the musical drivel on offer locally, and inspired (not dictated to) by the '77 punk rush, they set about to change things.

Whatever their divine guide, The Enemy certainly achieved that goal. Eventually mutating into Toy Love — Godzone's peerless pop product —

The Enemy, Beneficiaries Hall, 1978

they created a lineage in Dunedin, which, even 5½ years on, continues to bear bastard sons.

As The Enemy's trail blazed its way through to Auckland, a host of chubby cheeked young hopefuls rose from the ashes. The Clean were thrust from under The Enemy's wing and fresh-faced converts at Kaikorai Valley and Logan Park High Schools formed Bored Games and The Same respectively.

When Knox & Co. returned as Toy Love in 1980, these three bands (cheeks now firmly in) were carrying the local flag.

For a while Bored Games led the pack, but faced with such obstacles as being denied parental permission to play hotels they eventually succumbed to brick wall bashing and split in late 1981.

▲ Wayne Elsey   ▼ Shayne Carter

Graham Downes, The Verlaines

As remnants of the band joined The Same's remains in The Chills, The Clean had begun to make inroads further north.

With the experience of a forgettable national tour firmly behind them, the brothers Kilgour had the initiative to seek broader horizons. After months of pestering they were finally granted a midweek stint at the Gladstone Hotel in Christchurch, and as we say here in cliche land, the rest is history.

A liaison with Roger "where's the Red Label" Shepherd was struck up . .

Flying Nun Records was born, and The Clean went on to release three consecutive top twenty records through 1981-82.

Such an achievement by an independent set-up bordered on blasphemy within the confines of the New Zealand record industry and indeed Flying Nun ran advertising posters with cartoons of big biz 'n' belly record execs worrying over this new threat from the underground.

The outlet provided by Flying Nun totally rechannelled the direction of local music.

Of the 19 records released by Dunedin bands since 1981, all but one have come from Shepherd's flock — and the Idles don't count for much anyway. (Ha!)

Although failing to appreciate that the best Kiwi music of this decade has come from this city, those who derisively tag the Dunedin music scene as incestuous need only to trace the band trees stemming from the early 80s to substantiate their claims.

Jeff Batts of The Same and Wayne Elsey of Bored Games — both early defectors from their respective camps — got The Stones rolling in 1981. In the meantime, Martin Phillipps teamed up with original Clean bassist, Peter Gutteridge, retained a couple of Same colleagues and founded The Chills. Craig Easton, Phillipp's former guitaring partner, ended up with Graham Downes' Verlaines and by the time Downes (who incidentally used to play along to Sex Pistol's records at parties) had trimmed the band down to a trio, he'd been joined by ex-Chills bassist Jane Dodd who left her old band as two Bored Games members moved in. Alan Haig drummed for The Chills, then The Verlaines, then The Chills again, and . . . so it goes on.

One critic termed it "continual cross pollination", I'd be more inclined to go for total confusion.

Early on in their career Sneaky Feelings described it as a "cosy little scene" that they had difficulty breaking into.

Nevertheless that band, along with The Chills, Verlaines, and Stones,

UNEDIN MUSIC

PHOTOS BY CAROL TIPPETT AND PAUL ROBERTSON

Critic
JULY
1984

ost-Enemy
e Dunedin
ng Nun in

a learning
spiration.
eatles-Love
s and The
ting to be
ted to be
sychedelic
wn all the
"Dunedin
gh now a
r reference
ds.

ve endured
l changes,
ompile the
ls of the
with their
peaking at
arning the
18 months
lipsed its
20 in only
. With an
d for the
are set to

and similar
but single,
was voted
le of last
s and only
em in the
new E.P.
-Nun")
ssify, such

nduted a
but recent
e invigor-
ssful raid
confirm a

Martin Phillips, The Chills

in these modern times, and living,
breathing being, John Collie,
drummed on the band's debut single,
recorded in Auckland earlier this year.

Look Blue Go Purple proudly lay
claim to being Dunedin's first all-girl
band. Annoyingly coy at first, the
band has sharpened up considerably
and their femininity itself means they
occupy an original niche that is all
theirs — even if they "don't sweat," as
put by a rival band member.

If medals were given out for gut-
busting gigging, The Rip would
probably have enough to lead any
Anzac Day parade. Weary of their tag
as Dunedin's perennial support band,
The Rip have branched out on their
own with a recent recording stint in
Christchurch which will hopefully
culminate with a self-financed release.

The Clean, live at the Rumba Bar, Auckland. L - R: Robert Scott, Hamish Kilgour, David Kilgour. ▲

The Verlaines, Auckland, 1982. L - R: Alan Haig, Graham Downes, Jane Dodd. ▲

d. L - R: Robert Scott, Hamish Kilgour, David Kilgour.

heir debut
nite being
nell, will

halt last
Elsey has
ar trio, the
ys were
lsey and
e Carter,
a only a
-up. The
eventually
usual step

Although the music remains unden-
izably distinctive, the target of most
young Dunedin songwriters isn't so
alien — they simply want to write good
songs.

The refusal to adhere to trends
(enter and exit Netherworld Dancing
Toys from the tale) and a respectful
nod towards classic structures means
people aren't losing sight of their roots
— or their honesty (take out The
Idles).

It also means enough great songs to
make you dizzy.

The Doublehappys at the Empire Tavern, Dunedin, 1984
PHOTO: BRENT WILLIAMS

The Stones outside the Gladstone Hotel, Christchurch, 1982:
Jeff Batts, Graeme Anderson, Wayne Elsey
PHOTO: TERRY MOORE

The Doublehappys at the Dowling Street steps, Dunedin, 1984
PHOTO: KAT SPEARS

Me and Wayne halfway between Kaikōura and Picton, Doublehappys tour, June 1985
PHOTO: JOHN COLLIE

It sounds like . . . the Double Happys

THE Double Happys takes its spin on the tour circuit from next week.

The band is heading for Auckland, Wellington and Christchurch as well as a few spots in between and while in Auckland hopes to do the mixing stage of its new EP.

The Chills returned to Dunedin several months ago and while here the Double Happys took the chance to nab some recording gear and make a start on the record at Radio 1's eight-track studio.

Shayne Carter said the EP will include four live standards – Nerves, Needles and Plastic, Moss Monster and Some Fantasy. The ever-popular I Don't Wanna See You Again has been dropped from the intended release, as the recorded version was not a good one.

"It's probably far more representative of the band than the single (The Other's Way/Anyone Else Would). It sounds like the Double Happys," Carter said.

ODT JUN2 5th

THE DOUBLE HAPPYS, a band who have a lot of trouble keeping their feet on the ground, are left to right Wayne Elsey, Shayne Carter and John Collie. They have but one Flying Nun single to their name, but have a reputation as one of the brashest and most good-humoured touring outfits.

Our next venture is a disco at Zanzibar, who have picked up the sponsorship for our dancefloor show, on Thursday 13 June. One week later Dunedin double trouble comes to Varsity with the Double Happys in Shadows (2 flights of stairs above the Cafe) on Thursday June 20. They will also be playing at the Windsor the weekend after.

The Windsor line-up for the next month or so includes some great acts.

June 14, 15: The Bats
June 21, 22: The Double Happys
June 28, 29: The Chills in Space - a live rendition of their very successful on-air radio show in March. The cast and the plot are expanding rapidly so come dressed for the occasion.

Reco

It was Nick Cave's *First Eternity* that inspired a writer to warn of the Leonard Cohen revival undeniably played part in shaping an artist ing apart, but he's never on the hysterics practice and his ilk. Instead, misery were delivered monotone, sometime such regret and resig his music could verge bearable. If Leonard Co drown in his misery you ing down with him.

But the overwhelming cholic air of which made sics of 'So Long, Mar 'Suzanne' is nowhere t on *Various Positions*, C album for six years. The resignation seems to loped to the point wi has given way to wea ness. Once Cohen wa wrists right in front of y hed worry about putti stains on your carpet.

That's not to say there odd great line. "Here's who forgive what you do fewer who don't even toast anyone would rhyme that couples up with 'stand by her'.

But the melodies here ly unmemorable and does Cohen threaten t nation of potent lyric an ful tune – a marriage at best work. It all seems towards the conclusion Leonard Cohen revival a to start here.
Shayne Carter

The Doublehappys get airborne again this weekend. Anyone wanting jump about to lots of loud music should head for the Oriental.

ODT MAY 29th '85

Drinks break filming 'The Other's Way' clip, Christchurch, 1984
PHOTO: JOHN COLLIE

John Collie steps in for Herbie Fuckface at the Roslyn Woollen Mill, Dunedin, 1983
PHOTO: JEREMY FREEMAN

Wayne and his 'Rock on NZ' T-shirt at the Doublehappys' second-to-last gig at Shadows, Auckland, June 1985

a sex symbol when he was an actor, all chiselled and brooding, but when he sang with Say Yes to Apes he was an overweight boy with bum fluff, an odd, eccentric youth who sang enigmatically and played obtuse guitar under a mess of uncombed hair. But in fact it wasn't Say Yes to Apes on that poster. It was the Gorillas, a collection of some of their friends.

Call it ego, call it conflicting philosophies, but there wasn't enough room in the Cartilage Family for both Peter and me. Kathy and Lesley stayed out of our politics, knitting and jamming their own songs on the side. Peter complained that I played too many chords, and I was sick of being bossed around. We said adieu to each other, and went our separate ways.

Peter forged his own path. Obviously he would. His résumé reads the early Clean, early Chills, the Great Unwashed and Snapper. He did seminal recordings with a drum machine, songs he boiled down further into an incantatory minimalism based on the stuff he loved, like Suicide and Can. There were overdriven keys and guitar, no bass, and they sizzled together as one. Peter sang like the devil, a sensitive devil, and his voice croaked as he sang the observations he'd always kept for his songs.

Snapper predated a sound that overseas bands like Loop, Stereolab and Wooden Shjips would use later on. Peter was the master of the modern one-chord mantra. For a while that sound was trendy, but Peter went beyond trends. The only trend he had was his one, which he went at again and again and again. When Snapper played they blazed, at least until the drugs that Peter took wore him down, because he always took twice as much as anyone else, and, no matter how stubborn you are, that will eventually get you. His body began to suffer, and I was shocked one day when I drove into Dunedin and caught sight of him in my rear-view mirror. He was hobbling along on crutches, looking about eighty-five.

The younger kids in Dunedin had a nickname for all the older junkies who gathered for coffee at a bakery on a corner across from the Botanical Gardens. Crusties, they called them, and Peter was king of the Crusties. The pharmacy for picking up methadone scripts was in the mall just over the road.

I heard rumours in the 2000s that Peter was in trouble, that he'd been committed to a psychiatric ward after an incident involving the armed offenders squad. Pete's obsession with guns and war had turned into something more ominous. He'd been seen wandering around by the needle exchange in Moray Place carrying a rifle.

I have two photos from 1991 that were taken in Dunedin before a gig to celebrate the tenth anniversary of Flying Nun. It's from a studio at the local university radio station, where they've gathered various Flying Nun luminaries. There's Bob Scott, David Kilgour, Martin Phillipps and myself, and beside us is Peter Gutteridge. Peter had gatecrashed the interview, and he was seriously pissed off that he hadn't been invited. Flying Nun had had enough of him by then and he'd become persona non grata.

In the very first photo everyone's smiling; everyone that is except Peter, who looks stoned and very annoyed. In the next photo, David Kilgour, who has known Peter for years and been one of his most loyal friends, has his hands around Peter's throat and is pretending to strangle him while the rest of us laugh, and you can see everyone thinking, 'Oh, Gutteridge.' Gutteridge looks pissed, even while being mock-strangled, because he's not in on the joke. But David's action speaks for all of us, because Peter could be frustrating and sometimes you really did want to strangle him. He could be a burden, because like all junkies he was myopic, which only exaggerated the way he naturally was, and not in a way he could use creatively.

I last saw Peter in 2011. He'd come up to Auckland for a holiday and he visited my house in Te Atatu Peninsula out west. He stayed for a night, and we had our first decent conversations for at least a decade and a half. Peter had weaned himself off methadone by taking magic mushrooms, and while I was amazed that he'd achieved this—he had always seemed the most committed opiate user I'd known—I appreciated how he had done it. To free yourself of addiction, you have to flick a great switch and turn on a big light to see in a different way. Psychedelics can do this, because your ego is subsumed and the rationales you use to hurt yourself can disappear. On psychedelics, you might even realise that, as a collection of molecules, you're just part of a wider flow around you.

That was a stream that Peter plugged into anyway whenever he taped down a key on his synthesiser and the sound filled his house as he wandered about his day, smoking, noodling on his piano and guitar, reading war books.

Shamans realise that music, like life, comes down to vibration, pulse and soul. The rest is interference and human traps, like ego, organisation and politics.

I was happy to see the old Peter, because he had a spark, and the same dry humour, but he was still a pain in the arse to play with. We tried recording some tunes at my house, but Peter was back to his old tricks and I quickly realised my role in this recording was to be his engineer. He listened politely while I tried an idea, but I could see it took an effort. Soon we were back to Peter going, 'What about this?' and saying to me, 'Push record.'

In 2014 Peter passed through Auckland on his way to America. A record of his old drum machine tracks was being put out in the States, and he was off to do some solo gigs. It was his first time outside of New Zealand. He'd never got overseas when most of us had. But he could only blame himself.

I heard Peter was in town and sent a message to a mutual friend he was kicking around with. I'd been given tickets to the New Zealand Symphony Orchestra and I thought Peter might enjoy it.

The other guy came instead, which I thought was a shame, because as Mahler's Ninth Symphony played out with its unutterable poignancy, and I sat with tears on my face, I knew Pete would have loved it too.

The Clean were in New York at the same time as Peter, but they were reluctant to let him guest because they knew Peter would take over. Being in Manhattan must have been a big deal to Peter because to him it was Mecca, home to the Velvets, the New York Dolls, the Ramones, Suicide, and the original punk scene that had given him a lot of his cues. In LA, he caved in to some of the temptations that Hollywood had to offer.

Maybe he figured he'd seen enough, because when he returned to New Zealand, a few days after being apprehended at the airport because of his strange behaviour on the plane, he killed himself.

I was a pallbearer at Peter's funeral. David Kilgour and Chris Heazlewood carried Peter too, fellow guitar slingers, who, at one time or another, had played in Peter's band. When it came down to it, we were all on his side.

A small group of us took Peter out to be buried by the tranquil inlet at Purakaunui, and as we laid him down and covered him, David threw in twenty dollars because Peter was always bugging him for money.

I thought back to the last time I'd seen Peter, when we'd sat in the sun looking out over Waitematā Harbour.

Peter had told me about a book he'd read, a New Zealand novel called *Wulf*, which he said he'd really liked. I read that book after Peter died, and it had the same repetitive, incantatory air that Peter used in his music.

I hope you're still out there Peter, feeding the cosmic vibration.

In the mid-eighties, around the time of their *10 O'clock in the Afternoon* EP, the Verlaines were my favourite band. They were on a high wire between two opposing buildings, a bridge between classical and punk. They may have used the same barre chord the Clean used, the one where the two little strings were left open so it rang like two guitars, but they also applied lessons from Graeme Downes's studies, like baroque melody lines, odd time signatures, complex dynamics. Neither influence obscured the other.

Onstage, Graeme was a mess. His white shirt and black fringe were soaked, his face was screwed up and red. Tracks like 'Burlesque' and 'The Ballad of Harry Noryb' took heaving twists and turns. Graeme did quiet/loud long before Nirvana or the Smashing Pumpkins did. The unpredictable shifts in his songs inspired me and I used some of those devices later in my own tunes.

Another of my favourite musical observations comes from a *New York Times* critic who, writing about Bach, described Bach's chord choices as 'unexpected yet inevitable'. Graeme made those kinds of choices too.

But it was the rhythm section that completed his band.

Robbie Yeats was a red-haired drummer and a native of Gore, a little town not known for its hope. I liked Robbie from the time he shared a joint with me outside a pub when we were both about eighteen. Robbie was passionate and good-natured—at least, he was when he wasn't drunk. Then he could get sour and start grumbling, but that was a condition I could relate to too.

I didn't get off to such a good start with the bass player Jane Dodd, because I'd told her I didn't like hippies.

'But my older brother's a hippy!' Jane shot back, genuinely hurt.

I'm sure Graeme fastidiously plotted the music, and told his band where everything should go, but when Jane and Robbie put it there, they were invested. They told their own part of the story. It was a world away from reading charts.

All great bands have that, where their collective energy is bigger—the Clean, the Chills with Martyn Bull and Terry Moore, the Beatles, Booker T. and the M.G.'s, and whoever else you have to name. The individuals drive each other into a space beyond a singular conception, where someone thinks of something the other hadn't, and then a new dimension appears.

I had that in buckets with Wayne Elsey, in our band the Doublehappys.

Wayne's been dead for over thirty years now and there's a lot of him I don't remember. Specifics about where he lived and what he did, with who and when. He died in a train accident when he was twenty-one. That's the conclusion. I still carry him in memory, and a lot of people do. It's remarkable, and touching, that what Chris Knox described in a eulogy as a 'short, sweet life' could leave such a vivid impression. When I think of Wayne he surpasses memory, and becomes almost a feeling. The strength of that feeling, even now, shows how important he was to me.

Three years ago someone slagged Wayne off on the internet. They even made a joke about the way Wayne died, and it was bewildering that someone would bother to do that, especially after thirty years. I wrote to this person to defend my friend, which only brought more abuse. I left this person to their small life in a caravan park near Thames.

It shocked me that there was someone who even disliked Wayne, because I know no one else who did.

Then again, I fell out with Wayne for a short time myself, after he left school and Bored Games. I thought he was a poser and he thought I was obnoxious, or maybe it was the other way around.

After I left school, I shared my first flat with Wayne in a place above Terry's Bookstore. My room was windowless and minuscule, with barely enough room for a bed. It was an ideal location for creative masturbation, and projectile vomiting if I got too drunk.

One of our flatmates was the flyspray snorter from Cumberland

Street. He'd make half-baked suicide attempts on Saturday nights, and on Sunday mornings we'd have to wipe his blood off the kitchen knife to carve our bread.

Our other flatmate was Chris Hughes, the boy from Opoho who'd been a friend of the Same. Chris could get cranky, and he was always getting beaten up on weekends, because he'd be drunk and would tell the wrong load of carboys to fuck off. His curly hair and glasses and the fact he got beaten up when drunk meant I always lumped him in with David Mitchell, the wild guitarist in the 3Ds, who I met a few years later. Dave had the same physical characteristics and the same modus operandi.

Chris was a staunch supporter of the New York Dolls and the Stooges, even though he donned a three-piece suit during the week and politely served people at a camera shop. His laugh came from so deep in his chest it almost had an echo. Chris suffered an aneurysm in his twenties, and spent his last few years in a vegetative state before he died. I visited him once in hospital, and I told him I loved him, and although his eyes were milky I thought I saw him smile.

In our flat in the main street, we drank and played records loudly. We'd break Codral cold tablets in half and chew the yellow pseudoephedrine centres, then we'd speed and go all night. Sometimes Wayne and I went for midnight drives in the van he used for his job—aimless, jokey meanders under the starry Otago sky. We picked up a hitchhiker near Mosgiel once, around one a.m., and because we could, we dropped him off fifty miles south at his house in Kaitangata.

One of our favourite records was the Gordons' first album, and their song 'Spic and Span' smashed around the house. The Gordons were from South Canterbury and all their songs were chants against the zombies around them. We played the early Fall records a lot too. Mark E. Smith yelped 'Pay your rates!' almost like it was a reminder on a Post-It note. We loved the perversity of the Fall's sound, how fucked up it was and how purposefully unpopular. Mark E. Smith had a good range of sweaters.

A year later, in 1983, when we were both free agents, Wayne and I decided to form a band. We may have made the decision at a party where we sat on top of a tall closet, with our heads almost touching the roof, softly spitting on the back of a duffel coat worn by a person we didn't like. That was a template for the Doublehappys.

We thought we'd just have two guitars, and not bother with a bass. The Cramps did that, and they were another of our favourite bands.

The early Cramps records—*Psychedelic Jungle, Songs the Lord Taught Us, Gravest Hits*—panted with sex and heat. They had a song called 'Under the Wires' which celebrated obscene phone calls. There were none of the schlocky Vegas-isms they used later on. We never saw any videos of the Cramps, so our mental impression of them was based on their album covers, where they glared out like creatures from the deep or a gang at the back of the alley.

Drummers can be difficult. They're nearly always the weirdest member in the band. Drummers are like soccer goalkeepers— the eccentrics out the back. So Wayne and I dispensed with a drummer. We used a drum machine instead, built into a budget Casiotone keyboard with three useable beats—fast rock, slow rock and samba. In tribute to these limits, we christened our drum machine Herbie Fuckface.

Herbie presented his own set of problems, especially live, where we couldn't turn him off. We'd kick but miss the off switch and instead he'd speed up or break into a waltz or a happy foxtrot. We also bust a lot of strings at our gigs, which was the price you paid when you played on crappy guitars. My record was four strings in one song, when we were supporting the Gordons at the Captain Cook Hotel. *Ping ping ping ping* they went between chorus, verse and bridge. Herbie had a particularly disastrous gig at the same show, interjecting with unknown rhythms we'd set off with our feet.

We also got into abusing the audience at our gigs. Well, I did. Wayne was always slyer and quieter about it. It started off as a joke—telling our friends to fuck off was just a bit of banter, a bit of Johnny Rotten—but when I was drunk it could take a sour turn. Telling your mates they were a bunch of wankers was fine, but it wasn't so good said to a room full of strangers.

I'd behave the same way at post-gig parties, where, even drunker, I'd reel around spouting an aggressive and confused version of what I really thought.

I guess I can map that hostility, can trace the reasons why I was so confrontational, back into my childhood—but it just added to the impression held by an increasing number of people that I was an obnoxious little prick who needed sorting out. At a gig in Auckland at the Windsor, I asked if someone could throw us a beer, and someone did: a full jug that drenched me head to toe. I could only laugh, because I'd asked for it, but it was a wonder I wasn't lit up. At the same gig, as a parting shot I told the audience I hoped they got run over later. I heard a gasp of horror. I still shake my head and shrink at the memory of that. There were many similar moments when my mouth and my resentment got in the way.

After Wayne died, all that ended. I became quiet on stage, reserved between songs, and, while I was and still am capable of expressing my thoughts, I usually keep the dark ones to myself.

There's a tape from a rehearsal we had with Herbie that still makes me smile in a way that none of the other stuff can.

We recorded it in late 1983 on a two-track machine in our practice room at the disused Roslyn Woollen Mill, just up the road from our old school. My parents had once worked at that mill, and they'd put me in the daycare centre across the road. I was a pre-schooler then, so I remember only the white-haired lady there called Mrs Snow, and busting all day because I didn't like the gloomy loos.

That tape has all that was great about the Doublehappys. Herbie pounding away, me and Wayne on teen punk guitar—not the bootboy punk; more the sixties punk, shredding, swirling and frenetic like the Velvets on 'Heroin' or 'Sister Ray', or chiming, deathly and half out of tune, like on 'The Black Angel's Death Song'.

Later, in his liner notes for a Doublehappys compilation, Roy Colbert wrote that this 'was the sound young people make when they're in love with the electric guitar and think other people are full of shit.'

That's what that sound was.

On a two-chorder called 'I Can't Say', Wayne lets rip, and his vocals are like a compilation of all the best bits of *Pebbles*. Wayne sang like a garage punk, slurring his words, liberal with his tuning. The disaffection in his voice told you he didn't care, but it also said that he did.

I had a song called 'Barbie Bites You to Bits', which is about attractive hairdresser girls who've decided they don't like you, because, even if I didn't go to a hairdresser, those girls were still around.

After that came 'Wrapped Up in Myself Again', which is a very good title. That had a Celtic lilt like the Velvets' 'Run Run Run'.

'Moss Monster' is lax, obnoxious rockabilly, like a Kaikorai Valley Cramps. There's also 'Retards on 45', which was our take on 'The Stars on 45 Medley', which was a hit at the time. It was a series of old chart-toppers strung together over an empty Euro beat, and Herbie did a convincing empty beat.

Our medley was a sarcastic mix of the Partridge Family's 'I Think I Love You', Donny and Marie's 'Deep Purple', and 'Don't Make Love to that Bottle Baby (When You Should Be Making

Love to Me)' which was the theme song for an anti-alcohol campaign. We scattered some of our own bits in, like—

Tick-tock tick-tock tick-tock tick-tock
Riiiiiiiiiiiinnnnnnnnnng
Time to get up!

I sang 'tick' and Wayne sang 'tock', in expression of our brotherhood. The second time around, we expanded on our theme.

Riiiiiinnnngg—time to get up . . .
And get fucked!

—which was a description of a favourite activity, often referred to as 'wake 'n' bake', as well as a message for the public.

There's also a version of our hit that never was, 'I Don't Want to See You Again', about a hairdresser girl who didn't like me. At the end of the song I screamed, 'I don't want to see you again', for minutes, until my throat ached, or my voice simply gave out. Wayne took off in a reverbed roar on his guitar, and his line was gorgeous, all regret and panic.

The tape ended with 'I've Got Something to Say to You', which was a bit of an anti-climax. It was a report on my social behaviour.

You told me I was bleeding at your place,
That I had cuts all over my face,
Well I got something to say to you!
I got something to say!

The defiance makes me laugh. The last thing the Doublehappys were concerned about was being likeable. 'Fuck you,' we said. It was a brave stance to take in our small, self-righteous town.

155

While the Doublehappys hoped to project that we didn't give a shit, underneath we did, which was the dichotomy that gave us our oil. Wayne wasn't a punk. Like Carey Hibbert, he was thoughtful and empathetic. Wayne read books, good, complicated ones with sentences you needed to read twice. His selection was the kind found in university syllabuses, not in the backs of vans full of old clothes. The lyrics Wayne wrote, under the noise, were insightful, like real literature, and when I look back on some of them now I shake my head at their precociousness.

When Wayne and I played together we never once discussed what we were doing. No one ever told the other what they should play. I didn't explain what the song was about and he didn't have to say either. We just did it. We knew. It was the most unspoken, organic relationship I've had with another musician. We were from the same place, with the same history.

Later on in my life, when I edged towards becoming a 'proper' musician, I'd listen, or not listen, to the Doublehappys. I was a bit embarrassed by their rawness: this was out of tune, that could have been more accurate, maybe that would've been better if it was recorded properly, but when I made those criticisms, I was missing what really counted—the juice. As someone wise once said, the only mistake you can make in rock 'n' roll is being too careful about it.

The Doublehappys crashed along in their own uncareful way.

In our first publicity shot, taken in the lounge at Lesley Paris's in North East Valley, Wayne and I stand inches apart, squirting each other with water pistols.

*

Our Roslyn Woollen Mills tape impressed some of the big wigs up in Auckland. Chris and Doug loved it, and Doug invited us on a tour of universities with three other Flying Nun bands. The

156

Chills were the unofficial headliners, because at that point they were blowing up. The other bands were the Expendables from Christchurch and Children's Hour from Auckland. And then there were the Doublehappys.

We'd decided to ditch Herbie—for a machine he was very unreliable. We found ourselves a drummer. This was John Collie, who'd grown up in the same street as Wayne in Glenross, just like Wayne's drummer Graeme Anderson from the Stones.

John had gone to Kaikorai Valley High School too, but he was so quiet I hadn't really seen him. He was a dreamy boy, good at art and tech drawing. His father ran Collie's Pharmacy, which sat exposed in the top Brockville shops and was always being broken into, it seemed more out of habit than any sort of malice. All of the Collies were swimmers and had well-developed chests—John, his two older sisters Bronwyn and Lynne, brother Geoff, and his dad. John's father was never a fan of our bands, because to him it didn't make sense. Mr Collie never came to a single Doublehappys or Straitjacket Fits show. My parents, all three, were way more supportive than that.

John was the quietest member of the Doublehappys and was probably overshadowed by the skites up front. But he carved his own niche, full of idiosyncratic asides, like his weird little guitar riffs and his insistence that Genesis with Phil Collins was actually worth hearing.

I never heard it.

When I asked my boss at 4XO for time off to do Doug's tour, he refused. That's when I left and went on the dole. It's probably the best decision I've made. At work, I was always being warned about the state of my hair or trousers. I'd felt compromised working there; so much of it, the big voices, the behaviour, the inane music, went against my punk rock ideals. I was supposed to find City Council meetings interesting, but to me it was a bunch of dull old duffers self-importantly passing bylaws and building drains. I was

157

treated with great condescension by these people, because I was obviously a boy, and I shudder at the square look I had to adopt just to get through the day.

'I heard you were abusing people at the Empire,' my boss would say to me on a Monday, because he had tentacles all over town. I didn't have to wear that anymore, the same way I didn't have to wear the mustard-coloured trousers from Hallensteins or the sports jacket from Bob Campbell's that I loathed.

When I left 4XO, I started wearing mascara and fingernail polish, which looked better when it got chipped, and I wore my hair any damn way I liked. I grew it out to a mullet that went off in a thousand directions, and I'd grab big handfuls of peroxide and just chuck it on at the back. I did it because I could. As some people have noted, it looked like I had a skunk on my head. 'Party at the back,' others have said. That haircut became even more famous when I put it in the clip for 'She Speeds'.

Whenever the *New Zealand Herald* or some other paper compiles a list of the greatest New Zealand mullets, mine is always near the top. It became an object of ridicule, but the people ridiculing it wore Hallensteins trousers and sports jackets, so they can all go take a jump.

I also lost a lot of weight. There had been a day when we'd gone to Christchurch to visit Roger, and a group of us were frolicking in the surf at Sumner. David Pine was there. David was in Sneaky Feelings, who were relatively new on the Dunedin scene. Sneaky Feelings were always a step aside from the rest of us, because they were nervous university students from middle-class backgrounds. I was never a fan, despite David writing some killer tunes on their first album. The band's nods to 'proper' musicianship were off-putting, as was their drummer slagging off the Stones. He'd said they were Neanderthals. The same drummer skited that the latest Sneaky Feelings track had hints of 'Philly Soul', but I could never hear it. To me, he was deluded. The early Sneaky Feelings gigs were entertaining, though, because they'd have fights on stage and someone was always running off in tears.

David Pine was Sneaky Feelings' diplomat. He worked the counter at the Governor's Café in town, where we all went before making mischief on Saturday nights. David got along with everyone. He went on to become a real-life diplomat, and eventually the ambassador to the Philippines.

He wasn't diplomatic that day in the surf.

'Don't worry, we're not going to drown,' he said, 'because we can use Shayne's spare tyre.'

It was true. All the booze I'd been drinking, the toasted cheese sandwiches I'd get from the café across the road from 4XO, and the junk food I subsisted on all the rest of the time lay in a ring around my middle. I was embarrassed and starved myself for months.

My new slimmed-down look worked to my advantage, although some people mistook me for a junkie. My cheekbones came out, and I assumed a workable profile. Girls' eyes often used to drift past me, but now they paused to have a look. If I was going to be fully rock 'n' roll, then my cheekbones would be a part of it.

On the cover of the first Doublehappys single, flanked by my two starved bandmates, I'm the skinniest in the band.

The university tour, named the Looney Tour, with the Chills, the Expendables and Children's Hour, was a month-long dream. Partying with your mates, getting drunk, smoking loads of pot, ridiculing audiences, and playing searing rock 'n' roll, ticked every one of my boxes. It's like you're in a bucket and people keep pouring in fun.

There were over twenty of us on the road, and a dog called Gonzo. We'd only just met Children's Hour. They were from Auckland and they'd been talent-scouted by Chris and Doug, who'd wandered past their practice room one day and heard their musical thuggery. Children's Hour played a cacophony, a bit like the Birthday Party, and their singer Chris Matthews got drunk and snarky, which was a fun part of their show. Their red-haired bassist, Johnny Pierce, wore mascara, and usually a black blazer and trousers. Johnny was a talented sportsman, and although he didn't talk about that, there were hints in the doubles tennis matches him and a mate played with me and Wayne at the end of the tour. A few years later, Johnny hanged himself in the band practice room.

The Children's Hour guitarist, Grant Fell, was Māori, and when he played with his feet set firmly on the ground, swinging his shoulders side to side, he made a cutting sound.

Bevan Sweeney, the drummer, was like a male model version of Jesus but without the beard, and women throughout the universe drifted off in his pale, come-to-bed eyes. Like his band, his drumming was muscular and aggressive.

Children's Hour were our kind of people, and we were their people too.

The Expendables were more considered. Jay Clarkson, their singer and guitarist, was the only woman on the tour, which never seemed an issue—but only Jay can tell you about that. Rock was a mainly male domain then. Female performers were usually found at the lighter end of the spectrum, but Jay could hold her own in any musical setting. She was an innovative guitarist who used unusual chord shapes and strange progressions which she'd hover across in a weightless, distanced voice. She was almost a new school Joni Mitchell. Jay always had her own sound. I saw her play recently with her new band the Containers, and the name suited her music perfectly: cool, contained, with the usual pointy corners.

The Chills were the biggest name on the Looney Tour. Their early classics had worked their magic. Martin Phillipps had overhauled his entire line-up, a habit he'd continue for the next umpteen years, but the band was polished and together and they did justice to his set of songs. From the factory line of golden boys, Martin was the most golden of all. People were getting excited overseas, and there were plans to take the Chills to the top half of the world.

The Chills were always being given the best slots, when the crowd was its most lubricated and responsive, and the rest of us started to get annoyed. The Doublehappys were usually first to play. We couldn't argue, because we were the newest band and we hadn't made a record, but in Wellington the Doublehappys made their protest by smoking so much hash oil that we joed out on the table in the backstage room so no one else could use it. I'd become very good at getting out of it and passing out on tables or on the floor at someone's party. Wayne, and sometimes John, could do that too. After our nap on the table in Wellington, we had a meeting where everyone aired their grievances.

It didn't undercut our togetherness. The Flying Nun thing was catching on, and there were hundreds of people at the gigs, despite none of the bands being played on the radio. It was a pure and uncontrived popularity, a time when student radio barely existed. We were playing music that the kids, the sharper ones anyway, could relate to, and although we were never so noble or missionary, it was an indigenous music, when so far there hadn't been a lot of that. Maybe the Māori bands playing reggae, but even that music seemed based on Bob Marley. Our music described who we were and our place of emanation.

'These people aren't living in the real world,' announced the New Zealand head of CBS in an interview, sadly shaking his head.

At the end of the Looney Tour, the Doublehappys recorded their first single, 'The Double B Side', at Lab Studios in Auckland, with Terry Moore as our producer. We also recorded a Windsor

Castle gig, and five of the tracks we'd played, including 'I Don't Want to See You Again' and 'Big Fat Elvis', were released by a Scottish label on a live EP called *How Much Time Left Please?* several years later.

'Big Fat Elvis' was another of our hits that never was. I'd first seen Elvis in the film *King Creole*, when he performed 'Trouble' standing on a table, which was all I needed to see. I'd also read Albert Goldman's biography of Elvis. It was an outrageous, slanderous book full of inaccuracies, mis-observations and pseudo-professorial jealousy. But the theme of a great artist who'd lost his way filled our song 'Big Fat Elvis'.

Wayne played thick slabby chords, while I sang—

Big Fat Elvis was dying daily
Big Fat Elvis doesn't know what the past means
So I have to explain
To Big Fat Elvis
Isn't what he should be
I say, hey Elvis
You gotta listen to me

You've gotta kick the lot
You gotta stay away from God
Or you're a goner Elvis

A few months later we got a friend to paint a backdrop we could use at our final series of gigs—a giant, sweaty Elvis in his rhinestone Vegas suit. Above that was the red Doublehappys logo, which we'd based on the style of the lettering in a poster for *Apocalypse Now*.

Wayne's song 'Anyone Else Would' was heavily influenced by Lou Reed's *Berlin* album, which had become one of our favourite records. The bleakness, the hopelessness, the couldn't-care-less of it all. Wayne's song told the same story that *Berlin* did, of lost people doing 'booze, pills and barbiturates and . . . anything at all'. Ours was a less glamorous take than Lou's, but in its own down-home way it was equally decadent. It's one of Wayne's best tunes. The way his guitar slides down as he sing-talks in a bruised, punk sadness. 'Say what you mean, mean what you say, say what you mean, mean what you say!' went the chorus, becoming more assertive.

Martin Phillipps, Jay Clarkson and I sang backing vocals, but because we did a long 'Say-ay-ay-ay-ay' and ended with 'Say what you mean', we were finishing the words the opposite way to Wayne—but we didn't have the time, or the patience, to fix it.

Predictably, my song was based around A, E and D, and it held those chords all the way through, but I sang different melodies around them so it felt like different parts with a verse, a chorus and an outro. That became a trick of mine. It's a good way to make a song feel together and keep up its momentum. To the listener, it still sounds like separate bits.

'The Other's Way' was a song about another girl who, although she wasn't a hairdresser, still didn't like me. I played amateur slide guitar as an overdub, tuning my guitar to a chord and only just reaching the notes. But it wailed like an ambulance. Wayne played a fat lead break, because he had a bassier tone to fill out our vacant bottom end. My guitar stayed trebly and crappy on top.

'The Other's Way' still sounded like pop. Its most memorable lyric turned out to be the bit repeated at the end: 'If you wanna know the meaning of meaningless, then I'll see you on the seventh of May.' That was something I'd said to the girl who didn't like me. I'd told her I might be free the next week on the seventh, but that made no difference to her, her life or her itinerary.

I still see that line being bandied about on obscure Internet forums or as a pop reference on social media. I think it's because the line, with its date, is unusual and specific, so it's the piece that pops out and that people remember, even if they wouldn't have a clue what the seventh of May is about.

We designed the cover in our old red, black and white. Red made sense, because it was the colour of the Doublehappy firecracker. On the front, the band leaned forward through a label-sized hole. The back cover was a photo of us doing the same, but taken from the back.

I look nineteen, skinny and lovely, with a floppy long fringe, dressed in cut-off gloves and a sparkly glitter skivvy I later wore for the Straitjacket Fits video 'Hail'.

I can't speak on behalf of the other two.

When 'The Double B Side' came out, despite it not really capturing our thunder, we were stoked to hear ourselves on vinyl.

I was seeing a young woman from Auckland who'd come down to study arts and law at university. A perk of living in Dunedin was the annual tsunami of beauties from the north who were always more fashionably dressed and better presented than us Dunedin scruffs. This girl lit up the room. I thought I'd experienced love during those desperate teenage fixations, or in the midst of a hopeless rebuttal, but when you're run over by the real thing, you realise how short of the mark your other delusions were.

She'd come along to a Doublehappys lunchtime gig at the university, and she'd been impressed by one of our songs. 'Choking on Lovesick' was a song that girls from Remuera didn't often get to hear.

Choking on lovesick
S-I-C-K

Sick sick sick sick
In fact I think I might even be choking it
It's all over over to you-oo
It's all over to you-oo

That was the sum of it. She told me later that Carey Hibbert had talked to her, too—Carey was no fool—and it had become a close run thing. But I'd managed to get in the same car as her, one night after a party.

What a lovely, and kind, young woman she was.

This was the girl I lost my virginity to. When I was twelve, I boasted that I'd lost my virginity to a girl in Halfway Bush. I gave myself a hickey on the shoulder, because that was as far as I could reach, but I was busted by someone in the playground who said, 'You could have given that to yourself.'

I kept my exploits secret after that.

The Auckland girl was my first real love and my first serious relationship. We were together for two and a half years. She supported me in the time after Wayne died, when I went off the rails.

We promised each other that if we ever separated we'd get together in our sixties and do a boat trip up the Nile, because our sixties were as far away as the Nile.

Instead, our relationship ended in our early 20s, when I kissed another girl at a party. A guy ran off and told tales to my girlfriend, which he backed up with a carefully plotted sob story, so she left me to go out with him. After she left, I sank right to the bottom of the river.

We travelled to Christchurch to make a video for 'The Other's Way' on a budget roughly equal to the other video budgets around, somewhere between zero and a hundred dollars. We drove up with our friend Jeremy Freeman, who was now our manager. Jeremy was dark-haired, gay, well-dressed, a little camp—he may have tried kissing me when we were both drunk, but the memory is on the underside of a blur. Jeremy lived up North East Valley and he zipped around in a little white sports car, and he may have gone on to make a lot of money. I don't think he had any managerial master plan for our band, although he did help book gigs and arrange travel, and he once smooth-talked a store owner into lending him a video camera to film us over a weekend. Jeremy fell more and more in love with the zoom over those two nights, and most of his footage is unwatchable. He did keep the camera still long enough to capture regular versions of 'Elvis' and 'Anyone Else Would'.

We filmed the video for 'The Other's Way' in a warehouse in Central Christchurch. The cameraman was a friend of Roger's called Robin Neate. I'd made one video before which had been broadcast nationally on *Radio with Pictures* for 'Happy Endings', a Bored Games song I'd written about Marilyn Monroe.

I'd become obsessed with Marilyn Monroe in my mid-teens after seeing a picture of her body in an Elton John songbook. In the photo she was wrapped in a blanket beside the words to 'Candle in the Wind'. It struck me as gross and sad that she was still being exploited in death, and that someone thought it was a picture worth taking. Marilyn was an innocent surrounded by dogs. I felt she needed to be protected, even by a sixteen-year-old in Dunedin decades after her death. That protectiveness was a feeling she aroused in a lot of men—Norman Mailer, Arthur Miller, the Kennedys and a million others—all seduced by her little girl lostness and the way she went *boop boop de boop* while strumming a ukulele in a tight black dress. Maybe wanting to protect a vulnerable woman was something I'd learned at home.

Who cares about Marilyn Monroe
That's not who they saw
They just saw the Barbie doll
With feelings best ignored
Who cares about Marilyn Monroe
For years now she's been gone
We destroyed the Barbie doll
But we can carry on
We can carry on . . .

It was very earnest, but then again so were my feelings about Marilyn. She pushed all the buttons of nostalgia, lust, the desire for fame, the yearning for glamour, fantasies of another place and time, and the harshness and cruelty of people.

When Bored Games shot the video for 'Happy Endings', we also did a one-take shot for another song from our EP. It was filmed in a giant safe where we hung Glad Wrap from the walls and off our guitars. With the lights, it was a dazzling, economical effect, and we utilised the trick in our clip for the Doublehappys.

In the video, clear plastic clung to underfed torsos. Under the lights, the sweat had collected and cooled, and because the warehouse was freezing we entered the preliminary stage of exposure. We fought this off by drinking copious amounts of beer. Somewhere through this, the camera stopped working so Robin had to run off to find another one. Maybe it was a super-8 camera, because there was no sound sync, and in the final footage our lips don't match the song.

'The Double B Side' was released to the usual insightful domestic reviews.

'I wish there was a Flying Nun band that could actually sing or at least play in time, but I guess that's part of their charm,' snored the man in the *Christchurch Star*.

'The blending of chorus line vocals with faster guitar riffs in the second B-side "Anyone Else Would", would make it my pick,' stumbled someone in the *Midweeker*.

'Well presented with photos, graphics and lyrics,' enthused the *Southland Times*.

'Another neat Nun number,' said someone else, as thousands dashed off for the store.

I've always found the standard of rock journalism in New Zealand to be pretty desultory. There's a handful of good writers, but I rarely get asked about a lyric or the construction of a song. It's all, 'So where did you get the name from?' or 'When did you last play Hamilton?' I'm hardly ever asked about my craft, what I spend all my time doing.

I continued with my own rock reporting and started doing reviews for *Rip It Up*, where I rubbished new releases by John Cale, Leonard Cohen and the Cure. I let Iggy Pop off, but that was his greatest hits. I wrote for *Rip It Up* on and off for several years, and later wrote a humorous column for the magazine as a character called Buffy O'Reilly. Buffy was a mixture of me, Eccles from the Goons, Ignatius from *A Confederacy Of Dunces*, and Pee-wee Herman. Buffy was a naïve idiot who stumbled around the New Zealand music scene, taking pot-shots at people I didn't like.

'Ray Columbus is an old fart, but a small one who causes titters around the table,' Buffy said. I didn't actually dislike Ray—he once offered Straitjacket Fits a publishing contract, and the few times I met him he was supportive and friendly. But the fart analogy was too good to pass over.

'Joan Baez went out with Bob Dylan, but so did nasal whining,' Buffy wrote.

I'm sure Buffy gave Mike Chunn a stuffing.

Eventually I was busted on nationwide TV. After criticising the presenters of a music show—something about their adenoids—I was exposed as the mind behind Buffy. There were small-town howls of outrage, so I eventually packed him up. It wasn't safe to be rubbishing all my contemporaries, when I was part of the same minuscule scene.

That didn't stop me writing an overview of the Dunedin scene for the university magazine *Critic* around the time of 'The Double B Side'. I big-upped our record but elsewhere I may have been more critical.

'Promotional video must rank as one of last year's most embarrassing,' I wrote about the Sneaky Feelings single 'Be My Friend'.

'Big crowd-pleasers who've yet to produce a decent record,' I said about Netherworld Dancing Toys, a nu soul band crushingly popular with students.

'Brewery-sponsored vinyl slobber by loathsome pub hacks,' I noted sombrely of Rockylox.

'Stodge rock by dated metallists,' for the Idles.

'Their only vinyl stab, hearing it explains why,' about Broken Models.

I wandered around Dunedin feeling misunderstood, wondering why people didn't like me. I was only paying homage to the *New Musical Express*.

I wrote a good review for the Verlaines, who I made a cameo with for their video for 'Death and the Maiden'. Anyone wanting to see me humiliated only needs to look at the video, where I dance like a dork on a chair.

In the same *Critic* article, and even though I was in favour, I said that Look Blue Go Purple were at first 'annoyingly coy'. From a distance, this strikes me as a little sexist. As if everyone should be up there flopping out their cocks. I still had things to learn from the feminist wave going on around us. The movement in the eighties said a lot about equality and folk having the right to do what they chose with their bodies, about the objectification of people, about their duties in designated roles.

I'm sorry, a young man would say, staring sadly at his Roman sandals.

I think I'd given up on the world beyond my circle. Even in that circle, it was hard to get along. I had no excuses for a lot of what I did, even if I was so drunk I can't remember what it was, but I was upset about things and my powerlessness to change them. Nothing was what it was cracked up to be. I was flailing upstream against conservatism, violence and fraudulence. The reliable institutions were unreliable. There were cracks in my family and home. There were cracks in me too but I was too young to see them, so I battled on, railing against what I saw as others' assaults on decency and fair play. Often, without knowing, I battled myself. Music became a symbol of purity and escape, but even that could be smeared by copyists and fakes. Music could be perverted and twisted and used for power, or for maintaining the status quo.

Music meant more than that. To me, it was about spirit, attitude and a sort of faith, almost like life and death. I couldn't stand to see it sullied.

The Doublehappys often failed to back up my lip. We were too loud, and all the broken strings meant our pauses were as long as our songs. A song would rock, but then we'd be changing a string for the next five minutes and the momentum would be lost.

'Of course, Shayne Carter ended up abusing the audience,' said *Critic*, about our support with Hunters and Collectors.

After we filmed the clip for 'The Other's Way', we went to a trendy Christchurch bar. The crowd were dressed in club gear and dancing to new romantic songs by Spandau Ballet, Duran Duran, ABC and whoever did 'Send Me an Angel'. They ponced about in Lurex, tent-sized pants and obnoxious, heavy hairspray.

The eighties was a terrible period aesthetically. It's only in retrospect that the eighties is celebrated, at ironic parties by people who weren't there at the time. The shoulders pads, the pinks and greys, the mullets not as good as mine, the plastic music with flanged guitars and the rinky-dink Pak'nSave synth lines. The empty greed of yuppies. You can see it, too, in the blank glass towers they built in Auckland that everyone's regretted since.

All that trucked past us. 'Getting Older' or 'Burlesque' said more to me than Duran Duran posing on a yacht.

The Doublehappys talked about the club scene in our song 'Needles and Plastics'. It ran for five and a half minutes. 'Fat cunt in a studded belt,' went the opening line. The word 'cunt' was taboo, but we still stuck it in. The description was based on a real-life character from Zanzibar.

My God he thinks he's something else
When he's just another zombie probably made out of needles and plastic
White, white girl in a black, black dress
She's only pretty as in much of a mess
She's just another zombie probably made out of needles and plastic
It's a shallow, sickening sideshow
I don't think that I'm right, I don't think that I'm right
I know that I am
So I say hey!
They're all made
Of needles and plastic . . .

We filmed a video for the song in Chris Knox's front lounge, in front of our giant mural of Elvis. Chris did it in one shot and his camera bopped along with a bunch of our friends, who were on their knees throwing balloons and pretending to be a stadium crowd. My personal highlight was doing a star jump off an armchair, then I started laughing and lost my balance and fell back into the chair. But I still kept strumming and sneering. Wayne joined me on the armchair at one point. We pretended to duet like the Eagles in their twin lead break at the end of 'Hotel California', then we went back to sneering.

That video captures the things the Doublehappys were about. Our friends' hands stretch out to grab us, like we're a Dunedin Sound version of rock stars, but with a swing of the mullet we shake them off. At the end we don't know what to do, so we collapse in a three-man pile.

The Doublehappys lasted eighteen months. Shortly before our last tour we had a recording session at the student radio offices, Radio One, where I'd been employed, first selling advertising—well, sending out other people to sell advertising—and then as a news editor, which was a cruisy gig because we never had any news. They'd thought I'd be a good person to have on board because of my previous experience in radio. Martin Phillipps and I had a night-time show there where we played sixties obscurities like the Seeds, the Creation and the *The World's Worst Records*.

The Doublehappys recorded four tracks for an EP called *Cut It Out*. We were photographed in our undies so we could make an insert for the EP where people could cut us out and turn us into paper dolls. I'd drawn costumes to put on the dolls—a Gary Glitter space vest and platform boots, a Freddie Mercury jumpsuit, a Mick Jagger ensemble with a lump in the groin, and some ripped-up clothes like Sid's.

Cut It Out was recorded with Rex Visible, an Auckland musician we'd met on the Looney Tour. It was Rex's idea to have the two guitar amps facing each other so that the mics picked up the weird harmonics between the two guitars, the noises that neither guitar made, the bleed that was part of our sound. The record is the closest we got to how we were live—ramshackle, with lots of spill, like shooting a water gun into your bandmate's face. Wayne and I had two songs each. One of Wayne's was 'Moss Monster'. It might not have equalled the take from Roslyn Woollen Mill, which was more desolate and snotty.

His other tune, 'Some Fantasy', became an epitaph. The Verlaines recorded the song for an American compilation years later, because Graeme rated Wayne's words—

I don't believe that fatalism is an end in itself
Between the bottles, the sun will still rise
It seems the good must surely go to heaven
And I ain't got a thing to worry about
Because, complacency told me not to bother
And hypocrisy told me something else again
Twenty-four hours a day, seven days a week
A misery
Some fantasy

—sung over two dumb chords. The next verse was testament to his love for his girlfriend, and it's more optimistic, but heartbreaking. They're lines with an emotional comprehension beyond that of most twenty-year-olds. Wayne would have written a book.

We recorded 'Needles and Plastic', and my girlfriend played Modern Lovers keyboards. My other song, 'Nerves', was an epic based on the Verlaines' twists and turns, an attempt at sophistication, with quiet, loud passages, an anthemic end, and

173

pseudo-poetic lyrics. It was a hint of the Serious Stuff I'd try later with Straitjacket Fits.

Martin Phillipps, Jay Clarkson and the Chills bass player Martin Kean joined me on the vocals for the outro. 'If this trip's love, can I get off?'

For most of these tracks I sang at the end of my range. It could get too much, like someone bawling and complaining right in your ear. We edited a live track of 'I Don't Want to See You Again', because I couldn't hear it without blushing. But it was also a deliberate ploy. By pitching my vocals to an extreme, the song grew more exciting. It made you sound completely committed, like you were being overcome, or drowning in what you said. That approach worked more often that it didn't. The way Graeme Downes looked when he was about to pop his head, or how Otis Redding tore at the word 'tied'—but my biggest rowdy influence was an album called *Little Richard's Greatest Hits Live*.

Little Richard probably made dozens of records called *Little Richard's Greatest Hits Live*, but the one I loved most was recorded at the Okeh Club in Los Angeles in the mid to late sixties. It doesn't matter that it was recorded years after Little Richard's heyday, because to Little Richard his heyday never ended. His between-song monologues are hilarious—he's boasting, flipping, going off in a flood of surrealistic nonsense. For outstanding stream-of-consciousness, he equals Derek and Clive.

My favourite bit is when he interrupts a song to blabber, 'An' if you got on a wig like sum people say I got ahwn and this-is-my-own-beautiful-hair whadda ya do with it fellas? TAKE IT OFF!'

'Take it off!' roar the men in the crowd, because, like Little Richard, they love this punchline too.

And then Little Richard returns to pounding the shit out of his keys, and probably 'Tutti Frutti'. As Nik Cohn pointed out in his classic book *Awopbopaloobop Alopbamboom*—named after a

174

Richard Penniman song—Little Richard had one setting and that setting was Extreme. Little Richard didn't do soppy ballads. He just hurtled on like a madman in a gospel holler that woke the dead. Even Prince paid tribute to Little Richard, with his funky little pencil moustache.

There's a lineage that goes Little Richard, Jimi Hendrix, and Prince—Little Richard with his outrageous bouffant, Jimi with his pirate dandyism, and Prince doing 'Dirty Mind' while wearing bikini bottoms. They all had the same wispy moustache and they all took what was shocking and outrageous about black music and put it in a context that even old whitey could dig.

'You Keep On Knocking' by Little Richard is one of the most unstoppable rock songs there is.

When I was in Straitjacket Fits and we had major label cash behind us, we stayed at the same motel on the Sunset Strip that Little Richard lived at. Apparently he had a room on the fifth floor and he could sometimes be seen in the bar playing the piano. Our manager Debbi Gibbs said to me one afternoon, 'Oh, guess who we saw in the lift? Little Richard.'

This was the same Debbi who was once lucky enough to see Michael Jordan play basketball and had said, 'He's pretty good, Michael Jordan, isn't he?'

Out of all of my friend's achievements, being in the same lift as Little Richard is the one I most admire.

The Doublehappys had an excellent tour in the middle of 1985. Despite the broken strings and people complaining about the volume, it felt like we were going up a level. We had new influences too, like Big Star, Nikki Sudden, the Laughing Clowns and the German band Can. Our Elvis backdrop looked great, wobbling away like a big fatty, and we even laid off rubbishing the audience. Our popularity was growing, and because people obviously liked us, and took us back to their home for parties, we realised a lot of them were on our side. John was drummed in now, and Wayne and I could discuss what we did even less. We spent most of the time in our van, laughing and smoking pot.

'I've got blood in my THC system,' Wayne announced between Kaikōura and Picton.

At the gigs Wayne wore a T-shirt I'd made for him with 'Rock on NZ' painted on the front, because that was one of our private jokes and something we called out between songs at practices and into the microphone at shows. We meant it sarcastically, but we also meant it for real.

I had a badge made up with a cartoon of Wayne's face drawn by Chris Knox. It was a better drawing than the ones I'd done of him. The image was from an old Stones poster, where Wayne has his lips pushed out and his eyes squeezed shut, looking all cheeky and irreverent. I loved that badge and I wore it all the time.

When we got to Auckland, we stayed at Debbi Gibbs' father's house in Parnell. At this point Debbi was the boss at the Auckland student radio station Campus Radio. The Gibbs' house was like nothing I'd ever seen. It was made out of money that didn't exist in Dunedin—maybe you could get it if you sold Brockville and a quarter of Halfway Bush. Debbi's dad was a multi-millionaire who'd made his fortune buying companies and then selling them off for massive profits. Bendon, Securitas, ten percent of Telecom—he had a hand in all of that. The Gibbs' house was endless, with roofs the height of clouds. There were cupboards and corners everywhere, stuffed with food and prosperity. A table I thought was glass was actually crystal. Art sat exclusively on the walls. There was a sauna in a block downstairs, and when you pushed a button on the wall the wall slid open, like in a James Bond film, and then you flopped directly into an outside pool the size of St Kilda beach. You'd bake yourself to boiling point and then tumble into cool, deep water—it was a delicious way to tire yourself, reserved for the wealthy and privileged.

One morning Wayne pushed a button that he thought drew back the curtains in our room, but it actually set off an alarm. Within a couple of minutes, Securitas men were crawling around the backyard. We skulked away from the house and went off to get our gear for the last gig we'd ever play.

Those last few days were weird. The gig at the Windsor turned confrontational, and I ended up running the audience down. I got even more blind drunk and carried on at a party, none of which I remember, apart from a memory of three people standing in front of a white cupboard glaring at me, a man and two women, each of them holding a cup.

Wayne was in a strange mood too. He kept saying that people didn't like him. John and I couldn't work out where that was coming from.

The next day, we mixed our record at Progressive Studios. Some friends who'd been with us the night before came into the control room and shook their heads.

'You've gotta watch it,' I think one of them said.

We finished our mix in a pool of shame and self-loathing. The next day we went to the Auckland Railway Station with our tails between our legs, and then we got on the train.

*

I don't remember much of the day Wayne died. It's a very bad dream which runs in a different time, slowed down like you're drifting through a swamp. There's a fog around the borders, a Vaseline on the edges, like a picture or a film you slowly pull into focus and revisit time and time again. The sound is a mash-up, like a reused cassette where the old sound hasn't been wiped properly, so it sits behind the new one, jabbering and garbled, and none of the recording makes sense. The mix is a layer of confusion—laughter, idle chatter, a call through a speaker, the quiet in a carriage, the soft conversation—a shout!—the explosion of wheels on a bridge.

It was a crisp and bright winter's day. June the 25th. Maybe we had a bite at a downstairs café in Customs Street on our way to the station. When we boarded the train, the day was fading and Auckland was still and pretty—gold, pink, vivid—in the weak setting sun.

We sat in a gently lit carriage and had a couple of drinks. If we took the edge off, we might be able to sleep in the bunks I'm sure they had on the train. Wayne was halfway through *Under the Volcano*. We were on the Northerner that ran overnight, virtually the length of the North Island, all the way to Wellington. We still had two shows to play back in Christchurch.

Somewhere around midnight, around Taumarunui, we snuck into the part between two carriages, possibly to smoke a joint. According to John there was another young man with us, someone I've forgotten. But I have an impression of him now, maybe dark-haired, dressed a little straight, a similar age to us. I can hear him in the middle of the tape saying, 'I'm sorry for what happened to your friend.'

He melted away after the accident. I wonder who he was, if he saw what happened or played any part in the aftershock, or if he carried a longer shock with him, like John and I did, for years.

Wayne and I, probably high and looking for fun, stepped out of the train and down the passenger steps leading up to the carriages. We must have opened the door to get outside. I remember we were on the bottom step, facing each other as usual, me looking south, him with his back turned to the direction we were going in, and we were both leaning out, holding on to a handrail each, the ones that lay vertically either side of the door. We were both laughing as the wind shook us around, while the countryside stood further out, black, lightened by fog. There was the comforting chug of the train, though it might have been roaring. Maybe Wayne called out something, but it ended mid-sentence.

There was an explosion and a thump, and the violence of the train wheels on a different-sounding track. I was hanging outside the train, almost parallel to the side of the carriage, yet somehow I still held the rail. I could feel I was going to fall, but then John, who had stayed inside, swung out and grabbed me and dragged me back in. I don't know how I held on to that rail. It was a death, or life, grip.

Wayne was gone. John and I looked at each other and all around. We gabbled things, panicked. There'd been a splash of wet in my face when the boom hit, and I was spitting fragments out of my mouth. There may have been blood where we were.

We staggered back into the carriage and John pulled the emergency cord. There was a screech of metallic brakes. The conductor came through and we told him there'd just been an accident, and our friend had disappeared, and he looked serious and told us to stay right there.

John and I must have sat in our seats facing each other for half an hour, and we groaned and moaned, although it was all too new to cry. We were afraid we could be busted for smoking pot, so we made up an alibi.

Eventually an older man, an out-of-uniform sergeant, came through to where we sat, and he looked serious too.

'We've found your friend a bit back, on the banks of the river. Unfortunately he's died.' Then the sergeant said, 'You'll have to come with me.'

'We shouldn't have been hanging outside the train,' I said to the train conductor.

'We've all been young and stupid,' he replied.

We were taken to the Taumarunui Police Station and a uniformed policeman sat before us, behind a desk, writing the details down.

He told me I had blood on my face.

The detective sergeant from the train came into the office and told us that, while he knew there had been marijuana involved, he was going to let that go.

We were driven to a motel that the police said they would pay for, a pungent Barton Fink room, grim and moist with the scent of mould and people.

Somehow John and I slept for a few hours. Before I got between what felt like hospital sheets, I washed the last of the blood from my face.

The next day we were taken to a courtroom for the initial coroner's report. The policeman in the dock mispronounced Wayne's name, and I might have called out that it was 'El-cee', not 'El-zee'. Wayne had died from massive, unsurvivable head injuries—I can't remember the exact description, but it was technically and emotionally violent. He'd taken the impact of the abutment of a bridge that he was far enough out to hit. His body had slammed into mine and knocked me out of the way, cracking two of my ribs. There was a television report later that said a person had died, and that another person with the one killed had been lucky to survive.

The police were reluctant to show us the body, because Wayne was a bit of a mess. He was identified by the scars between his fingers and toes that we told the police he had.

Barbara Ward, Chris Knox's partner, drove down from Auckland to pick John and me up, and I'll always be grateful for that. It was a typical act of kindness. Hours later, when we arrived back at Hakanoa Street in Grey Lynn, Chris came out and greeted us at the letterbox, and he gave me and John a hug.

'You poor bastards,' he said, and then we were led into the house.

Back in Dunedin, we fell around in grief. There was a procession of people who stared into the short distance with tears in their eyes. At a gathering at the Phillipps' house, I broke fully for the first time since the accident, and bawled for minutes. Roger Shepherd was there and he put his hand on my shoulder, while the rest of my friends carefully orbited me like I was a planet that, for now, shouldn't be touched.

'He's just crying,' somebody said.

I can remember, at another time, meeting Martin's father, Reverend Donald Phillipps, in the street, and telling him that my father had died.

'Life goes on,' said Donald, and I was bit offended then, but I grew older and realised he was right.

There was another gathering in our upstairs flat in George Street, where for weeks the sewage had been running directly into the alley. We couldn't work out where the sludge was coming from. I got drunk and angry at Martin Phillipps, because I had to blame someone.

'All you care about is your band,' I said to him, a comment stemming from jealousy and my residual resentment of him poaching some members of Bored Games.

That was an unfair thing to say, because Martin was thoughtful and always the person who remembered birthdays. The Chills had put up the money to fly John and me back from Auckland.

Another night, a group of us were at Lesley's house in Chambers Street, and someone put on an episode of *The Young Ones* to cheer us up. Horribly, it was the episode where Vyvyan sticks his head out of a train and gets decapitated. 'Turn it off,' someone snapped, as a headless Vyvyan staggered around the carriage with spurts of blood spewing up from his neck.

We went to the Elseys' place. Mrs Elsey, a tall, slim women who dressed in seventies slacks and continuously sipped wine, spent a lot of time sighing, and her breath caught like Aunt Helen's had when Aunt Helen had described her father. The booze ran out at the Elseys and John, Wayne's father who ran a car yard in Kaikorai Valley, pulled some liqueurs out of the garage we used to practise in—sickly peppermint or licorice-tasting liquid that felt like chalk. I got so drunk I fell off my chair. I felt embarrassed afterwards, afraid I'd offended Wayne's grieving parents.

'They understand,' I heard through a friend, but I never went back to their house.

At the funeral in the chapel at the Andersons Bay crematorium, I was one of the people who spoke. I remember looking over my shoulder at the buffeted and bleak Tomahawk Beach, its grey waves rolling unknowingly in the wind. I repeated an inspirational quote I'd read in a small calendar book that students at Kaikorai Valley High were given at the start of each year so we could jot down period times and homework reminders. One quote from Ralph Waldo Emerson said, 'Whoso would be a man must be a nonconformist. Nothing is at last sacred but the integrity of your own mind'—and I thought that was perfect for Wayne.

Wayne's girlfriend Nicky sat hunched in the front row at the funeral, small and broken like a sparrow. She was unable to talk to anyone, and she didn't say a word. She came to none of our gatherings when Wayne died; she stayed at her parents' home and grieved. It would have been unimaginable for her, because her and Wayne were in love.

Wayne was cremated, and there's still a small plaque for him in the rows above the crematorium.

I can remember standing on the front lawn at Caldwell Street with my father, in the hours after Wayne's funeral, and I told my dad I loved him, because I needed to hear him say that back. He may have, but I'm not sure, because that was a feeling he found difficult to express.

Days later, there was the dinner with my family, and I had a few drinks and for the first time I described the accident. Once I started, I couldn't stop. The details came spilling out, one dreadful piece after another. No one said anything. They just all looked sad, with their eyes filling up. Mum came around the table and rubbed me on my back.

'I heard we almost lost you too,' Wayne's mother had said to me that drunken night at the Elseys.

*

John and I should have got counselling, but we never did. We struggled with the trauma in our individuals ways, John more quietly, me by drinking harder. My relationship with the Auckland girl ended in the strain. I swam in the black for at least two years, possibly longer.

Somewhere amid this, John and I formed a new band. It took us a while to regroup, but I think we thought it was the right thing to do. We had unfinished business that had been shockingly interrupted, and I'd learned that life could be brief, that it could end at any time. There were no scales of justice decreeing what was and wasn't fair. You had to do what you had to do, while you were still around to do it.

Perhaps John and I thought we had to achieve something on behalf of our friend who was no longer here. The music we eventually made was filled with inspiration and fire.

I believed I survived the accident because I still had a mission, but then, Wayne's life was incomplete and he'd had his mission too.

Maybe my theory was half right.

But these were the motivations behind Straitjacket Fits.

Part Two

Burn It Up

I found some relief through playing with the Weeds, a casual group that never practised and whose members were all quite skinny. The bass player Bob Scott (a.k.a. Norbert) and his flatmate Michael Morley started the band as a diversion around their flat. 'It's D, A and C,' they'd tell me before every song, just before we played it live.

Bob has written a million tunes with the Clean, the Bats and the Weeds and he's formed a million bands with relatives, flatmates or someone he's met in South Dunedin. Bob is always writing a song. He has a million cassettes and he's done a million paintings, always in primary agricultural colours and usually featuring men with the same-shaped head as his. He is the resolute centre between the Kilgours in the Clean, and Dunedin music's most serious unofficial archivist. The best thing about Bob is that everything he does is idiosyncratically him, and he doesn't care what anyone else thinks.

Michael Morley had come to Dunedin from Napier with his friend Richard Ram. We always got the pair mixed up, because they were both immigrants from the north who wore the same jerseys and had the same springy brown hair. Michael and Richard played in a duo called Wreck Small Speakers on Expensive Stereos, who were like Cabaret Voltaire stuck at Dunedin wharf. They used awkward grooves, bass and a malevolent synth. Later, Michael went even further out and formed the Dead C, whose music was as dark and as base as a Ralph Hotere painting. Michael's early paintings often echoed Hotere's. Hotere had a studio just up the hill in Port Chalmers, and Michael would visit to share whisky and old jazz albums.

Alastair Galbraith was another musician who painted. He was flatting with Bob and Michael when they formed the Weeds. Alastair's music was more reverential than theirs. His early band, the Rip, had a song about music called 'The Holy Room', which he sang as a raw-faced schoolboy with a painfully trebly guitar. Later, Alastair refined his music with a pastoralism that reflected the open spaces he recorded in—lonely baches by the sea, the upper floors of a musty, deserted warehouse.

Alastair and I played games of chess in his warehouse. I often won, but one day I was lecturing him about a certain position and he said, 'But what if I did this?' and placed me in checkmate.

He and I once went to West Coast and managed one night's camping before being murdered by mosquitos. We took some acid, climbed a glacier, and looked down at a trail of tourists walking by the ice below us.

'Aw, ya dickwhackers,' I blurted out, in unnecessary Brockville fashion, and Alastair doubled over laughing. It was like Constable or Turner looking out and saying, 'Aw, ya dickwhackers.'

Alastair was sensitive, and he was always having his heart broken, like he needed that for fuel. He was crushed when Wayne died.

I don't know if Alastair was a fan of the Weeds, because the Weeds were idiots. John Collie, who also needed cheering up, formed a twin drum crew with the Weeds' original drummer, Chris, while Jeff Harford rattled a tambourine. The Weeds dressed in women's clothing, with makeup, tight tops and glittery dresses.

We once played the Dunedin Town Hall in our undies.

Word of this got back to Dad and he said, 'Now, what's this I hear about my son playing in the town hall in his underpants.' Then he laughed and looked proud, because it was a play straight out of his disco playbook.

The Weeds performed in Auckland once, but our in-jokes didn't travel. We formed a human pyramid in the middle of our set—human pyramids were big on our scene then, as were trust games that involved falling off mantelpieces—but the Aucklanders just stared. They didn't understand the power of a 3-2-1 formation or why we'd build one onstage. Dunedin is always ahead of the North when it comes to matters of cool.

The Weeds eventually recorded a single: 'Wheatfields'. On the cover we're shirtless, six weedy men with foliage on our heads.

'Feed The Weeds—Do They Know It's Christmas?' it said at the bottom.

'Do They Know It's Christmas?' was a big charity song at the time, raising money for Ethiopia.

Needing bucking up, I got back into football. Bob Scott played too—he was a clever player who giggled when he set off on a tricky dribble. Graeme Downes was in the same team with us, Mornington FC, with our light blue shirts and club rooms close to the top of the Mornington Hill.

Another friend, Alan, played too. Alan was a drummer and a bit like Paul Baird, in that he was a big boy who liked banging things. He also had a drug habit, and sometimes before we went to practice he'd go into the loo and bang up with a needle. One night, he reeled out after an obviously strong hit, then he went to football practice and played like a maniac. Our coach was so impressed he put Alan up two grades for the next game, but in the light of day Alan was exposed, and soon he was back to playing with us.

I was quite good at football, because I had speed and a Stanley Matthews swerve that Lindsey Hudson's father taught me as an eight-year-old. I played as a winger for much of my early football career, and when I got older I plotted behind the strikers.

Mum enrolled me with Roslyn Wakari, the club at the bottom of Brockville Hill, when I was five. She'd come to my matches but watch from her car, because it was always so cold in the mornings. The roughs in the turf were frozen and left red, keening scrapes on your knees. For a while Mum tooted her car horn whenever I got on the ball, which I asked her to stop doing because it put me off my game.

Roslyn Wakari was one of Dunedin's oldest clubs. Its soggy changing rooms smelt of liniment and tired boots. Long-dead players with translucent eyes and settlers' moustaches stared out from the old team photos hung along the hall.

My primary school team was one of the best in Dunedin and went undefeated for three years—will-o'-the-wisp Brockville boys, with Hiku out the back. Our striker was a chubby, blond-haired boy called Graeme Laing, the son of the famous swimming coach Duncan. Laing didn't do much except score—lots and lots, every season. Even then we were aware that football strikers, like rock stars, are born not made, so Laing was left to his tubby seagulling and his gargantuan hunger for goals.

I gave up football in my teens but picked it up again with Mornington, and then again in my thirties when I found a footballing fraternity in Auckland. I played for old-man teams then, for Western Springs, and we'd come up against former All Whites who had slowed but still retained their skills. Fred de Jong would come on, score a couple of headers, then go back off again to talk on his phone.

I remember the trajectory of the ball—the one that scores the goal or splits the defence—just as vividly as any rock 'n' roll moment. It's like a tree falling in a forest or when you've killed a song in the practice room. The fact that it happened is enough. One of the best things I've done in life is play football.

Football has other similarities with music. Finding answers on the fly, the Zen-like application, the camaraderie—football teaches you to trust other people, and sometimes when I pass a song to the other guitarist I'll think, 'Here, you have the ball.'

When you play team sport you learn its central maxim—that it's always the other team who cheats and throws in from the wrong mark. They score goals they don't deserve, while your creations are noble and devoid of fluke.

It's amazing how well you've played and how much the opposition stank.

Sport is also a great theatre where people stop pretending.

The other side are the people you say things to that would get you hit on the street, or who you kick so hard that if you did that on the same street you'd end up in court.

But at the end of the game, the enemy becomes human again; in fact they're just the same as you, there for the same joys of kicking a ball, and you shake their hand at the whistle, and think, 'Ah, they're all right.'

Then again, I've met some total fuckwits out there.

Soon after Wayne died, I went to a show at Sammy's with my Auckland girlfriend. She'd been given free tickets because she knew somebody close to the band. The band was called the Party Boys and they were a collective of famous New Zealand musicians—Neil Finn, Dave Dobbyn, the drummer Rooda, and my old nemesis Mike Chunn—and they were on tour, making lots of money playing old party hits in front of a Coruba banner. This offended every part of me. I got drunker and more belligerent as their set wore on.

191

'Cheer up, Sleepy Jean,' chirped happily from the stage.

I was blacked out when we went backstage, even though I was still walking. That's the worst part of being an alcoholic: when you're mindless but still going around. Of course, I challenged every one of the musicians to a fight—Finn, Dobbyn, Rooda and Chunn. I wanted to punish them all, which was ridiculous, because at that point I wouldn't have been able to fight my way out of a soggy Coruba carton. I was ejected, and my girlfriend cried, and I felt rotten about that.

It was a continuation of a trend that had been running for a few years now. I'd greet touring bands as a one-man alcoholic welcoming committee, then pass judgement on them, to them, after a gig. Once, when I was working at 4XO, I was smart to the Screaming Meemees and the Dance Exponents in a café after a show and their manager complained to the station. I also got kicked off a judging panel for Battle of the Bands when I told a covers band they sucked and that they wouldn't win it. Ironically, with me off the panel, they did win it.

Another night, around the same time of the terrible Sammy's gig, I was rude to the singer Sharon O'Neill, and a man I knew from Brockville said that if I didn't zip up he'd take me outside and do me. I was snarky to Jordan Luck a couple of times, which is risible, because Jordan is an affable guy. Once, in Auckland, I went to his house in Ponsonby and I sang 'Darling I'll Say Goodbye' to him, just that, for about ten minutes.

Poor old Jordan. Another time he turned up innocently to a party at Hakanoa Street and Chris picked him up and carried him out of the door.

My crowning glory came a few years later when Straitjacket Fits opened for the Australian band Hoodoo Gurus at the Dunedin Town Hall.

It was in the early days of Straitjacket Fits, and relations were strained because John Collie's partner absolutely despised me. She seemed to resent my position at the head of the band and whatever I meant to her boyfriend. At the town hall, she threw a bottle at my head. Andrew Brough, who was just as munted, added to the spirit by randomly smashing another bottle on the floor. The whole thing turned into a riot and our brawl spilled into the Hoodoo Gurus' dressing room, where they'd been quietly waiting to play. We ignored them and continued our scrap, although I may have paused to gobble some of their hummus.

After the gig, near paralytic, I went back to the hotel where the band were staying with their road crew. Doug Hood, who was promoting their tour, was there too. They were all watching *Pee-wee's Big Adventure*. They kicked me out of their room but I stayed on the veranda and banged on their door, crying, 'Let me in!'

When we went to collect our gear the next day, the Town Hall manager said, 'You stupid cunts.'

There was a clause in the contract that said the support band had to help load the PA out, but we ignored it.

On one level, the bands I insulted were the icons we had to shoot for. Anyone above us needed to be warned. I was a junior Johnny Rotten calling out the fakes. It gave me fuel in a perverse way because, then, I had to back up my lip. But I was also a young drunk who would let loose on whatever was in front of me. Sometimes it was a band who were popular and successful, when maybe I feared that I'd never amount to much, continuing the Brockville trend. So I'd have my say, even where no one was asking.

My run-in with Neil Finn was the beginning of a small grudge match that has simmered, quietly, for years. I saw him in Europe once when we were both on tour, the first time I'd seen him since the Party Boys gig in Dunedin, and I told him I wasn't drinking anymore, probably because I wanted him to realise that I was actually okay. He smiled and said, 'Oh, that's a shame. I thought you made a good drunk.'

Neil was always magnanimous and never confrontational. I think he felt above that.

That didn't stop me in the early 2000s, when I'd started drinking again and was up to my usual nonsense. I'd gone to a party at Neil's son Liam's place, and, because I was half cut, Liam annoyed me.

'Don't you know who Liam is?' a girl said to me, which really got my hackles up. My antipathy increased when Liam said he couldn't get me a beer because he'd run out, and then he returned with a fresh one for himself.

When I saw Liam at another party a few weeks later, I pointed a few things out. I don't remember any of it, although I'm sure it was based on the conclusions I'd reached after seeing the two older Finns, Neil and Tim, play together at the Regent Theatre. Neil was the songsmith but Tim came across as less calculating—his music seemed to come from a more compelled place. Neil could write a melody, but a lot of it seemed based on a vague, middle-class angst. I couldn't hear his struggle, or any real blues.

Liam was offended by what I'd said, as any son hearing his father put down would be, and this led to him saying in the *Sunday Star-Times*, when asked about his fellow APRA Silver Scroll songwriting nominees, 'Really, I don't care who wins, so long as it's not Dimmer. To me Dimmer just sounds like Shayne Carter trying to be Marvin Gaye, but he's left out all the Marvin . . . he sounds really gay,' which is a line I'm sure he made up in his practice room. Liam's comment did not go down well with New Zealand's gay community.

'Get back to me when you've written a tune, Shorty,' I should have replied, but didn't.

I met Liam again a couple of years later in Texas when he was chasing Kelly, the bass player in Dimmer, and he was fine then, modest, even a little unsure of himself. Kelly later married the drummer from Crowded House.

In the mid-2000s, Bic Runga asked me to sing backing vocals on her album *Birds*. Bic had sung backing on a couple of Dimmer tracks, and she liked my way with harmonies. This also felt like a good way to get revenge on Sony, who'd dropped me after the first Dimmer album and whose general manager used to stomp around his office going, 'But he can't sing!'

Yeah, well, I can't sing well enough to be asked to sing by your biggest artist, buddy.

Neil Finn was in Bic's band too. It was an ensemble of famous New Zealand musicians—Bic was always canny with her team selections. Neil brought all his skills to the record, arranging, advising and playing piano. During our tour he never said anything about my run-in with Liam, although word occasionally drifted back to me from mutual musician friends who said they'd been at the Finns' and that people there weren't impressed. But Neil was friendly on tour, and we had some decent chats. The Flight of the Conchords were supporting Bic—this was just before they made their HBO series—and Jemaine gave me a CD of Mitch Hedberg. I might have given him *Why Bother?* by Peter Cook and Chris Morris. I may also have told Brett, who'd played keys with the mainly white dub band the Black Seeds, that I couldn't stand white men pretending to be black. I was a bit pissed. It was an undiplomatic thing to say.

I did actually feel like Marvin when I sang with Bic, or at least one of Marvin's backing vocalists. In a live video of Marvin playing in Europe, the bloke parked between the two women singing background parts seemed to be onto a very cool gig—just looking sharp, pointing a finger and dropping an 'Oooooh' in the middle of a number. It's a challenge to hit an angular note without any run-up. But singing three-part harmonies with Anika Moa and Anna Coddington, two songbirds with a supernatural ability to be in tune, was a pure, sensual pleasure.

Bic's band let her down, because most of us drank too much when we went on the road around New Zealand and Australia. Not always, but often enough to be disrespectful. Later, in Europe, Bic ended up firing the band, maybe on the advice of her mum. I didn't go on the European tour, something about there not being the budget—but I wondered if it had anything to do with the night when I got back from a gig in Nelson and played a Dimmer demo at obnoxious volume in my room. I looked out the window and there was Neil standing on a balcony across from me, holding up his palms as if to say, 'What the fuck?'

The next morning I looked out the same window and saw Neil standing by the hotel gate with Bic, gesticulating firmly. Even though I couldn't hear any words, I was sure he was complaining about me.

One night I got slaughtered in Wellington, and Bic told me I looked like a drunk uncle.

After our soundcheck in Christchurch, I was walking up some stairs and I heard Neil giving an interview around the corner. The interviewer was asking him about me, and referring to a line from the *Listener*—something about Carter being 'New Zealand's greatest, most natural rock star', a quote that sometimes got bandied about.

'Well, I'm not sure if he is New Zealand's greatest rock star,' said Neil sourly, although I'd never seen him at one of my gigs.

The bass player in Bic's band was an Australian called Conrad, from a group called the Devastations. We clicked from the first time we spoke, and he was a favourite in our party. Conrad has a stutter, so it can take him a while to make his point, but his point is usually worth it. He is tall and slim with rock-star hair, and always well presented in stylish op-shop clothes. Unfortunately, he has the male Australian habit of leaving his shirt open to the bellybutton. The New Zealander in me was always thinking, 'Do your shirt up, mate.'

Conrad thought that Neil didn't like him either.

He'd been staying at one of Neil's adjunct houses in East Auckland with Riki Gooch, the Trinity Roots drummer, who was also guesting with Bic. Neil loved Riki, but he ended up asking Conrad to leave without explaining why. As revenge, Conrad performed an act of self-expression in Neil's shower, hoping to clog his drains, and I do wonder what mental picture Conrad used to drive his dreadful effort.

Later, we were waiting for our luggage at Melbourne Airport when Conrad ran into his Melbourne pal Mick Harvey. With his work on the Birthday Party, the Bad Seeds, P.J. Harvey, and his own music, Mick has an impeccable résumé. Neil bounded up to say hi but Mick just blanked him, which both Conrad and I enjoyed.

I still see Neil occasionally. We have a lot of mutual friends, and his wife, Sharon, is a cool woman. Neil invited me to a dinner party at his palace just last year, because I was staying with Don McGlashan, and it was civil and relaxed and all of the guests were interesting and accomplished. Neil was nice. Mike Chunn was there, and he gave me a hug. Sean Donnelly and his wife Joanne were seated to my right at the table. Neil and I ended up sitting opposite each other, which felt a little awkward.

Neil made some light comment to me about mothers, but he didn't realise that mine had died recently, and I could tell he was a bit embarrassed.

Yes, of course he knew Beethoven's late quartets, he said later, a bit defensively; he had all of them on vinyl. But he didn't know who'd played it, or whenabouts it was recorded.

In 1985, when I was in the Weeds, the brothers Jefferies rolled into town. They'd come down from New Plymouth and rented a flat in the Coronation Street terrace houses in the middle of the university hub. The Jefferies brothers were intense—Peter very intense, and Graeme even more so. They didn't eat, barely slept and lived on cigarettes, coffee, pot and a huge amount of intensity. They were both over six feet tall and had twenty-seven-inch waists and talked in very deep voices. Peter's voice was deep, but Graeme's was even deeper. When Graeme spoke, it was like Ian Curtis's singing, except Graeme was talking. Graeme always stood too close to you, and when he said something an obscure amusement would play along his lips. He had a screwball sense of humour. Graeme and I fell out later over a woman, and he ignored me after that. Perhaps I became the subject of a couple of his songs, but I never took it personally, because I felt that this was all a part of love and war.

The Jefferies brothers had started out in a band called Nocturnal Projections, and now they were This Kind of Punishment. Both of these bands were class. Because the brothers were so obsessive, their songs were beautifully arranged and well-ordered even though they recorded them on nothing bigger than a four-track. They'd bounce tracks carefully and their music sat just so. Graeme played masterful guitar on a handsome Flying V. Peter's singing was tuneful and emotional, his drumming often majestic. To the Jefferies, it was music, music, music, and music the way I liked it. They played no game but their own. They didn't have any time for phonies or putting it on. Peter would dismiss all of that instantly with a flick of his cigarette.

The Jefferies' intensity was too much for some people. They didn't want to hear Peter's explanation of how he'd eliminated a certain EQ or stuck a mic somewhere—his descriptions were so long and full of detail you could hear his mouth getting sticky. But I felt inspired and challenged by Peter, and I often sat on the edge of a precipice at his table, hoping I'd done it right. It's good to be answerable to an equal who keeps you accountable.

Both the Jefferies liked my stuff. Peter said he'd seen a Doublehappys gig that had made him feel levitational.

I don't care about the opinions of critics or record company people or people who go to the gig for a beer. The respect of my peers is what matters to me, because they're the ones who know. You can see people who've sold millions but they don't have that respect, and you can tell they feel sick about it.

One Sunday, Peter came around to my upstairs flat in George Street. There was an old laundry room out the back that we'd converted into a rehearsal space, and, although it was tiny, it was a convenient place to jam. I think our idea at first was to muck around with a bunch of songs, some of mine, some of Peter's, but instead we worked on just one tune.

'Randolph's Going Home' is one of my greatest songs, possibly the greatest. I feel free to big-up it, because it really is that good. 'Randolph' makes people cry, and I think it has a kind of nobility that has always moved people. Obviously it wasn't contrived that way. My one purposeful attempt at writing a hit was absolutely shit. I can't guess what the public likes. Popular opinion often eludes me. It's time, not other people, that tells you what your best work is.

'Randolph' is one guitar and drums, with an overdubbed guitar in the chorus. When that extra guitar comes in, it's overwhelming—lonely, dissonant chords that at the time I felt like I had invented. That chord change from a weird E to a weird B is the deepest switch I've written. The whole atmosphere in 'Randolph' is otherworldly, and when the chorus hits the song goes to the sky. The other chord progressions mystify me. I don't know how I wrote them—they just came out, one combination of strings, minors mangling majors, leading to another. If ever I felt that I'd divined a song, 'Randolph' is the one.

Peter put on a stately beat as funereal as the tune. When we got to the end, he suggested repeating the last two lines of the chorus. Peter's obsessiveness took over then, and he made us work on that song for close to two hours, which, to me, was forever.

I'd written the song for Wayne. Randolph was another short-lived nickname I'd given him, probably when he was being a ponce. The song referenced one of our favourite Velvet Underground songs. And it laid out all the events of Wayne's death.

The sergeant says he's just back there
So come with me
And somewhere Randolph's gaily singing 'I'm set free'
Set free
Lonely, lonely like a mother's cry
This anger seems the only thing that never dies
Never dies

And Venus lies alone
Fanfares fade into drones
Line up to cry, cos Randolph's going home

It's not that I'm big-headed
Sending myself letters
It's just that no one knows myself better than me, me . . .

And Venus lies alone
Fanfares fade into drones
Line up to cry, cos Randolph's going home

At the end I'm singing as hard as I did at the end of 'I Don't Wanna See You Again', but everything has built to this point and it's the only dynamic to end on.

At first, I thought the words in the second verse were a bit self-obsessed, but then I decided they intensified the feeling of loneliness.

The next day Peter said we had to record the song. He'd put up the money, whatever it took, as long as we got this tune down. We carried a four-track into Chippendale House, a collective arts space in downtown Dunedin.

I sang the song in the stairwell, with its harsh natural reverb, which suited the vocal because I wanted it to sound cutting and toppy, like John Lennon singing through his nose.

I wrote the B-side, 'Hooked Lined and Sunken', in half an hour. Harmonies stacked up on a dreamy chorus, which may have been a nod to 'Out of My Hands' by This Kind of Punishment.

It was Bruce Russell who suggested the cover image for the 'Randolph' single. It was one of the last illustrations from the book *The Little Prince* by Antoine de Saint-Exupéry, where the Prince falls from his planet like a rock.

The single came out at the same time as the single by the Weeds, but they were markedly different records.

It was also Bruce Russell who recommended Andrew Brough for our band.

Bruce had replaced Carey Hibbert at my flat with the handy laundry room and half-polluted alley.

We'd started Straitjacket Fits in early 1986, as a three-piece, with a bassist called David Wood.

David Wood had turned up on my doorstep one day and said that someone from Sneaky Feelings had told him that John and I were looking for a bassist. He seemed nervous and edgy, as David usually did, but he also acted like this was only a pop-in for him and he had somewhere more important to go. Maybe he was wearing his purple tartan flares, because he was always well dressed with a tad too much pizzazz for the dour Dunedin streets. He was another immigrant from the North Island who'd come down to play with a band called Working with Walt, and his fretless bass guitar was as flashy as his flares. He sometimes missed the notes, but David didn't care because a fretless looked more snazzy. Eventually he got it fretted, maybe at the suggestion of Peter Jefferies.

David projected confidence and certainty with his bass, and a lot of the time he was also certain about the records and people he liked, his appearance, and the food he cooked with care. But he seemed to have a wavering opinion of himself. The abrasiveness he kept in front of that was a big fat bluff.

Straitjacket Fits played their first show, as a trio, on the back of a trailer on the university lawn where Dad had once given his lecture. John had borrowed some drums off Sneaky Feelings and they fell off the back of the trailer halfway through our set.

Richard Steele, a coworker at Radio One who may have worn Roman sandals, guested on sax. One of the songs was called 'Green-Eyed Fevered Lines', and Richard wailed away on that like a foetal Pharoah Sanders.

I'd tried a few tentative steps in songwriting before Straitjacket Fits. I'd jammed for a bit with David Kilgour. He was like Gutteridge in that he liked simple songs. He probably found my songs too complicated, and maybe he didn't feel comfortable with their emotionalism either. I can remember playing him one of my upset songs on an acoustic in my lounge, and the stridency of my singing reeked as much as the foetid lyrics. David Kilgour didn't say anything, because David plays it cool, but I felt enough shame for us both.

I'd been flatting with David Kilgour and his partner Gen a bit before then, with our band war a thing of the past. Tony had turned up to that flat one day in 1986 to tell me that my brother

Kristen had been born.

I moonlighted as a drummer for George D. Henderson's band the Puddle for a time, although I couldn't really drum. I tried playing standing up, so I could maybe coordinate my kick drum and snare hand better, but it didn't help. For a guy with rhythm, I sure had none with the drums—but playing George's songs made me appreciate how fine his music was. Nothing flashy, just George softly intoning through his thin blond beard, flicking his hand at his fretboard like he was shooing a fly, singing of drug dreams and Christmases in the country. George is a singular songwriter who's rarely got his due. A few years back, I was fortunate to see the English band the Clientele play, and I saw George there. It was beautiful to watch him hearing his music played back by a group that he'd inspired.

In between my session muso outings, I picked up my first conviction. I'd been caught shoplifting some Camembert from the wanker at the twenty-four-hour dairy. When he stopped me, I put my arms out all innocently and said 'What?' as thickly as I could, forgetting I had the cheese under my armpit, so it dropped out and rolled on the floor. That was a dumb move, but we hated the wanker at the twenty-four-hour dairy. He was an ex-cop who was always being sleazy to my girlfriend. We saw stealing from him as a justifiable crime. My girlfriend and I were Maid Marian and Robin Hood, sticking it to the oppressor.

We took turns nicking cheese and other deli items from the Wanker, but I was the one who got caught. The Wanker put me in a policeman's headlock, dragged me out of the shop and pushed me up against a wall. A mysterious crowd of rugby thugs materialised out of nowhere and stood around me, keeping guard, daring me to run and making the odd disparaging comment. They probably grew up to be police officers, or wankers with their own shops.

I received a court summons. I was familiar with the procedures there, having reported on them for 'Live from the District Court' 4XO, so I was worried. I dreaded seeing my old media buddies from the wrong side of the box. I was also concerned about the presence of school children, because they were often in the public gallery on social study trips, brought along by their teachers to be discouraged from turning into criminals.

Not only was the gallery full but it was packed with kids from Kaikorai Valley, including two of my former teachers. When my credentials were read out—Shayne Carter, twenty-one, unemployed of Dunedin—I could feel them tut-tutting from the bleachers. My teachers had always suspected I would turn out like this.

My duty solicitor lamely offered that I spent my 'days writing songs', and when he said that, it sounded like a total waste of time. I was so broke I paid off my $120 fine in lots of $5.

At Straitjacket Fits' second gig at Sammy's, I was back to being a rock 'n' roll prince. Doug Hood had offered us a support slot with Wilko Johnson. This was before the episode with the Hoodoo Gurus at the Town Hall, and Doug still thought he could trust us.

The Sammy's PA was excellent, and I could hear everything pristinely, including David Wood's backing vocals.

Yeah, of course he could sing, David had told us back in George Street; in fact he'd been the singer in one of his old bands. But you could never hear his vocals properly through our weak practice PA. We hadn't figured out that you could turn the guitars down, but even if you did, John hit so hard you would have had to turn them back up again. These were the days of the volume wars, when it was every man for himself.

I finally heard David sing at the gig at Sammy's. It shocked me at first, because I didn't know what it was—a horrible moaning, maybe a weird frequency in the mid-range that the sound man hadn't wrung out yet. It sounded like a seal barking. But it was David—adding his two cents to an already glorious chorus. He was never allowed on the microphone again, and his place there was taken by Andrew Brough.

Andrew had sung and played guitar in the Orange, where Jonathon, my old mate from Bored Games, played bass. They'd released an EP on Flying Nun, so Andrew was already known for his singing. Andrew had had choir training and his phrasing was perfectly rounded, and when he sang he sounded like golden syrup. He had glasses and red hair and he wore either black or white skivvies. He also had a paisley shirt and a blue shirt, which he rotated because he couldn't be bothered with fashion. This would have offended David. It did offend David.

Andrew seemed a good fit for our band, because I really wanted to have harmonies and another singer, like in the Beatles. The first time Andrew stepped on the mic and played his round, Revolver guitar, we knew we'd hit on a sound.

From the start, Straitjacket Fits caused John and Paul arguments, where people had to decide which singer they liked best. I was just happy that in our band I was obviously John Lennon and that I'd never have to sing 'Maxwell's Silver Hammer' or 'Ob-La-Di, Ob-La-Da'. Paul McCartney was a tidy bassist and all that, but a lot of the time he was a drip. 'Helter Skelter' was just him mimicking wild rock 'n' roll.

John Lennon's first solo album was a lot more me, because of how caveman it was with its baseness and its soft and loud brutalities. It was one of Phil Spector's best productions as well, because, like Lennon, Spector had turned his back on everything he was famous for and kept the tracks fundamental. His only obvious touch was a Buddy Holly slapback on the vocals. Ringo Starr drummed the shit out of that album, and like Lennon and Spector he took it back to level one.

Lennon had his own 'Fuck you', but with whispered tracks like 'Love' it could sink into a listless, perfect romanticism. Lennon was one of the best double-tracking vocalists—so accurate with his twin takes that you could hardly tell there was two of him, even when a song was quiet and his ghost cruised to the front. I loved that Lennon had songs called 'Love', 'Help' and 'God', and that was all they said. He said, 'When you're drowning, you don't say "I would be incredibly pleased if someone would have the foresight to notice me drowning and come and help me", you just scream.' A dumb conclusion can have genius in it, and even a sort of opposition to its conclusion—like 359 degrees on a compass, where the opposite ends almost touch. The way laughing can sound like crying.

The item list at the end of Lennon's song 'God' kept running, and it was full of resentment and bile, but at the end he found a light. Lennon chewed you over and then sang you the loveliest lullaby. That range really influenced our band, as did the picking guitar and the sliding stereo needle noise at the end of 'I Want You (She's So Heavy)'.

That was what Straitjacket Fits were after—a polluted sort of beauty. We had our own individual takes on what that was, and our own way of hearing it as we deafened ourselves in the practice room.

Andrew preferred it cleaner, with flecks of wild guitar. He couldn't stand his songs being twisted. He was very particular and would get upset with any discord. He'd write all the notes out, point at the sheet, and say to David, 'No, this is what I want.'

He'd look at me sometimes when I was wearing a T-shirt that revealed the protruding veins on my arms, and he'd say it was too much, but Andrew was blunt like that, even about other people's bodies. The Abrupt Brough, I used to call him.

But my songs, like my veins, could be too much. I wasn't afraid to let it go. When I was putting together a song with a band in the practice room, I preferred to let it run and to make mistakes, because that could lead to discoveries, ones you couldn't make on an acoustic in your bedroom. There's a huge difference between standing in the rehearsal room with a full band blazing and humming to yourself in front of a heater.

I let people play what they wanted, because I could always amend it if I didn't like it. I'd learned from playing with people like Wayne and Peter, and even from playing football, that a team effort can open you up to another dimension. People are at their best when they're invested, and you achieve nothing by standing over them and telling them they're shit.

On the other hand, if it wasn't working, I was just as capable as Andrew was of pulling the plug. Even a football team needs its captain.

I don't know what David's and John's motivations were. Essentially they wanted to rock. I think David was the one who most wanted to be a rock star—you could see that in the way he dressed and scowled and purposefully wriggled his bum. We called him Rockin' Ron, after Ron Wood from the Stones, because that was how the Wood we knew was.

I think we all fantasised about being rock stars, even if in the indie world that was like saying you'd coshed a granny. I'd been obsessed with Marilyn and Elvis and I liked to read *Vanity Fair*. All the glamour and the parties—the sassy women, the classy men, their underlings who gave you whatever you wanted. It was a fairytale, far removed from being on the dole in Dunedin. But for now, that fantasy was what we had, while we sang about parties in George Street.

I wrote diaries in my Straitjacket Fits years, and I'd always held on to them because I thought they might be useful one day. Maybe I could even use them for a book. But they're boring. I couldn't bring myself to look at them again. A girlfriend once found those diaries while I was away on tour, and she said they were boring too.

The diaries described the sharks circling around as our band got bigger, and the overseas trips, and the escalating excitement—but mostly it was me moaning about my family, my neuroses, how I went there and then there, and then I did that, and someone said this, and barbecues, and bookshops, and movies, and mountains of personal drudgery. *Twin Peaks*. Picking up a fungal infection in Australia. 'Oh, I wish I could be happy.' 'I may be writing this on a different continent, but I'm always in the middle.' I don't need to read what I was thinking, because I was the one who thought it.

I scanned through the diaries about five years ago. It was like being force-fed a 1,000-page city council report on drainage. It was that dreary and that compelling—the same issues, names and theories repeated every week. The only real value I got from reading them was that they made me realise how you spend life chewing over the same problems and finding things to trip yourself up with. It didn't matter that I was good-looking and at the peak of my powers, singing all over the world in a hot rock 'n' roll band. I was still an expert at pulling myself down. Nothing—my songs, my success, my relationships—was ever enough. You're blind to the ride around you.

A few weeks ago, I thought about those diaries again, with their dribbling, repetitive paragraphs, and I went out the back and burned them.

I kept scrapbooks as well, and they're more useful for drawing a map of my early life. I was always an enthusiastic scrapbooker. Later I wrote a song in Dimmer called 'Scrapbook', but that was about a woman who broke my heart and not about all the pictures I had of trotters.

In the end, I prefer the prejudice of memory. Unlike other prejudices, this one has substance because the memories stay around for a reason. Janet Frame explained this beautifully in the book *Janet Frame in Her Own Words*. I like that the book is in her own words, not the words from other people saying what they thought of her. 'The thing which prompts you to sit down and write must be something that haunts you,' she says. 'You observe it even without knowing it and then it comes to mind, it comes to mind again and you look at it and it comes to mind again.'

Janet Frame's is one of my favourite autobiographies. I admired the way she wrote so astoundingly about unglamorous Ōamaru and buffet lunches in Princes Street. I could relate to what she said about writing—how you're haunted by fragments that you make into pieces of art.

Janet Frame also knew the same psychiatric wards haunted by some of my family.

*

Just like my diaries, the details of Straitjacket Fits can get tedious. Like the day Andrew beat me in a chess game on a flight, and I was annoyed because it was the only chess game we'd played. I'd brought my queen out too early, which Andrew advised me of later, and I was always behind him after that. The modest way he said 'Checkmate' at the end was powerfully understated. It was a match of obvious symbolism, like the day I defeated Neil Finn at table tennis while we were working on Bic's album *Birds*.

Our first big tour was with Look Blue Go Purple at the start of 1987. I remember standing on the pancake rocks at Punakaiki, wearing the half-moon brooch I'd bought from the German hippies up the road. I remember someone changing a lightbulb in Ardmore Road in Ponsonby and the whole suburb going out—there'd been a coincidental power cut. That was in the flat where the Exploding Budgies and Bird Nest Roys lived, with other boys and a whole new squadron of girls. David Mitchell from the 3Ds flatted there, and he'd always be arriving with a new cask of wine or a case of beer or carrying fresh bruises after another drunken bashing. His glasses were constantly broken. Sometimes he'd fall asleep under a house in Parnell and walk home the next afternoon.

The people at Ardmore Road all loved 'Randolph's Going Home', and they'd play it while we drank in the sitting room and sit there and look at me. *Pee-wee's Big Adventure* was on high rotate in the same lounge, and at the time it was wild to watch a character that outrageous yet that innocent, and we'd cry out to each other, 'Would you look at this guy!'

We met the Skeptics. They'd shared the studio they built with members of the Gordons, who were now calling themselves Bailterspace. Both bands were at the heavy end of the spectrum, the Skeptics more pointedly so. The Skeptics were an amalgam of samples, brutal guitars and odd, misplaced rhythms. Their singer, David D'Ath, seemed a little spacey and very self-contained. He'd pull out t'ai chi moves when he sang, and even though it was a bit hippy I couldn't dismiss it as easily as that.

David D'Ath died of leukaemia in 1990, when he was just twenty-six. He left a very unique record; in fact he left several unique records.

Our tour with Look Blue Go Purple pulled in sizeable crowds. We were taking off. The Chills had visited England, and the press there had conceded to their sound. The music writers would still make sheep jokes though.

Back home we partied on, buoyed by our ascension. We played host to touring bands and got them back to our places for parties and falling off mantelpieces. The international bands were too cool for that, but when the Bird Nest Roys and Goblin Mix came down, they were the first ones up on the ledge. Goblin Mix was

Dave Mitchell's new band—their song 'Travelling Grave' was one of the tunes of the year.

Hunters and Collectors came to a party in Liverpool Street, and they knew what was happening, because they covered the Clean's 'Anything Could Happen'. Mark Seymour stood around holding a Steinlager and enthusing about our scene.

The Go-Betweens attended a party at mine in George Street, and Grant McLennan had a pash with my flatmate Ange. The Go-Betweens' drummer, Lindy, was after Graeme Downes—who looked a bit like Robert Forster—but Graeme was already taken.

Robert Forster sat in a chair in the corner, and at first he tried to be alternative and enigmatic. He said something Dylanesque—Bob or Thomas, take your pick—that was supposed to be cutting, but it was so pretentious that I laughed in his face. I said something like, 'I'm not an *NME* journalist or someone in London, mate.'

Robert was fine after that.

I had a fruit bat preserved in a glass jar of formaldehyde that I called Boris. Boris sat on the mantelpiece scrunched up in his glass jar with a pissed-off look on his face. 'If only I could get out of here,' he always seemed to be saying, brooding in his jar. Someone had stolen Boris from the Med School Library and he'd ended up with Dad. Dad had passed him on to me, so now he was a sort of family heirloom.

I'd positioned Boris on the chimney of a long plastic model ship so that a light shone into his jar, lighting him from underneath like Boris Karloff. The model ship was on our mantelpiece. At the party for the Go-Betweens someone knocked Boris off. The glass shattered and there was an immediate stench, as Boris, holding his rigor mortis, rolled along the floor.

Free at last, free at last.

The Go-Betweens grew up in Brisbane, Queensland, which was as fascist as South Africa, and, because they were the freaks in their town, we recognised them straight away. The Go-Betweens were our people too.

The Faction weren't. They were a three-piece synth band who'd backed Nico when she played a bummer show at Otago University. Nico had looked ruined, like a chain-smoking Gloria Swanson on her own Sunset Boulevard. The Faction appeared to be chancers, and when they came to my place after their gig they acted like Englishmen who thought we were waiters. Two of them scoped out my bookcase, which was full of a lot of sixties and seventies subjects, and they told someone else that I was a Neanderthal. Happily, I never heard of the Faction again.

In 1986 I upgraded my guitar to a Swedish-made left-handed Hagström. It had a beautiful varnish and funky machine heads. You can see that guitar in the 'She Speeds' video, below my mullet. I paid it off like my Camembert fine, five to twenty dollars a week, and I was so enamoured with it I put it at the end of my bed with the case open so it was the first thing I saw every morning.

I loved that guitar the same way I've loved all my guitars, even the $130 Maya and the Crimson teardrop one, which didn't work, but which I still mimed on in the clip for 'The Other's Way'.

My Hagström was stolen at a Straitjacket Fits gig in Sydney. I also had my ruby red Les Paul nicked from a venue in Sydney. That had been disastrous, because that time they took Andrew's guitar as well. We'd hastily found replacement guitars, but they were strangers to us, and the whole show felt like playing underwater. Simon Someone Who'd Signed The Cure had flown in especially from Capitol Records in LA for the show, but Capitol didn't sign us. Always take your guitars with you, especially after soundcheck in Sydney.

I got burgled in Auckland in 2008, and they took my guitar as well. It was a rare sixties Gibson SG that I'd scored from the left-handed shop in Pasadena and it still had the original pick-ups. It's probably sitting under the bed of some kid who gets it out once a month to play upside-down versions of 'Smells Like Teen Spirit' and 'Enter Sandman'. I complained about the theft on National Radio and a private detective offered to help me find it. She said she'd heard about a guy in West Auckland sitting on a collection of fifteen hot guitars. Why would you need fifteen guitars?

My SG was never recovered.

My connection with my guitars is intimate and deep. They've gone into battle with me, and they symbolise every victory and defeat. Guitars have always been there, and whatever the outcome they'll be there the next day as well. Hopefully.

I feel like a warrior when I strap on my guitar. The fretboard wears my blood, my sweat, my most private thoughts. My oil gets ingrained in that wood. I know every part of that guitar, and it knows every part of me as well. My guitars are my only material possessions that matter.

I have a photo on my wall of my current guitar—a blazing black seventies Gibson SG with a paint job that looks like the work of a failed spray-painting apprentice in Green Island. It may have been hot at one point too, because the serial number has been sanded off, but that's so far back in its lineage I'm not exactly going to give it back. I wouldn't know who I'd return it to, and I'm not going to talk about it on National Radio. Dad gave me that guitar. Maybe it came into his hands at the same time as Boris the Bat.

Now that Dad is dead, that guitar is more important to me. I didn't play it for years, because the neck was loose and it kept going out of tune, although I used it once in the studio on Andrew's shoe-gazey song 'Such a Daze', because I could bend the neck so it sounded like a whammy bar.

I once lent the SG to Robbie Yeats, who's left-handed, so that he had an electric to puddle about on between his regular gig as the

Dead C's drummer. No one from the Dead C cared if the guitar went out of tune. Robbie said to me one day, simply, 'The neck snapped off.'

But he got it fixed, and the guitar has stayed in tune since. I really love that guitar.

I've never been a collector or a gear snob who pulls a guitar off a wall and says, 'Oh yes, and I used this one back in 1991 for the bridge to the chorus in "Cast Stone".' I can't afford a collection, and I like to keep my company exclusive. I'm not one for having affairs.

I don't put my guitars through lots of effects boxes, because I don't like to sully their tone. I use a Hotcake overdrive pedal, and a Cry Baby wah pedal that doubles as a volume pedal that I also use as a filter, to sweep through frequencies. I added a Boss Sustainer pedal in the early nineties, because Dean Wareham used one of those when we toured with Galaxie 500, and when you kick it in on top of the distortion, the guitar goes up a level and the notes you hold turn into sweetly accurate feedback. But that's it. Why cart around a pedal when you're going to use it for thirty seconds as a gimmick? I'd rather just think of something more interesting to play.

Great guitar playing uncovers a subject boiling inside that bursts and bubbles over. David Mitchell and I always agreed that Lou Reed's lead break at the end of 'I Heard Her Call My Name' is a sublime lead break, because it had that uncontainable energy and, also, every note in it is wrong. Turns out that Reed copped that from free-jazzers like Ornette Coleman. The jazz players have been an influence for me as well. When I first heard Thelonious Monk, he felt like a brother, because the sour undertow to all his notes is exactly how I play my guitar too. The burn behind John Coltrane's saxophone inspired me as well because, like Hendrix, beneath the virtuosity was the spirit that really mattered.

Miles Davis was a master. You could hear it in the way he'd choose one long note instead of twenty, and that one note would say it all. *Tribute to Jack Johnson*, *Sketches of Spain* and a box set of the *In a Silent Way* sessions are big records. The outtakes from *In a Silent Way* are just as good as the official LP. It sounds like he's inventing ambient music.

One of my favourite guitar moments is by Neil Young on an obscure early nineties EP called *Eldorado*, which were mixes or outtakes from his album *Freedom*. Before the bridge on 'Don't Cry', there's a snare crack and a thick, phased guitar crashing in that sounds like the bottom of the earth dropping out. It's very heavy and fucked up. I love that piece of guitar.

I liked Rowland S. Howard's guitar on the Birthday Party's *Bad Seed* EP, too, because it was like the bluesmen, from deep in the woods.

But lots of the guitarists who've inspired me are the ones who've always been nearby. Alec Bathgate, David Kilgour, David Mitchell, Graeme Jefferies, Heazlewood from King Loser—a flotilla of talented players, each with their own voice. I was a fan of Keith Levene's guitar tone with PiL, and I can remember talking about it with Jed Town on a footpath outside the South Dunedin Town Hall while the Gordons played inside. Jed's band, the Features, were on the same bill, and Jed—another excellent guitarist—was using an aluminium guitar just like Levene's.

I learned later that Keith Levene modelled his sound on the German guitarist Michael Karoli in the krautrock band Can, and Karoli became another favourite of mine. His lines had a particular, austere architecture. It was a very European, non-bluesy way of playing guitar. I love blues—Howlin' Wolf, Muddy Waters, Son House—but I don't like modern bluesy guitar, because it's over-polished and clichéd and it sends me to sleep. Most of the great blues players played out of tune anyway, and they never had chorus on their amps.

Hendrix played blues, but he played it in a way that all the people who ripped him off don't. He didn't play lines to impress another customer in a guitar shop. My favourite Hendrix record is *Blues*, which is always sitting in bargain bins for $6.99 because every song on it goes for eight minutes and Hendrix spins off into unknown corners of the universe. But you can't be a rock guitarist and not love Jimi.

I worship at the altar of whoever played rhythm guitar on James Brown's 'Sex Machine'—the insistence and fineness of that riff. Why change chords if the one you're on is doing so well?

Steve Cropper from Booker T. and the M.G.'s is another class guitarist, all precision and economy. He's like Hubert Sumlin with Howlin' Wolf. Cropper and Sumlin both give the song only as much as it needs, as any good player does. It's not about showing off the scale you've slaved over back in your room. When I hear someone going 'widdly widdly', I think, 'Nice, you know a scale.'

My own favourite guitar moments on record would probably be described by some people as 'a bunch of noise'. The instrumental in 'Crystalator' and the end of 'Cast Stone' by Straitjacket Fits are definitely noise—but it's personal, deeply felt noise. With both of those lines I had a vague plan when I started out, but I was happy to ride as a passenger. I didn't know where those lines were going to take me, and I couldn't tell you half of the notes I played—I was going somewhere into the ether, where you mix with the ghosts of dead relatives and friends and blues players. I was just following my fingers. The lead break to 'Cast Stone' sounds like a wounded big cat in the middle of a train tunnel. 'Crystalator' is gone too, somewhere wild and alien.

But I also enjoy the lead break in the Dimmer song 'Smoke', because it's so little and pathetic.

Every decent musician transcends their influences. You take it in until it comes back out as you. There's your own voice. When we recorded the first Straitjacket Fits EP, that's where we were at—sure of how it should go and how it should sound, and by then we sounded like nobody else.

We'd stumbled on our template by accident. Andrew and I could harmonise in a way beyond most of our contemporaries and we countered each other with chiming and roaring guitar. We had an advantage over a lot of indie bands, because we usually sang in tune. I liked Prince then as well—the poppiness and sleaziness in some of my vocals was partially due to him.

Straitjacket Fits had two songwriters, who, mainly because of punk or what followed, had been writing their own songs for years. Each songwriter kept the other one on his toes. We were only twenty-one, but that's an ideal age for making great pop or rock music, because you're at your sharpest physiologically and you haven't been worn down by all the tiresome outside factors.

We had an overwhelming sound. You could see it in our crowds.

*

When Straitjacket Fits ended, people would often describe us as the Band That Nearly Made It. We were the group that had scored the big American deal and should've been Far Bigger.

But a lot of our gigs did make it. In the crowds we played to, even those that numbered just in the dozens or hundreds, I know that there were affected hearts and minds. Anyone standing in that room was lifted or transported and felt the burn. That's what all great rock bands do, and the Straitjackets were often a great rock 'n' roll band. I don't need some publishing guy or music critic or a sales chart to tell me if I've made it. I did make it. And so did my band.

Still, I have the list of excuses that any kid rolls out when they've been told they could have done better—our geographical dislocation; the fact that our music was, mostly, outside of trends;

217

our mismatch with a major record label; our weird music that we never got on top of in the studio.

The world was so much bigger then. It took three weeks for a letter to travel to New Zealand from London. It was no good touring the northern hemisphere for a few weeks every two years, because by the time you went back again a blazing gig had been forgotten and you'd have to start all over again.

When we released *Melt*, our strongest, most cohesive album, when we were at our peak live, it was lost in an ocean of grunge.

We struggled in the studio. If you're a stranger listening back to our records, you might even wonder why there was any fuss.

There wasn't an obvious precedent for our band—for producing bands like us or listening to bands like us, because a lot of our songs, even with their pop centres, were angular and eccentric. We tried things that made our songs less reassuring and probably more uncomfortable, which counted against us commercially while making the music, to my mind, better. But we didn't have the production savvy to translate that sound in an artificial environment. We were always better live.

If you want to be a big star you have to really have to want it, but I always felt ambivalent. I was a punk rock kid from Dunedin who liked weird bands like Thinking Fellers Union Local 282 and the Strapping Fieldhands, even if I read *Vanity Fair*. I couldn't relate to the industry; couldn't get excited about a box addressed to Barry Manilow in an Arista office. Something smelt rotten at the core, and in order to get past that you couldn't be holding back.

When we talked to the Arista people, we'd sit opposite them and wonder who they were. They were thinking the same about us. We found that a lot of Americans couldn't understand why you wouldn't do anything for fame, like going on Rock of Love or dropping your trousers so everyone could take a look—but I wasn't willing to prostitute myself for fame. I didn't want to be famous for doing shit. There were other people who were happy to do that job.

The songs we put on the first Straitjacket Fits EP, *Life in One Chord*, were the best in the first set we wrote. We recorded the EP in the Lab Studios in Auckland, which was out the back of the music store where I'd bought my beautiful Hagström guitar. The Lab was run by an Englishman called Bungalow Bill and his shop was called Bungalow Bill's. Bill was a Geordie, and a total Beatles nutter.

Terry Moore was the in-house engineer who produced the record. Most of the songs worked. The only disappointment was 'All That That Brings'—it was a standout live, but it didn't suit the choppy twelve-string acoustics we used in the studio and it came out sounding lumpy.

Andrew contributed 'Sparkle that Shines'—a winsome, classic tune with a lovely melody, like all of Andrew's songs, and he sang it like a choirboy in a raggedy op-shop cardie.

'She Speeds' and 'Dialling a Prayer' remain Straitjacket Fits' most well-known songs—those, and Andrew's 'Down in Splendour'. People often pick 'She Speeds' over 'Dialling a Prayer' and hold it up as their example of what Straitjacket Fits were about, and 'She Speeds' was definitely promoted as being superior to 'Dialling'. But that's like Fox News hammering away at one point until it's eventually accepted as truth. I always preferred 'Dialling', because that song is a tank. It works whether you play it with a band or on an out-of-tune acoustic, and its instrumental section predates art noise bands like Sonic Youth. But 'Dialling' is better than any song Sonic Youth ever wrote. It has an unexpected structure and verses that never repeat. It uses quiet/loud like the Verlaines or the Gun Club, and it cooks the whole way through, right from the stuttered opening guitar note, which might be a version of B.

'She Speeds' is a vital song. The chord change to the chorus, from E to D, is almost as good as the one in 'Randolph'. It feels

219

like the wind changing direction. The little bridge that connects the first chorus back to the verse is a songwriting nook that to this day I'm proud of, even if it's a subliminal effect. It's a well-mapped song, and organic, and it makes its own journey. I don't like songs where you can predict the chord changes—you need to be braver than that.

'She Speeds' was inspired by the actress Miranda Harcourt, who I'd kissed in Dunedin and once again in Wellington. My feelings for Miranda were never as extreme as they appear to be in 'She Speeds', but the character in the song, like her, had better things to do. I remember sitting across from Miranda at a table in the Robbie Burns hotel, her with her springy red hair, and she was eating an avocado with a spoon for dinner. She'd told some of her friends who might be turning up that they'd recognise me, because I looked like a criminal. Miranda was going through her Bad Girl phase. She was fresh back from Sydney, where she'd gone armed with a book of Katherine Mansfield short stories and a jar of twenty-cent pieces. She'd heard they could pass for Australian coins.

John did the cover for the EP—one of his disturbing Dali-esque paintings, of a melted, misshapen man jogging past a barn with a phallic pitchfork leaning by the door. The predominant colour was a sickly, uncommercial pink. For the photo on the back cover, I built a set in my lounge and filled it with teddy bears, guitars and a giant cardboard phone.

When *Life In One Chord* came out in October 1987, it set off the big alarms.

The record got excellent reviews and made the top twenty. It even reached England and both *Melody Maker* and *Sounds* made it their singles of the week. At the start of 1988 we went to Auckland and played with some other bands on a barge parked in the harbour, our new reputation in tow.

I watched Sneaky Feelings play and decided that that was one of the things I wasn't going to do. It was like an entire band of McCartneys doing George's lesser tunes. Straitjacket Fits were going to be sharper than that, so we went on next and smoked the stage.

Brough and I held opposing views on Sneaky Feelings. Once, Andrew came along with a song I didn't like—I thought it sounded too much like Sneaky Feelings. 'But I like Sneaky Feelings,' said Andrew, and that was our difference right there.

We were invited to open for the Pogues at the Powerstation, and the place was packed and seething. Sweat and alcohol slid down the slimy walls. The air felt delirious and a little dangerous, and people in the audience were waving Irish Independence flags, so I wasn't going to muck about with that.

Shane MacGowan skulled long glasses of red wine all through the afternoon and to the end the night. The barely dressed women backstage turned out be hookers, and because I was naïve I felt a little shocked.

There's a missing demographic in Dunedin. Often, it seems like a town made up of students and the elderly, who, back in the day, you saw sitting on buses or wearing their old-man hats, smoking roll-your-owns or trotting off to have lunch in South Dunedin. The people in between, somewhere between twenty-five and forty, disappear into the suburbs or shift to somewhere bigger.

When I returned to Dunedin in 2015, after nearly three decades of living in Auckland, I saw it in a way I hadn't as a young man. The land, the stillness, the inky horizons, the cold foreboding ocean banging on empty coasts. The bald green hills smudged by a watery light.

James K. Baxter said the reason New Zealanders harbour an innate anxiety is because the land and sea around them can be intimidating, and I believe there's a truth to that. Reminders of your mortality and insignificance lie all around you.

The Otago Peninsula is like a Sibelius symphony, or 'Pink Frost' by the Chills. You can feel the land vibrate. I hear the landscape in a lot of Dunedin music, in the strange, angular pop songs, and in the beautiful and bleak melodies. The uncompromising terrain around Dunedin is magnificent, but when I was twenty-two I didn't appreciate that. It was all I'd ever known. There was nothing exotic in shivering on a beach or freezing at the top of a hill.

I wanted to be in the middle of It, sitting in smoky rooms full of cool people or walking through concrete canyons with interesting shops. I wanted a page in *Vanity Fair* or *Melody Maker*. So we joined the great northward drift and packed up and headed to Auckland.

Debbi Gibbs offered to become our manager, because she had the same eye for an opportunity as her dad. Debbi was smart and organised, which helped, because we were all of the first and none of the second. Maybe Debs also had something to prove to her dad, because she seemed determined to forge her own way. She'd always say 'Ohhh myyy Gawwwd' about anything, even if it wasn't outrageous, and I still imitate that, to her face, to this day.

The world was opening up to the Flying Nun bands. There were rave reviews in Britain, and nerdy boys in American fanzines were writing about our records with a zest and perception beyond most of the critics at home. The mainstream in New Zealand, the radio stations and the music industry, still didn't touch us, so it seemed obvious to just hop over them.

In 1989, a lot of the Flying Nun bands were at their peak. But that year the New Zealand Music Award for Best Group went to When the Cat's Away, an all-woman collective who dealt exclusively in covers of seventies hits. It was only when we left and came back, vindicated by success in the northern hemisphere, that people changed their tune and went, 'Oh, we always thought they were great.'

We wanted to use Auckland as a springboard, and we felt jealous of the Chills, who were filmed sitting on the London tube in their video for 'I Love My Leather Jacket'. London was Mecca then. Before that, it was Sydney, where it became a Kiwi tradition to go to Kings Cross and die of a heroin overdose. After London, New York was the place, then Berlin. A couple of years ago, people were discussing Istanbul.

I got a flat in Ponsonby with Ange, who'd also moved up from Dunedin, and Gary Cope. Our flat was a downstairs dump in College Hill with the landlord, an architect, stomping about upstairs. The architect reminded me of the wanker at the twenty-four-hour dairy, in that he was an older man who sleazed around my girlfriend, although the architect was better dressed. He tried to sue us for damaging his flat when we shifted out, but the flat had been damaged before we moved in, so we won our day in court.

Gary saw the architect in the foyer afterwards and asked him, 'How does it feel to be a loser?'

Roger had also relocated to Auckland and had rented an office in Queen Street, which was still affordable then, and Gary was working there, mostly doing the accounts. I was broke, and I managed to get part-time work at the office as a receptionist. I wrote press releases, banging too hard on a typewriter. I'd learned to type two-fingered on a springy old Olivetti at 4XO. I'm bashing the shit out of my MacBook Pro right now.

I worked because I had to eat. The dole was $105 per week. Before we left Dunedin, Ange and I had shared a flat in Pine Hill—I thought of the chorus to 'She Speeds' when I was walking to the Pine Hill dairy—and we nearly starved in Pine Hill too. I was so poor I had one pair of shoes that my other flatmate had given me. They were half a size too small. Ange and I ate baked potatoes and boiled rice. We still managed to get slightly drunk, because you could score bottles of McWilliam's Port for $4.95, so I'd eke out one of those over the Friday and Saturday nights.

But someone dobbed me in when I was working at Flying Nun, and I was called into Social Welfare.

Auckland was another world, ten times the size of Dunedin, with food from all over the world, trendy clubs, and a mix of brown and white people. It had foreign vegetation and citrus in backyards that smelt thick with humidity. Everything was lush. I hadn't really seen Indian people before either, and it was too cold down south for most Polynesians. There was also a flood of beautiful women in Auckland, and I was a fan of beautiful women. Once, a therapist said to me that I was a collector of women, and I felt appropriately cheap.

When I quit drinking at the age of twenty-three and didn't drink for thirteen years, it was at the height of my rock 'n' roll years, and I was touring and being the spunky lead singer. Stylish women would come up to me and say straight out that they needed to sit on my face. But I was usually in a relationship, and sober, and I turned most of these offers down—ninety-nine percent of the time.

I learned early on that empty bonking wasn't worth it, because, for me, fucking someone is never casual. There's too much heat, and residual feeling, for that.

I had two loose years, both during periods when I was drinking. But one of those times was when I first came to Auckland, when I realised I could pretty much have anyone I liked. That was an exceptional power, especially for someone with shaky self-esteem. I noticed a pattern where women would simply hover nearby. Unlike men, they wouldn't approach. That's what I found, anyway. They would position themselves in your sight line instead, so you could see them.

The guy who stole my girlfriend from Auckland came up to me

at a welcoming party and said I should watch it, because all of the people at the party were taken.

'Be careful,' he said, insinuating a beating, which was golden coming from him.

I had another loose year, around 2005, when I was drinking again and sharing a flat with Dion from the band D4. I was probably in a mid-life crisis and I couldn't afford a sports car. Both of us were single and lonely.

Dion and I would get pissed and make up broken blues songs like 'One Man, One Fork, One Spoon', because that was all Dion had in his house when I first shifted in.

Dion helped run a club night called the Black Luck Club, where we played rock 'n' roll and soul records. My DJ name was Keith Miller, which was the worst DJ name I could think of, and I'd write up a self-important DJ sign to stick on the front of my booth: 'QUIET PLEASE!! DJ Keith Miller in session. NO REQUESTS PLEASE!!'

The Black Luck Club was full of women, and I put myself about for a bit. I wasn't as hot as I was when I was younger—who is?—and I could feel the fade-out of the ageing screen queen creeping up behind me. But I was more famous then, and that has its own kind of power.

None of the looseness worked. The jacket never fitted. I'd think there was somewhere better, but I'd get there and think exactly the same thing. So I'd get restless and move on to the next chapter, the eternal bachelor recycling his old delusions.

Mostly I've been in a string of relationships that last two to four years, and then I leave, or I make them leave, because no matter where I am, it's never enough.

*

My mother told me that the reason I didn't have successful relationships and was always getting my heart broken was that I 'always went out with those dolly birds'. She told me I needed a solid woman with wide hips who could bear me children. Then again, Mum liked my eccentric girlfriends, the ones with troubled backgrounds, because, it's obvious to think, she related.

She wasn't so fond of my partner who was an actress—the last partner I had before Mum's death—because she thought the actress was faking. It was true that the actress hid some dark self-doubt behind a jolly facade. She was from a middle-class suburb in Auckland, where everyone acted polite, and when she met my friends from Dunedin she was upset by how uncouth they were and the coarse way they interacted. Tex Houston's name for me is 'Cunt'. David Mitchell was back from England when he met my girlfriend, and he probably called me one too. Dave was half drunk at soundcheck.

When Peter Gutteridge stayed for a night at the house the actress and I shared in Te Atatu, he would have done nothing to improve her impression of my friends, not Gutteridge with his straggly hair, shuffling gait and missing teeth. He did score a few points, because he knew a lot about herbal remedies and books. But she obviously thought her and I were different people who belonged with different sets. Her father, a businessman, pressured her to give up acting and maybe find someone who wasn't a musician. Even though he was friendly, I think he was stressed by the idea of an unreliable income. But acting brought her validation. Happily, she still does it, successfully.

When the actress moved out, she took most of the furniture in our house. One man, one fork, one spoon. The cat she had, that we both loved, got accidentally poisoned and died a few days later.

She'd been hatching Monarch butterflies when she left, and they hatched in front of me as I sat sick and sometimes crying on a deck chair on the porch. The butterflies were born into a furious wind, and most of their still-wet wings were torn, so they bobbled about pathetically on the porch, listing to the side, struggling on scrawny legs. I'd take them and put them by the plants they liked, which didn't do any good. All of them died and rotted.

Her father came around and sprayed the edges of the property with weedkiller so that the weeds would die and so his daughter could claim her bond. Two days later, a hedgehog crawled out, and that died in front of me too.

These all felt like obvious messages, and I looked up to God and said—yes, I get the point.

The whole time the actress was with me, she had a text message and email relationship with a young author whose novel she'd once reviewed. He knew a lot about art history, and didn't mispronounce 'Degas' the way I did. The author had contacted her after reading her review and asked her if he could borrow one of her lines, which I thought was an odd request to make, because he was an author, and surely he had his own lines.

When the actress was walking out, I said to her, 'I'm going to be pissed off if you go and have an affair with your penpal.'

She did go and get together with her penpal—Clayton, who wrote the novel *Wulf*.

After the success of *Life In One Chord*, we felt the pressure to record a follow-up. It was important to strike while we were hot. But we'd used our best songs on the EP, and we were pushed into making an album that we weren't ready for.

Hail was a real let-down. It just wasn't very good. Our weird little songs wriggled around, sounding messy and one-dimensional. Even the song 'Hail', which we'd had big hopes for, got lost in a studio mush.

There were some decent tunes. Our songwriting chops were too good for there not to be. 'This Taste Delight' was ethereal with big harmonies between me and Andrew, but it felt dulled down in the studio. That song was inspired by my love for Big Star's record *Third*, a record with glacial, ice-flow tunes called 'Holocaust' and 'Big Black Car' that played on the point of collapse. I didn't like Big Star's more up-tempo stuff, because it sounded old-hat, like the Raspberries or the Byrds. Years later I saw Alex Chilton play in London, backed by a band called the Posies, who were turning his songs into bar-room boogie. I wanted to yell out, 'Play the slow, depressing one!' because Chilton belonged on the outside, not in the middle playing party music. He produced records by Tav Falco's Panther Burns, who were nearly as mean and primeval as the Cramps. He produced *Gravest Hits* by the Cramps too, their first and meanest record.

'Grate', the first tune we'd written as Straitjacket Fits, worked on *Hail*. The line 'Your skin crawls to escape my hand' is one of my strongest images. 'There is cold steel and it is grating' went the hook, about the distance of a lover. We also recorded a blistering 'So Long Marianne', which went out as a first single as a double A-side with 'Hail'. The lead break was a world away from Cohen's folky strum.

But the rest of our songs fell flat. They were decent ideas we couldn't unravel. I think we all tried too hard—Terry Moore as the producer, and the band as well. John nearly broke down trying to keep in with the click track. 'Life In One Chord' has no ride cymbal on it, because it was out of time. Then again, this was the period when the Jean-Paul Sartre Experience were, at their producer's insistence, recording their drum parts drum by drum, cymbal tap by cymbal tap, even though Gary Sullivan is one of New Zealand's best drummers. But with the rising stakes, everyone thought they needed to get 'more professional', which was an attitude that only worsened as record after record was drained of its blood.

In the middle of the *Hail* recording sessions, we agreed to do a gig—which was a mistake, because we were in the wrong mindset. When you're recording, you're listening to the music in an analytical way and you don't do that onstage. There, it's one big rush where you set your feet in the middle and turf it out. The gig was with the Headless Chickens in front of several hundred people at the Powerstation and the Chickens made us nearly irrelevant.

The Headless Chickens were at an apex then, and probably felt like they had something to prove. Their sound, with its On-U Sound samples and forward-looking art-rock turns, was more contemporary than the rest of the Flying Nun canon. They were a bit like the Skeptics but more accessible and direct. They knew they'd kicked our butts at the Powerstation, and so did everyone else. No one did that to Straitjacket Fits.

We retreated back to the Lab and kept going with our awkward-sounding record.

Andrew contributed two songs to the album, one fast one and one slow one. That became his pattern. Altogether he wrote seven songs for Straitjacket Fits, three fast ones and four slow ones. Fans of Andrew sobbed after he left and said that Andrew was bullied into silence, but he was by far the slowest writer. Sometimes I thought he was a bit lazy. He never seemed to try that hard with his words, which could float about in a cloud of non-specifics. Andrew said later that this was his version of lyrical Impressionism, which, even if it's not true, is a very good excuse.

I'd get pissed off when the same people said that Andrew had our best tunes, because he wrote seven songs in four years. I wrote about forty, and I thought my return would be pretty good too if they were narrowed down to seven.

But Andrew's role in the band was important. His harmonies, guitar, and pop sensibilities did a lot to shape our group. I liked Andrew. He was smart, cultured in an unpretentious way, with a twisted sense of humour. He was as unforgiving as the rest of us, but he also had the quickest temper—snapping sometimes and barking at the stage crew or others on the periphery. I always found it ironic that his public image was that of the gentle altar boy set upon by the bully Carter.

When my dad was having problems with his mental health, he joined a support group at the university. One night he was talking to another man in the group and telling him about his son being in a band. This man said that he had musical son, too, who was doing quite well now with a group called Straitjacket Fits. It was Andrew's dad.

I love that image of our dads together at the depressives club, making their big discovery.

Andrew got depressed sometimes too. He probably felt underappreciated being in our band, and that must have been depressing. 'I really like Andrew's song,' David would say, and John would say the same thing. Andrew's songs had easy melodies that you could latch on to, but I think he struggled with confidence, and he probably felt overshadowed, especially out on stage where I'd get right on the mic while he held back, picking away in his glasses. It was usually my picture they put in our reviews.

When Andrew left and formed his own band, Bike, he made one poppy, chiming album called *Take In the Sun*. Then he seemed to disappear.

He did an interview once where he said that whenever he wrote a song, he would wonder what I'd make of it.

I think of Andrew with me on his shoulder, saying it wasn't right, or sneering that it didn't rock hard enough—I don't like the thought of being inside his head like that.

I agreed to do a cameo in one of the first Bike music videos, where they're travelling around and miming to their song inside a caravan. I played a cop—and grew a moustache especially—and at the end, I pull their caravan over and write the band a ticket.

I was in a bad way while we were recording *Hail*, in a pit with all my drinking.

After our album was wrapped, I finally did something about it and went and sought help.

When you face up to an addiction and stop destroying yourself, it's because you have no choice. You can only turn your life around if you're scared, or shocked, into action.

I was scared. Scared that my life was opening up, and there was me pulling it down. I was finding it harder and harder to live with myself, with how little I'd remember, with how nasty I could be sometimes to people I liked and who didn't deserve it. I was rude to two people one night, women I respected and who had always been friendly. One of them said to me later that it was like I was striking out against something I was afraid of, and maybe she was right. Perhaps it was wrapped up with my mother. I don't know. I was too drunk to tell.

I got off alcohol by taking a psychedelic drug, just like Peter Gutteridge had when he'd kicked methadone. I tried Ecstasy for the first time. E was still new, and this was the real McCoy. I wrote about the experience later in the Straitjacket Fits song 'Headwind', which had a lead break that tried to describe the lid of a skull coming off.

Saw truth explode
Through false windows
It caught and lifted the hood
Caught and lifted like I never thought it would
Killed the pretence and it unmasked all the fools
And I'm seeing in full circle—360 degrees
I find no need to fight

These things crawling inside
like slaters on dead wood
Nothing's forever so make sure it's good
High as vertigo goes
Funny how things come to a head
Laughing at sick jokes
I don't have to

My experience that night was as transformative as psychedelic experiences are often hyped up to be but rarely ever are. When the E kicked in, I was overwhelmed with foreign feelings—positive ones, like solidarity and empathy. Gone was the murk and resentment I usually fell into on alcohol. I realised that other people weren't my enemy, that they were fellow beings in their own vessels, dragging along their own crosses. I felt an oceanic sensitivity, and a regret, for the way I'd often been. To ignore this and charge on regardless would be an act of self-sabotage.

At the height of my trip I ran into David Mulcahy, the guitar player from JPSE, in a bar. Dave had seen me out the night before, when I'd caused the usual stir, but all he said was, 'You don't seem very good, Shayne.'

I nearly cried when he said that, because it was supportive and forgiving.

The same night, I was down to do a solo performance at a late-night cabaret out the back of K Road. I didn't think I'd be able to go, but Rupert and Peter from the Bird Nest Roys told me not to be such a chicken, and they offered to come as support. They stood on the stage beside me with their arms folded, looking staunch, like Public Enemy's 'Security of the First World' flanking Chuck D. They were just as high as me. I bashed out some bitter tune with lyrics I couldn't relate to.

The feeling of that night stayed with me. I didn't drink for another thirteen years.

I enrolled at an out-patient alcohol treatment centre, tucked away down a driveway in the plush suburb of Newmarket. There, I talked to a Dutch counsellor called Willum and attended group meetings, where sixty-five-year-old nurses and men with ruined varicose faces told exactly the same stories about alcohol as mine.

I got angry when Willum told me he was leaving and that our sessions would have to end, because I thought he was abandoning me too.

But I came out of my treatment prepared to move on, with all of my wits about me.

Hail got good reviews—though usually four stars instead of five. It probably made us more hungry. When Rough Trade released the album internationally they combined the album with our first EP, and we could stand behind that.

In September 1988 we were offered a New Zealand tour with the Jesus and Mary Chain. We were excited, because the Mary Chain were one of our favourite British bands. Their 'Upside Down' single was spectacular, a ruckus with bashing drums that sounded like metal barrels and layers of screeching feedback. The feedback was the loudest feature. Their album *Psychocandy* was ferocious too, pop songs lashed with razors.

The Jesus and Mary Chain didn't say a word to us the entire tour, but the Reid brothers seemed to find it difficult to talk in general. They sat around on the other side of the hall, moping beneath their fringes, mumbling to themselves in Scottish.

A member of their road crew told us they liked our version of 'So Long Marianne', and the same guy came over at soundcheck before our last gig in Auckland and told David that William Reid wanted to buy his bass. David said that if William wanted to buy his bass, then he should ask him himself—but William never did.

We held our own with the Jesus and Mary Chain, and the New Zealand tour was proof to us that we weren't inferior to anyone.

We supported R.E.M. as well when they were touring their album *Green*. We weren't intimidated by R.E.M. either: we just went out there and did what we did. The American bands didn't overshadow us. Our songs and ideas were as good as theirs, maybe even more progressive. A couple of years later the 3Ds supported Nirvana, and they were just as good as Nirvana.

In early 1989 we went to Australia for several gigs. It was my first time overseas, and it felt surreal to stand in another reality.

The Australians were fashionable, I thought, but in an identikit way, with expensive gear from trendy Oxford and Chapel streets and a brazen display of flesh. The Aussies didn't go for the buttoned-up look.

Our tour promoter was based in Sydney. She invited me to stay at her house, and at nights, while her partner worked upstairs, she'd curl up on the couch opposite me and throw me seductive looks.

It was exciting playing to new audiences, because you weren't over-exposed or bogged down by your history. The Australians just took what they were given and seemed very grateful to be given it. They went crazy. There'd been a lot of pre-tour hype. We were bringing a form of rock to them that was different from the four-square rock they knew. But the fact that it rocked appealed to them and made us possibly the most popular Flying Nun band across the Tasman.

The reviews were over the top. The guy who wrote us up for the *Melody Maker* said we were the best guitar band in the world. The reviewer at the *Sydney Morning Herald* agreed with him.

When we returned to Australia a few months later the reception was equally fervid, and some of the reviews went even further. 'The inheritors to the Velvet Underground,' they said. It was a buzz to have our band written up that way, but Brough stayed abrupt, I stayed suspicious, and David usually made a smart comment. We carried on, convinced of our worth but sometimes bluffing a bit.

In the middle of 1989, Rough Trade put out our record and we were offered our first northern hemisphere tour. We thought it was only natural that we'd go on crushing everything in our path.

New York was the city of Marilyn, Elvis, *Vanity Fair*, Audrey Hepburn standing in a gown, chewing a pastry in front of Tiffany's. The yellow fire hydrants from *Taxi Driver*. The stoops before the buildings, like the set from *Singing in the Rain*. The city was bigger than my preconceptions. It was New York, and I'd grown up in Brockville.

Our gig at CBGB—the legendary CBGB, with the dirty stage and graffiti, and a toilet sitting oddly in the middle of the Men's— was, like our first show in Sydney, one of the best gigs we ever played. It was a part of the New Music Seminar, then the biggest alternative showcase in the world. A woman from Epic was there. Afterwards, while we milled about outside the club, someone leaned over and asked her whether she'd liked the gig. 'Very much so,' she replied.

Big international labels started sniffing around us then because we were only licenced to Rough Trade, and Flying Nun hadn't sorted out any contracts. At least a dozen bands from Dunedin were getting American deals. Tiny, irrelevant Dunedin giving indie to the world.

Bob Biggs from Slash Records had flown out to meet us in Auckland before we left, hoping to get to us first. A tall all-American guy, Bob had already signed the Chills and Verlaines, but that put us off because we didn't want to be part of a stable.

In Los Angeles, someone threw a pig-sized piece of paving

stone at us from an overbridge and it smashed just in front of our van. We heard that a person had been killed by someone doing that just the week before. I'd seen the guy holding the stone above his head as we were driving up, and I thought he was holding a giant leg of ham.

LA was trashy and weird, but it also felt familiar because of the movies we'd seen growing up. The guy at the PA company was Mickey Rooney's grandson. One of the first people I saw when I got to LA was the singer from Mötley Crüe, in a red bandana, driving past on a Harley with big ape hanger handlebars. He looked like a poser.

I thought I saw Arnold Schwarzenegger on Hollywood Boulevard, also riding a Harley.

In our LA hotel, at first I thought the American accents coming through the wall were on TV, then I realised they were coming from real Americans.

The refrigerator in the hotel leaked and in the middle of the pool there were two drowned cockroaches.

The Hollywood rock magazines, the ones they gave out for free in the shops that sold leather clothes and garish buckles, were full of light metal bands with poodle hair and sucked-in cheeks. We joked that these bands were all the same four people, just wearing different wigs. The oldest member of the band always looked a bit ashamed, arranging his face in a favourable way but only just holding up.

Onstage in San Francisco, I joked that it was ironic that a city most famous for its summer of love had a main street named Haight. I meant it as a throwaway but it came across as unfunny and abrasive. There'd been a giant earthquake the day before we'd arrived—freeways had collapsed on cars and a lot of people had died. People were shook up, and San Francisco was still rumbling with aftershocks. It was odd being in a large city where everyone had had the same near-death experience. It wasn't the time for poorly conceived jokes.

Haight-Ashbury was decrepit. The summer of love had curdled. Drug pushers in hopeful rainbow-coloured clothes muttered 'Hash . . . speed . . . heroin' through broken teeth, but we just kept on walking.

Detroit was the epitome of America gone to seed, with its tall sooty buildings and redundant diggers sitting in fields on the outskirts, like broken *War of the Worlds* machines. We were warned to go straight back to our hotel after the show in Detroit, because we wouldn't be safe on the streets, but instead we milled about with thousands of black people and no one there was bothered.

In America, I could feel the sharp divide between black and white. Different coloured people related to each other in a stiff and self-conscious way, and they were arranged separately in cities, with clear lines between the 'okay' areas and the 'dangerous' areas. The dangerous areas were always black. 'Oh, you don't want to go there,' someone with us was always saying. We weren't used to that. In New Zealand, people of different ethnicities co-existed and sometimes had families together and it wasn't a big deal.

Some goons abused us out of the car in Salt Lake City though, which was reassuring, because it was a touch of home in a strange and far-off land.

We'd visited a Mormon temple in Salt Lake City and it felt as plastic as an American Express card. But the cathedral in Cologne, Germany was different. It was the most amazing building I'd seen, with goths flitting around its base. When you went into buildings like that, you could feel the press of history.

In Europe, the people were respectful and polite. They'd bring out trays lavished with bread, cheeses and cold meats, and cases of free drinks. We weren't used to that in New Zealand, where ancient bar managers made sure we wouldn't disturb the three alcoholics sitting at the bar watching sports. Our soundcheck couldn't interrupt the 3:15 from Trentham.

The Europeans had a touring band circuit you could get lost in forever. Some of the bands did seem lost forever, as did the drivers with rough cigarette faces who drove the tour buses. Those buses smelt like ten thousand bands, and there were often used tissues beneath the mattresses of the coffin-sized beds. The toilets had a lemon smell that couldn't obscure the stench of urine. When the flush knob was working, the contents of the toilet were tipped onto the road.

One frosty day, we visited the Dachau concentration camp. In the reception area at Dachau there were photographs of sad, skinny Jewish people, sitting in baths full of ice cubes while uniformed Germans stood around them, writing on notepads. The ovens were blunt and revolting. Outside, an old Jewish man in traditional dress was walking around crying, picking his way through the tidy grass strips where the barracks and people once lay. Autumn drained the morning sun of any shred of warmth.

When we got to Berlin, the wall was coming down. We'd seen the East Berliners on the autobahn, puffing along in their fibreglass Trabants with black smoke blasting out of the exhaust pipes. Down at the gates of the border, East Berliners were driving out, punching the air through their open windows. Westerners stood around cheering. You could spot the former communist, because he or she was always pale, in dowdier clothes, and usually carrying bananas or video equipment—stuff you couldn't get in East Berlin.

We drove through some Eastern Bloc areas late at night, and the atmosphere by the road felt dangerous and suppressed. People were always reporting on each other. The problem with the Stasi.

Citizens with their bags packed, waiting for the knock at the door. In 1989, Berliners brought sledgehammers down to the wall, and swung it at with a fervour dedicated to decades of apartness and not being allowed to be together.

There were parties on the top of the wall, and I grabbed a fragment to take back to Aunt Nat.

We went on a subway ride running through a part of East Germany and outside the carriage it looked eerie and abandoned. There were still bullet holes in the walls of old buildings.

There's a picture of me with three friends standing in front of the Berlin Wall. Oddly for me, I'm throwing a peace sign.

We were sufficiently full of ourselves to give obnoxious interviews to the English press, because we thought that's what you did.

I told Rough Trade's magazine *The Catalogue* that the Rugby band Spacemen 3 were interesting but that they weren't as good as Snapper. One of the Spacemen 3 came to our gig and told me that he'd really enjoyed it, so maybe he hadn't read the article in *The Catalogue*. He was with his partner and bandmate Kate Radley, who he'd later write some of his Spiritualized songs about.

I also told *The Catalogue* that we'd taken care of business in Australasia, and we'd probably do that in England and Europe too. There was a picture of me and David in *Melody Maker* and we looked the part.

The head of Rough Trade, Geoff Travis, a modest-looking, headmasterly man in glasses, told someone we were naïve, and his comment got back to us. Geoff apologised, which many record company people did when they weren't trying to scare us. *Hail* went into the English indie top twenty but Galaxie 500 were always several places above us. They were our label mates on Rough Trade and we were put together on tour. At point we were being talked about as two of the most promising bands on earth.

Galaxie were fluid and graceful. Their guitarist Dean looked like a film star. He'd been born in Wellington but you couldn't tell it by his accent. He played long, languorous lead breaks that slowly stepped to heaven and he sang in a shaky falsetto. The rhythm section was a couple, Damon on drums and Naomi on bass. A lot of their lines sounded like New Order slowed down. Galaxie started when the trio had met at Boston University but now they were based in New York. At first, their records reminded me of the Christchurch bands, with their Velvet Underground chords and plaintive sadness, but when Galaxie played live they went beyond that. They were the most popular band on our bill, and by the end of the tour they always went on second. Someone told me I wasn't as handsome as Dean.

Geoff Travis said later in another interview that we'd been overshadowed by Galaxie 500, but that we'd probably learned a lot from the tour.

In London we partied with New Zealanders in big tenement buildings, doing bongs out of buckets of water. London was Mary Quant, black-and-white films with young men in drainpipe trousers smoking cigarettes, girls with thick mascara. It was a buzz to skip the streets that Jagger, the Beatles and Jean Shrimpton had skipped down in the sixties.

But after one gig we played, a man lay in a gutter with a pool of blood around his head, either unconscious or dead. He'd been beaten up by one of the bouncers. When someone called the cops, the bouncer—a tattooed, meat-headed man—ran off down the road. The man he'd hit was eventually roused and probably taken to hospital. The English bouncers were awful, like blow-ups of the Brockville bullies, sneering and barking orders.

Even though I was on a magic carpet ride, in between the exciting moments I still wrote the same complaints in my diary. That was the touring life—half miserable, half hardly believing you were there. I missed my girlfriend, and wrote her erotic letters that took three weeks to arrive.

Because their bands were being approached by record labels around the world, Flying Nun felt under threat and went into partnership with Mushroom in Australia. Mushroom couldn't really relate to the New Zealand bands, although the boss, Michael Gudinski, probably recognised the pioneering spirit that he'd had when he first began his label. But Mushroom seemed to be mainly conservative Australians dealing in the mainstream, and although we had some fans in the Melbourne offices, many of them didn't get it. They'd only heard the rumours and the rumble from the underground.

Mushroom brought a new efficiency to Flying Nun, and suddenly there were contracts being bandied about. We signed a contract for what was then a lot of money, while keeping our options open for the rest of the world. I suppose we felt some loyalty to Roger, but he seemed to get misdirected on the Mushroom trip.

When Roger went to base himself at the Mushroom offices in London, Lesley Paris took over at Flying Nun with her partner Paul McKessar. They had to become Mushroom apologists doing the dirty work, because the musicians were all their friends. I felt sorry for Lesley because she was stressed and at heart she's an honourable person. She had to be the bad news bearer for the new Australian boss.

Mushroom's A&R guy was a New Zealander, and he may have been a genuine fan of our band, but there was something smarmy in the promises he made, and our swords came to cross. In LA, I was seeing the singer from a popular Australian band. She was sharing an apartment with the A&R guy, supposedly as friends, but he was fond of her as well. When I went to her room in the apartment, there was only one bed. I got upset and asked her what the hell that was about. She said the A&R guy hadn't been able to book a room with two beds, but that was okay because they were friends and the bed was big enough for both of them.

A few months later, I was talking to the A&R guy, and, trying to smooth our working relationship and be open with him, I mentioned that I knew he had feelings for my girlfriend. He got offended and angry and he told me I didn't know what I was talking about.

We began writing a new album. I felt uncluttered and clear. I was sharing a flat in Grafton with Rachel Phillipps (Martin's sister) and her boyfriend Richard. They'd scored the place through the Methodist Church, because Rachel's father is a Methodist minister. The rent was very generous, way below the standard for a clean, roomy house in Auckland. Rachel always had the Front Lawn album on the stereo, with its beautiful song 'Andy' that Don McGlashan wrote about his older brother who had died. With their 'How You Doing' skit, Don and Harry Sinclair anticipated the Flight of the Conchords.

Rachel also had *There's a Riot Goin' On* by Sly and the Family Stone, and I grew to love that record. In my rock nerd top five lists it's near the top—the grimy funk of it all and the lonely lyrical bummers. On 'Time', it sounded like he was improvising while dying slowly on the mic. Sly Stone recorded most of the album alone in his studio through 1970 and 1971. 'Dance to the Music' and 'Everyday People' had disappeared in his rear-view mirror. The tracks on *Riot* were all muffled and boxy because during the recording Sly would invite women to his studio, snort more cocaine, then try to bed them, and to help with that he'd ask the women to sing a backing part, which he'd usually go back and wipe. He did that so often that the tapes started wearing out. It affected the record's fidelity. But he also did a lot of rethinking on his record, blowing a million dollars from Columbia Records while rotating his obsessive and often dismal ideas. *Riot* is a classic, answerable only to its creator. The music was shrouded in a personal despair. But Sly could still write a chorus. *Riot* leaks soul out of its bleak, black arse.

I developed new songs on a Tascam four-track cassette recorder that a friend in London had bought me and sent over. I'd never had such a sophisticated home recording set-up before. Until then I'd just record bits on a dictaphone, and if I was feeling expansive I'd play it back and record another layer onto a cassette tape recorder.

My room in Grafton had a lot of light and it was a fresh environment to work in. I felt a new positivity when I was writing—I wrote the songs with clarity and a growing motivation. The Tascam was good because I'd lay down one riff and build variations around it; it was amazing how many notes you could fit around one riff. The notes that sounded a bit off were often the best ones, because they pulled against the tide. 'Cast Stone' was like that—one riff with a dozen chords around it.

I wrote 'Cast Stone' about Wayne. I was still dealing with my grief. I was desperate for the song not to sound too earnest, or dishonest or manipulative, or as if I was taking advantage of a situation. In the end, 'Cast Stone' didn't sound sentimental—though, as with many Straitjacket songs, it trod a fine line.

'Melt Against Yourself' is a delicate tune, one of the prettiest I've written. It was about sobriety and a model I had a crush on called Rossana who, according to me, needed to lose her boyfriend. I liked how a song could be about one thing but equally about another. My lyrics often have a lot of ambiguity—maybe partly because I'm not quite sure about the way I truly feel. Or maybe I have a small fear of commitment. Really, I just like playing around with words.

'Melt' had off keys that stopped it being sappy and Andrew and I found a harmony that was one of the best we did.

I addressed sobriety more than once in the new songs—'Missing Presumed Drowned' was about how people could feel threatened when you were sober, offering you drinks and saying how much fun you used to be when you were drunk. It wasn't fun for me.

'Roller Ride', a discordant rocker with a fairground chorus, was about that too: 'And the view from the ground makes me blind to the thrill of the ride.'

The tunes I wrote for *Melt* were some of my strongest. I was at the top of my game. 'Bad Note for a Heart' became a single, although in the video we look awkward, and someone has put too much makeup on our faces and piled our hair high with hairspray.

The makeup and hair showed that we'd reluctantly go along with the industry people, because we didn't know any other way and we thought they might be right. It was part of their job to convince us that we didn't understand and that we needed them there to pull the strings. It's the same strategy that politicians use—making you feel afraid to make themselves seem essential.

It's a great irony of the music industry that musicians are controlled by people who don't have as much talent. One solace for the musician, to cheer them up as they're dashed against the rocks, is that everyone on the periphery would like to do what the musician does but they're mystified by the process. People in the industry liked to go home and tell their family 'And then we did this!' as though they were a member of the band. They liked to feel involved in the creation of our songs.

I didn't like being in a record company office, because often the people there would joke about how crazy a certain musician was. It was demeaning, as if the musician was a baby needing to be taken care of. The musicians needed help because they'd be hopeless otherwise. But this was just another control thing.

Later, industry people said I was crazy too—but only because I disagreed with them.

Record company people were everywhere now, sending faxes and discussing territories. All the Americans were called Randy, Chip or Todd, and they'd be wearing long shorts and buying us a drink. Most were masters of the bluff. There were hardly any female A&R people, because at record labels women were kept in middle-tier positions. It seemed to me that women were only ever hired to work on promotions because they were pretty, or to tap up a report after another testosterone decision.

Mushroom arranged a new producer for our record, someone who could make sense of what we did. The producer would cost tens of thousands of dollars, but money was no longer an issue. Mushroom were throwing heaps of it at us.

Gavin MacKillop was a Scotsman, only in his mid-twenties, and he'd produced records by Shriekback, PiL and Hunters and Collectors. We were interested in what a real producer did, but naturally suspicious. But Gavin was easy to get along with, and he'd often take the piss.

'Would you stop pouting,' he'd tell me if I was doing my guitar face in the control room.

Gavin dressed the music up in lots of effects that stay tethered to their time. Early nineties choruses, too much reverb. The record sounded produced. It's the curse of being contemporary or trying to be too modern. A day later, the trend is out of date.

Gavin also deconstructed the songs and put them back together, and I liked a lot of his choices. Our songs sounded unstoppable, but they also sounded shiny and expensive—which counted against us at that time, especially in America. *Hail* had made the college radio top twenty, but *Melt* was too smooth, unlike the rough, underproduced records from many of the other indies. It was a time of a conflict between the underground and the majors who, in the wake of bands like R.E.M., had realised the college radio circuit was worth a fortune. Big labels everywhere were dipping in and stealing indie bands. Scruffy boys and girls were moulded into pop stars, and dated Winona Ryder and Mickey Rourke. Nirvana were on the cover of *Rolling Stone* wearing T-shirts that said 'Corporate Magazines Still Suck'. Everyone was going grunge, playing seventies hard-rock riffs on big Marshall Stacks, which was popular with the majors because that was music they understood. The indies responded by getting more extreme.

I saw the same thing happening in Dunedin with Xpressway and bands like the Dead C. My old flatmate Bruce Russell, upset that a lot of acts were being overlooked or dropped by Flying Nun and Mushroom, formed the Xpressway label with Peter Jefferies. Flying Nun didn't help their cause by being slack with royalty statements and woefully missing release dates. Accountability was never their strong point.

Xpressway released cassettes from South Island artists that the American indie scene preferred. A shop in Hoboken had Xpressway releases in the window, not Straitjacket Fits. Bruce and Peter were very fervent in their thoughts about the industry, and Peter would sit and talk about how unfair it was, his mouth running dry. They fell out with Roger, even though Bruce had worked as Roger's assistant for a while, and the division grew deeper. The bands on Flying Nun were made to feel like they were sell-outs. I'd tentatively tell Peter about a plan I had, and he'd go, 'Really?' Then he'd flick his cigarette.

Perhaps to stay connected with Dunedin, I made a single with Peter in which I put a battery-powered toy Marshall at the bottom of a rubbish bin. We'd show them high production and international standards. I believed my friends in Dunedin more than I believed some guy in Manhattan. That guy would just tell you what you wanted to hear and pretend to know a lot about obscure records.

I also started playing occasional guitar with King Loser. King Loser could be a lethal band, even if they were usually too out of it to arrange their songs properly. I soon realised that Celia Mancini, the stylish, clever, part-Indian girl who sang and played bass and organ, was the band's best songwriter. She had more cohesive ideas than her boyfriend, Chris Heazlewood, but Heazlewood could definitely play a guitar. Celia also knew how the classics went. She had spent time singing ironic—but not ironic—standards in her covers band the After Dinner Mints.

Celia and Chris worked me out, and they could sense that I was floundering a bit between two contrasting worlds. They thought I needed cleaning with the devil's rock 'n' roll.

In a video of a show we played together, Chris and I are dressed in suits and Celia is in a see-through Playboy nightie. Lou Allison, a new arrival from England, is bashing away at the drums. Celia had picked the suit for me, a crisp brown polyester number, and, when I later got that suit couriered to America for *The Conan O'Brien Show*, Celia said that there were plenty of polyester suits in America. But she had a better eye than me.

In the video we're doing a cover of 'Live and Let Die', even though I'm not a big McCartney fan, and in the riff, which sounds better than the version by Guns N' Roses, Heazlewood and I are playing a dual lead break with our guitars behind our necks. It's a move I haven't seen before, at least not by two guitarists at the same time. It's one of the classiest moves I've been involved in, though I haven't tried the Hendrix backward roll that he did at Monterey. I've held off doing it because I might get tangled in my lead.

The Losers blew it by mistreating people. They acted self-involved and short-sighted. There wasn't too much empathy, but there was a whole lot of entitlement. If there was a dispute over the ownership of a guitar, then the Losers might take the guitar, because they rocked harder.

A few years after the Losers ended, Celia came up to me at a concert and it was only halfway through our conversation that

I realised it was her. She was going on in a ragged voice, but she could still make a hilarious point. I had a lot of time for Celia, even if she could be a pain. She had a big heart, and a fire, and she was always a loyal friend. I think she got a lot of bad press because she was stroppy, behaving in a way that men could get away with. Her opinions, on culture anyway, were usually suavely right.

Like Heazlewood and Xpressway, Celia thought it was wrong to do more than one take of a song. She was about purity, even if the song sounded nasty. That was the Xpressway ethos—the belief, like Chris Knox's too, that if it wasn't done on a four-track then it wasn't real. Chris gave me a hard time when the Straitjackets were in a big room making *Melt*, and I'd go to his house feeling apprehensive.

Improvisation was in and arrangement was out. I wasn't so sure where I stood, because a lot of great records and real songs had been made in proper studios. Sly Stone spent a million bucks on *Riot*. Music works whether it's made in a forty-eight-track studio or recorded with a knitting needle.

Heazlewood stayed on to become a dick. He played bass in one of the first Dimmer line-ups, and wrote 'Ace of Spades' on his scrawny chest when we played at the Big Day Out. He told people it was okay he was in with Carter, because he was going to 'fuck it up'. I wondered if he was jealous, or if he resented me for no longer being in the Doublehappys, who he'd idolised. He left Dimmer by rubbishing me on the internet, which hurt because he was showboating at my expense. I didn't speak to him for years, even after he'd apologised.

I let Heazlewood back in around 2014, a time when a lot of our friends were dying. We played together at a wake for one of our friends, Cameron, and we did Hendrix's 'If 6 Was 9', because the song felt relevant to Cameron, who had died in London. I loved the lyric about the white-collar conservatives flashing down the street, pointing their plastic finger. The words, 'I'm the one who has to die when it's time for me to die—so let me live my life . . . *the way I want to*' is close to a personal mantra.

Soon after, Chris rubbished the improvisatory band I had with Michael Morley and Robbie from the Dead C. I enjoyed that band. Carter, Morley and Yeats. Our publicity photo was a doctored shot of Crosby, Stills and Nash sitting around like hippies on a porch with their faces melted off. Musically, we'd get on lost highways, struggle for a bit, then discover a far-out place. The best thing about that group was that no one in it was scared. Heazlewood slagged us off on Facebook anyway, mercilessly. He's a skilled writer. He'd been a boy journalist back in Dunedin like me. Some of his mates agreed that Carter was fucked. Someone else said I was responsible for the worst improvisatory music he'd heard. I told that punter he could kiss my arse.

Heazlewood calls himself Cash Guitar these days, but I don't go to his shows.

I thought the Dead C were terrible when I first heard them in the early nineties. They had a number called 'Bad Politics' and it was their only catchy song. Bruce Russell could be a brooder, and with his dark, circled eyes he often looked melancholy. He was another intellectual, from Nelson, and was very well spoken. He lectured at the university.

Sometimes Bruce would perform poems he'd written. The usual poetic despair about being left languishing in the dust. His solo name was 'A Handful of Dust', after Evelyn Waugh's novel.

Michael Morley smoked pot and laughed at what he played, but only in the practice room. I think he enjoyed the objectionability of the Dead C and how they explored the same dark corners that his favourite paintings did.

Bruce once played a Dead C set supporting Sonic Youth, and

for some of the set he didn't even plug in his guitar. He just made noises with the end of his lead, sticking it into the wood of the stage. That was at the Theatre Royal in 1991. He was proud he couldn't play guitar.

I became a convert after seeing the Dead C play a set in the lounge at Michael's house in Port Chalmers. The songs were ridiculously heavy and every chord was wrong, and it would have laid me out if I hadn't already been sitting down. After that I became a believer, even if the last time the Dead C played I was ready to leave after two songs. I stayed on, which was the correct decision, because the Dead C, as they often do, became wonderfully involving.

The budget for the *Melt* album would have been enough to make a million records by the Dead C. We recorded it at flash studios in Auckland and Melbourne, where people brought you biscuits. We stayed in luxury apartments in Melbourne, with one big suite each. Things were laid out for us, and we beavered away studiously over a lot of time, getting the music right. We spent nine weeks recording *Melt*, which was a biblical period then.

One of my favourite tunes was 'A.P.S.', which we'd constructed from an old song. 'A.P.S.' stands for 'Awful Pretty Sight' but that felt a bit lame so I hid it behind the initials. I came up with the guitar riff while I was walking to the studio in Melbourne. It's good to write when you're walking, because the song has a natural step to it. Music gives you flashbacks, and whenever I play 'A.P.S' I can still see the street where I thought up the riff, like the rooms I also see where I've written other songs. It's almost like time travel—stronger and more visceral than memory—where you're transported to the place of origin. They say music is second only to scent as a memory trigger.

The riff for 'A.P.S.' is the kind of riff you can play forever because it never gets old. It aroused a lot of feelings, non-specific ones, something yearning, half forgotten. When I hit those notes, I'd have tingles in my stomach and goosebumps on my shoulders. It's one of the most powerful riffs I've written.

That was the power of music, where the instrument said something you couldn't. It explained the in-between feelings, where words might struggle. It's hard to put your finger on something that isn't really there. That's why people, often writers or painters, refer to music as the art of the gods, and even if that sounds pompous I think they're probably right.

We were in a club one night when the Pixies song 'Where Is My Mind?' started playing. The hook was immediately classic, so I snuck in something similar in the second verse of 'Missing Presumed Drowned'. The way the Pixies motif sustained itself may have influenced 'A.P.S.' too.

Andrew had three songs on *Melt*, including 'Down in Splendour', which I think everyone—the record company, the manager, the producer, Andrew—thought could be a hit. It was the only song on the record that might be a radio song, and I think it was always shaped as one. The video for 'Down in Splendour' was made by a young Australian called Andrew Dominik, who was beautiful, with angel's hair, and looked like he should be in front of the camera.

Andrew Dominik had had a drug problem when he was younger, but he'd cleaned up and his directing skills were obvious. He made several clips for us because we were one of his favourite bands. After he made 'Down in Splendour', he told Mushroom, 'Let me do a clip with Shayne,' even though he'd made Andrew look perfectly presentable in his Vaseline-lensed clip with the slow-motion shots of arrows going through apples, golden ribbons floating across the screen, and two lovers drowned in a swimming pool. In the clip I used the black SG Dad had given me, even though it was out of tune.

I added what I imagined to be a Pink Floyd lead break on the end of the song, although I didn't know Pink Floyd—and I used the black SG for that as well because it had a warm, round tone, and I could tune it between takes. I kept adding bum notes to the lead break and Gavin would say, 'No, not that one,' and make me do it again.

Andrew Dominik went to Hollywood and became a big film director, with hits like *Chopper* and *The Assassination of Jesse James by the Coward Robert Ford*.

'Down In Splendour' is probably one of our most popular songs because, even though it's a strong tune, the best one Andrew wrote for us, it was also the most traditional. Mushroom were keen to push the song, as were Arista when they picked us up later. The song became contentious in our band, because Andrew's sixties classicism bugged me. It seemed too retro to me when I wanted to be more forward-looking. I liked King Loser, Peter Jefferies and Fugazi. We all agreed on My Bloody Valentine, at least, because beneath the noise, which was attractive in itself, they wrote catchy songs.

That was what Andrew wanted. Catchy songs. It was supposed to help break Straitjacket Fits out, but it would split us up in the end.

There were now Shayne and Andrew camps, with each side backing their man. Old friends had a word to me about Andrew and his friends had a word about me.

*

We signed to Arista for North America. The A&R guy, another former college hero, could be charming and funny but he was also full of shit. He did a big rap for a documentary screened in New Zealand where he likened me to Bruce Springsteen and Bono.

'Shayne Carter has that kind of power,' he said, intensely, although he'd never seen our band play. He'd got on to us through the hype from other companies.

In San Francisco, he gave us pot from Mexico and it was the strongest pot we'd ever had. In our photo in *Rolling Stone* we've got big bags under our eyes.

The A&R guy had managed the Smiths—when they were breaking up—and he took me to a Morrissey concert at Madison Square Garden. People were throwing themselves at Morrissey. Their chins thudded against the stage. They were beaten by security and thrown back into the gladioli-wielding mob.

We thought Arista would be appropriate because they'd had Iggy Pop and Patti Smith back in the day, and the boss Clive Davis had signed Sly Stone and Janis Joplin when he was at Columbia. This was all news from Mars. Arista also had the Church, an Australian band who'd had an international hit with 'Under the Milky Way', and the Church were on Mushroom as well. The Church recommended Arista to us, and recommended us to them.

Iggy and Patti were gone by then and now Arista's big acts were Whitney Houston, Barry Manilow and an alternative band from Canada called the Crash Test Dummies. They had a hit called 'Mmm Mmm Mmm Mmm', which the singer sang in a deep, inexpressive voice.

Roger McGuinn from of the Byrds was making a record for Arista called *Back from Rio*. It was the worst record he made, because he was in a studio surrounded by idiots who were conning him into using their songs. He'd lost his confidence. I love the scene in the Tom Petty documentary *Runnin' Down a Dream* where, during the McGuinn sessions, Petty goes into the studio and chews those leeches out. 'I could smoke a joint and come up with three better lines than that,' he tells the record execs. He tells them what a great artist McGuinn is and that they're insulting him by asking him to play their crappy song.

Melt fell between the cracks in America, as did Straitjacket Fits whenever we visited the Arista offices and a uniformed man ushered us into a lift. It was in the same midtown block that Audrey Hepburn and George Peppard sat in front of in a scene from *Breakfast at Tiffany's*. Some of the Arista people were nice, including Kris, who smoked pot and let me stay at her house, and a bolshy promotions woman we codenamed Fluffy. But some of the people there reminded me of 4XO, wearing too much cologne and asking us if we'd like to be taken to a secret sex club in the meat-packing district.

Clive Davis came and saw us in New York after Andrew had left, when we played a small Arista party, around the time of the *Done* EP. Arista hadn't released that record because it was too rough, and between albums, although some of the songs were re-recorded for our last LP. I wore a Flying Nun T-shirt at this show, and said accusingly into the mic, 'This was released by Flying Nun,' and then we did a song called 'Whiteout'. It wasn't a very commercial song. I'd written it about the guy who in 1984 had gone into a McDonald's in San Diego and massacred the people inside.

Don't say it, I don't wanna hear
I've got my own stupid ideas
I've got a band playing crap upstairs
And a ringing in my ears
This is not enough
This is not enough

Clive talked to us after the gig. It was rumoured he put boot polish on his head, but I was careful to look in his eyes. He said to me that while we weren't happening quickly enough, they would give us a real shot.

Still, I look happy enough in a commemorative photo, in my Flying Nun T-shirt, tongue stuck out, half punk, half Māori challenge, Clive leaning in like a Don.

Melt was big in Australasia, and we were nominated for awards. The Australian critics went nuts for the album, even though our music was too weird for ordinary Australians. When we toured there, we were Sydney's biggest thing. Women offered us blowjobs. Steve Kilbey from the Church wanted to make a record with me, and the Church invited us on their tour.

Famous people came to our gigs around *Melt*, like Lemmy and Kurt and Courtney and Peter Buck. I sat directly opposite Sofia Coppola at a club, and she was alone and looking at me over her drink, but I was too shy to talk to her, even though I'd met her before through a friend. Lou Reed's wife gave me a filthy look at her party, because I'd stumbled on my way out of the bathroom— but my condition was due to jetlag, not drugs. Jim Jarmusch sat at the bar. The good-looking guy was Matt Dillon. Near Central Park I saw Yoko Ono walk past.

Our picture looked great on the cover of *Drum Media*— we were on the back cover as well—and I used our exposure to diss the Hoodoo Gurus. I remembered supporting them at the Dunedin Town Hall—how we'd brawled in their dressing room and eaten half of their hummus. I said the Hoodoo Gurus represented the plainsmen rock we hated.

We were better behaved with the Church, and their guitarist said we'd inspired him.

In Melbourne, *Beat Magazine* put me alone on the cover, where I looked handsome and interesting. Well, that's what I thought, but the other band members weren't that impressed.

We got to tour America again, but this time we had to go with the La's.

The La's were Scousers who'd had a hit with 'There She Goes', which was a good song, but I knew plenty of people with one of them. The rest of the La's set was skiffle, which the singer sang authentically. Their three-minute sixties songs already sounded reheated. While the British media was writing the singer Lee Mavers up as a genius, I don't think he cared, because he wanted to record everything on one microphone and he hated all his records. We didn't speak to the La's, because they were on pot, or—it was rumoured—heroin, so we'd just mutter at them when we passed them in the hallway. Neither us, nor the La's, could be bothered.

In Salt Lake City we were riding an open goods lift, and Lee Mavers was on the floor above us, looking over into our cage and pushing a button that kept stopping and starting the lift. I looked up and told him to stop doing that, and that was the only thing I ever said to the singer of the La's.

We usually blew the La's off the stage—because we could, and they were annoying.

Andrew got dark on the tour. He spent a lot of time in his room. At some of our own gigs, it was like he was giving up. I remember looking across him at Cleveland, where he was fluffing around on his guitar. After Cleveland, we had a band meeting and Andrew said he would try harder at the important gigs.

As if.

It blew up in Toronto. Andrew was on forty-five percent again, and when it came to one of his songs I thought he might try, but he just stood there humming and hawing. When he sang he was almost half yawning. Fuck that. I threw off my guitar and stormed from the stage—it got the biggest cheer of the night—which is the only time I've ever left in the middle of a gig.

In the dressing room, John and David held me back as I pretended to lunge at Brough.

Andrew told us that he didn't like touring, or practising, or recording, which didn't leave many options. It was no fun now. Unpleasant. Andrew didn't like the situation, and the situation with him was a drag. We couldn't write, and then we couldn't communicate one to one, and the walls came up and resentment grew like a vine around us.

Andrew left when we got back to Auckland. With our next EP we put out a press release: 'Yay, no more slow songs.' Some people were offended on Andrew's behalf, but he knew our form of humour.

Our A&R guy left Arista after we released *Melt*, and with that a lot of the enthusiasm for our band disappeared. It's the record company classic where you lose the essential cog in your support system. The A&R guy went on to become a successful restaurateur with franchise restaurants in New York and LA, and I didn't hear about him for ages, until early 2018 when the *New York Times* ran an exposé on him. He was accused of getting handsy with the waitresses and encouraging his clientele to do the same.

Our replacement A&R guy at Arista worked out of Los Angeles and flew out to see us in Auckland once, but the only suggestion he made to us was that our next record should sound like Nirvana.

I don't remember his name—it was either Randy, Chip or Todd.

It was when we had Arista behind us—with Clive Davis saying it was 'only a matter of time' and our A&R guy, in his usual extravagant way, predicting stadium tours while rubbing our backs—that the band fell apart. Andrew probably left because he felt he had to, and I can freely admit that what we'd had, a crucial part of our alchemy that set us apart from everyone else, was gone.

The band had become unworkable and we couldn't finish songs. We'd reached a creative impasse which made me realise that, no matter where you are with your band, it has to be fun being in it. There was no point otherwise. You may as well go do something else you don't like that pays you better money.

Maybe we blew it. That was the popular view. Andrew said as much in interviews later, where he figured we could have gone on to sell hundreds of thousands of records. 'But no . . . self-sabotage . . . self-sabotage,' he concluded, abruptly.

All the ducks were in a line when Andrew left: the big record company, the rabid international press, the way we could shake up an audience. We got used to people saying we were the best band in the world, and we thought they'd just go on saying it. Our press was entertaining—when Rockin' Ron wasn't being grumpy—because we weren't scared to say what we thought. The Chills may have been given the keys to Dunedin by the mayor, but I didn't want to be a band a city could be proud of, because that's not rock 'n' roll. We believed in rock 'n' roll, and that's what gave us our charisma. It was still 'Fuck you', but everybody loved it.

Straitjacket Fits never worked as well after Andrew left. We became a plainer rock band, even if I tried to make us weirder. There was the part of me that wanted to sell just 120 cassettes on Xpressway rather than a million like the Crash Test Dummies, and I wrote purposefully rough rock songs to prove we weren't just about 'Down in Splendour'. Our last album without Andrew was called *Blow*, and half of it did blow, because I couldn't stand behind half of the songs. We were pushed into making that record by the people around us, although the band were keen to move on as well, as quickly as we could.

I could see our popularity shrinking on our last tour of America, with Andrew's replacement Mark Petersen. We were on a package tour with the Jean-Paul Sartre Experience and the Bats, and the

Bats were by far the most popular band on the bill, because they were the band, the modest, honest band with the frayed edges, that the college radio audience could relate to. We were too rock and too rockstar, and now we were without the levity of Andrew in his glasses. That's what had made us different—the yin and the yang, McCartney and Lennon, the dark and relief—all that.

Self-sabotage, self-sabotage. Maybe we couldn't let ourselves win. I've always been useless at victories because nothing is ever enough.

At different points, Andrew and I ended up back in Dunedin, staging conversations with our friends like our dads had once at the depressives club.

*

When Straitjacket Fits did a reformation tour in 2005, Andrew didn't come. He'd agreed to it at first, but on the day he was supposed to fly, he didn't get on the plane. We'd all written prospective set lists for the tour, and Andrew didn't have any of his songs on his list. I said, 'Come on . . .'

When we were inducted into the Rock and Roll Hall of Fame in 2008, when Mum held my hand on the red carpet and wouldn't let go, Andrew didn't come to that either. There was a sort of Beatles press conference—an unpopular Beatles—and Andrew's chair sat empty behind a card that said his name.

I can respect that. You don't have to do anything you don't want to. Maybe Andrew couldn't stand returning to the scene of the accident, and torturing himself all over beside the smoking twisted metal. It was a pity, because the tour we did in 2005 was healing. It had none of the politics, no one else pushing in; it was just us, with our songs, enjoying one another's company. The simple, base pleasure of being in our band.

Before each of those shows, we'd gather in a huddle. No matter where we were in the world, we could always get into that same circle with the same three goobers staring back.

'Just remember, we're the Straitjacket Fits,' I'd say, and we'd go out there feeling untouchable.

It's a shame Andrew never got to hear those words, because he could have done with a bit of a buck up.

Mark Petersen had been playing in my girlfriend's band. She had a big contract with Warners.

Her and I were together for a few years after I gave up drinking, but I think we were quite different. She came from West Auckland, so I could relate to her bogan roots, but she also had a New Age side that wasn't me, because I don't like hippies. At this point, I was trying to figure myself out, as most people are when they're that age, but I was confused by my new sobriety.

I think I disowned a lot of my past and wiped the slate clean when a lot of it was still useful. I've spent a lifetime reassembling some of those parts, realising that some of the prejudices I'd had at seventeen, even if they were naïve or immature, were right all along. It's like I'd gone through a long tunnel but instead of coming out at the other end, found myself coming out right back at the start. I may have been trouble when I was younger, but my trouble helped me as well.

We got Mark in the band because he was proficient and he could sing and play anything. If you called out the name of a song he could play it, even if he'd never played it before. He was like a jukebox. But Mark needed to sort out his look. When he did his first gig with us alongside My Bloody Valentine in Australia, he turned up in a metaller's studded belt, daggy jeans and a Westy sleeveless T-shirt with a picture of naked women being harassed by panthers. It was an out look, especially when you're playing with the hippest band in the universe. I lent Mark a shirt for the next night's gig, and because his mullet was twice the length of mine and Rockin' Ron's, we told him, through a friend, that he needed to get a trim. We'd long abandoned the mullet. Well, I had.

Mark was hurt, because that was who he was and it had worked fine for him up until now. 'I can pick up a woman in my singlet,' he told me, objecting.

Maybe Mark's ability to play any song was a problem with us, because there wasn't enough of Mark in his playing. He'd stepped into something he hadn't helped create, and often he was following what I'd shown him. Later, in our reunion shows, he felt integrated into the band but at the start he may have been over-respectful. There was none of the disagreement that makes you good or the competitiveness that makes you better.

Still, though—the gigs with My Bloody Valentine through Australia in October 1991 went off. Some of the scenes at the shows were like Dante's *Inferno* or *Fellini Satyricon*, although I have neither seen the movies nor read the books so I'm only guessing they're the same. The gig in an old theatre called the Phoenician Club in Sydney was one of the best we played, because without Andrew we had something to prove. 'Whiteout' tore out the roof. 'Roller Ride' fucked with people's heads.

We were as good as My Bloody Valentine, although for a change we didn't feel competitive. They were cool, relatable people, because they were Irish not English and they didn't have to big up themselves. Kevin Shields seemed doubtful, and for him, as well, his records were never good enough, and he'd refer to them quietly or say how much of a mess his band was live. He was buzzed out because he'd met Chuck D in New York, or at least sat in front of him at a seminar. My Bloody Valentine had a million Fender Jag guitars with whammy bars, and they were all in different tunings. A young woman who looked like Sinead O'Connor played the flute.

I sent Kevin a Hotcake pedal later, because he'd trusted me with his $120. *Melody Maker* took a picture of us in Sydney, where our long hair is being blown in the wind on the same curve as the Opera House behind us. *Melody Maker* repeated their assertion that we were the best guitar band in the world, so we figured their theory would stick.

When you play a gig that goes off, or when you're in a band that rules, the exchange between you and the audience is close to egoless. Music is bigger than you. The sound is a separate entity, wobbling in the room. You're like a solider trying to carry it or a labourer digging it up.

When people say you're the best band, you might think that's an awesome power for a small group of people to have. But music is democratic. You lift the crowd, and they lift you, and everyone's just happy they're there.

I shut my eyes and try to connect with the song, because a singer has to find their song.

It's an incredible feeling to create a huge, beautiful sound, and that's why I'm a musician, but I'm content to do it at practice or to an audience of three. The knowledge that it happened is enough.

The roar of a crowd might be a buzz, but mostly it's background noise. I just dig in harder and think, 'Well, if you liked that, check out a bit of this.'

When we played back in New Zealand, goth girls would turn up at my flat carrying bunches of mournful flowers.

Someone declared their love for me in the personal ads in the *Herald*, then she somehow got my number and I told her in the middle of an awkward, pause-filled exchange that she should just come up and say hello the next time she saw me out. She did come and say hello to me, and that was all she said.

262

I've always been a crazy magnet, and I've always attracted stalkers. Demented people pick me out of a crowd and come up to me on the street. Straight people will never sit beside me on the bus, probably because I look like a criminal. The seat beside me stays empty, even when people are standing in the aisle. Only a crazy person will take that seat.

It's been disturbing and unfunny to be cast in other people's delusions. People are convinced you've been in a relationship or have somehow done them wrong. Two people have told me they wanted to kill me, including the man who told me while I was tripping that he thought he had to kill me because I was seeing someone he liked. He'd been a former drinking colleague who'd had the most miserable life, and the day after he told me this, he turned up on my doorstep with a taiaha, bent down on one knee on the doormat, and told me to beat him as a punishment. I didn't beat him. I gave him a hug. Later he molested a child and hanged himself in Fiji.

Another man threatened me and my girlfriend: he was her stalker. 'You sucked my cock!' he screamed at her in the video store, when he turned up there at midnight, the same time as us. Even if she had, that didn't give him the right. Then one day he fell through the roof of the gym and died on the floor where I played my indoor soccer. He was a lighting technician and a tradesman who'd been employed to fix a leak.

I felt bad about that, because I'd written a song where I actually wished death upon this guy, which is a dangerous game to play. I told my dad about the man's death, and my song, and the stalker— six foot four, in his forties—who'd been threatening to hire someone to break my girlfriend's arms. Once, he drove alongside her in his car, slashing a finger across his face. Dad said the guy should have fallen through two floors.

My sister Tash had a habit of introducing me to her friends who turned into stalkers. Another person became obsessed and travelled to Auckland from Dunedin to see me, carting her young daughter with her. She knocked on my door one night at nine o'clock and watched me eat my dinner. I felt sorry for her daughter. This woman went back to Dunedin and told half the town that she and I were lovers and that I'd stood up in front my family and friends at a meal and kissed her in front of my girlfriend. Creepily, she also befriended my mother and said she'd be a sponsor if Mum gave up drinking. Later, this person became obsessed with a member of Sebadoh, flew to America to see him and stood unannounced in his hall.

Things kept edgy back home. Sometimes I thought Mum and Tony saved their big arguments for when I came down, like a command performance. Warring couples are often like that, publicly displaying their pain so outsiders can see how hard it is for them.

One Christmas, Tony and Mum pushed each other's buttons in exactly the same order, and the whole family screamed at one another. I never usually screamed like that, but that day I screamed myself hoarse, because I was sick of it and so was everyone else. Tony fumed, puffing on a cigarette, and mum cried. Everybody looked hurt. It was really fucking dismal. I left feeling hopeless, and I also left a note under my mother's pillow that said, 'Please get some help for your drinking.' She did stop for a while, but then she started again. Whenever she stopped it was if she expected a celebration parade with balloons—but life keeps going, and you have to find your own peace in it.

Once, when she was drunk, Mum waved her arm around and said, 'Why don't you write a song about that?'

It hurt that a parent could be jealous. But they're just people too.

Mostly, Mum told customers at her shop how proud she was of her son.

Because I had money, I splashed out one Christmas and bought the family gifts worth more than a hundred dollars. I got Tony a large ornamental butterfly, the kind people put up on garden sheds in Auckland because their kitsch had become trendy again. I could tell Tony was let down, especially in light of the other presents I'd given—maybe he felt I'd placed him on a lower rung on the ladder.

'Ah-hah,' was all he said—the same way he'd said 'Ah-hah' when I'd shown him the words to that song about Jillian Humphries.

*

We recorded the *Done* EP with Tony Cohen in Melbourne. Tony had produced Nick Cave and the Bad Seeds' song 'Mercy Seat' which was a production masterpiece, a lesson in sustained intensity that rose like an incoming tide.

Tony had a drinking problem. We'd find bottles of Jack Daniel's hidden in strange spots in the studio, and he was constantly sipping Coca-Cola from a plastic cup and eating Disprins. Sometimes he'd be lying on the couch, holding his head, saying he needed a break. But Tony was cool. The versions he produced of 'Done' and 'Spacing' are better than the ones on the album.

'Done' was supposed to be hip hop. We based the beat on LL Cool J's 'Mama Said Knock You Out', which LL played on MTV once, backed by a band who'd taken their shirts off. That seemed like an exciting amalgam of rap with real bands, and no one has bettered that song since. Most rap/rock mashups are Adidas-wearing dudes looking self-conscious while talking to whitey. Whitey is usually covered in tattoos, looking tough and antisocial and playing the faceless nu metal that only Slayer are any good at. But we were hip hop fans. It was one of the most exciting developments around. It had the tenets that rock 'n' roll had forgotten, like protest, and weirdness—the way the sampled guitar in 'Illusions' by Cypress

265

Hill was weird, or the way the production team the Bomb Squad caused freeway pile-ups with Public Enemy. Hip hop was made by people looking in—the ones the industry were scared of. When hip hop wasn't protesting the lack of fine-looking women or the size of the bling, it was calling out a lot of people. Musically I think hip hop can back itself into a corner, but it can also break out again in an unexpected way. Someone like Kendrick Lamar surprises you with a sophisticated cut-up. All genres are like that—turning in and talking to themselves before someone lifts the conversation and breaks it out of its shackles. Hip hop is innovative in its sounds, where not much counts for a lot—the spaces and the weird little constructions built around them. Hip hop was also like the blues, where someone could take a basic template like a beat or a twelve-bar to tell their story.

Because John was from Glenross and David was Pākehā, 'Done' didn't sound very hip hop. Our rhythm section clumped through the verse. The chorus was supposed to be euphoric, like 'Dance to the Music' or 'I Want to Take You Higher' by Sly, but we ruined that too, with discordant guitar and continually clumpy drums. But it was still very singalong and the crowds still sing along with it.

I think I wrote 'Done' about Andrew.

Red lights flashing madly
And a stop sign, saying,
No more road to go—No!
I ain't run out of track
I got track and plenty behind it
Done
Good as done
Up and down and bounced like a see saw
Why are you sayin' why did you leave for?
Sad men suffer gladly

And this here ain't no matter of theory
Done
Good as done.

While we were recording, Andrew Dominik made the video clip for 'Done'. David wears a singlet but makes it look fashionable, and by the chorus I've taken my shirt off. I didn't really do this for the camera, because I like to strip down in the studio—singing is always easier in socks, with no clingy clothes on—but then again, I also had the confidence to go topless for the ladies. At the end of the clip my shirt's back on again.

'Spacing' later ended up on the album *Blow*, but it didn't really work there either. 'Spacing' could take off live, but in the studio it mooned about, writhing on the spot, linear, undynamic, much like the song 'Hail'. 'Spacing' is another tune with no template, so no one knew where to put anything or how to lock it together. But I always liked 'Spacing' live, because it was worrying and unpredictable, like a stalker.

'Whiteout' was dark too. When the song exploded in guitar at the end, it was so intense I'd puff out my lips, squeeze my eyes and turn my head to the sky—it was so heavy I could barely push it out, trying to do justice to its humanity and weight. The hair on my neck prickled whenever I played it.

I can't remember the fourth song on the *Done* EP. It was a floppy one with My Bloody Valentine vocals and it just wasn't any good, because I hadn't finished writing it yet. The A&R guy at Mushroom told me it was his favourite, and if we recorded it again it would make a great single.

When I was writing the last songs for Straitjacket Fits, they packed me off to America. The sojourn was arranged by our manager Debbi, who did it under the pretext of 'creating an environment for the writer'. I bullshitted Chip at Arista and said the trip might be good, because I'd get a chance to check out American rock radio, and Randy got all excited because it was about time I discovered the Stone Temple Pilots, Pearl Jam and the Red Hot Chili Peppers. But I wasn't going to listen to any American radio, apart from Howard Stern, who back then was relatively funny. The truth is I just needed to get out of Auckland.

I had just split up with my Westie girlfriend. She had met up with a fellow New Ager, a guy who was into burying himself in forests to find inner peace. He said he wanted to save the world. I've always meant to write to him and ask how he's getting along with that. But I needed to be away from my situation and the Lower East Side was way funkier than Grey Lynn.

On the stopover in Hawaii, I got taken out the back at customs. I get nervous talking to customs. Uniformed people made me anxious, and they can sense it. I was always getting pulled over at airports, which struck me as stupid because I'd be a fool to be carrying drugs in a guitar case, looking the way I did. They'd read my tedious diaries, and in Auckland I had to stand naked in front of two bored customs officers who told me to turn around.

I can't remember the name of the music publisher in New York. It was a big company and the people there spoke like the people at Arista, in friendly American accents that led to nowhere. The publishers tried to stick me in a box in their offices where I was supposed to be inspired and write on command like a grateful New Zealand slave. One day the publishers took me to the record store and told me to grab whatever I liked—so I did, in a pile so high that even they weren't going to wear it, so I had to put half of them back.

Instead of writing, I flew to LA to meet up with a woman I'd briefly met the last time in New York, when she'd come to the gig at the Knitting Factory. Jean and I drove up the Pacific Coast to see Thinking Fellers Union Local 282 in San Francisco—one of my favourite bands. They were awesome, although Jean leaned in during some racket and asked if the drive had been worth it.

Later, I asked Jean what the worst thing that had happened to her was, and although she found the question appalling, she told me something I only half heard—because I was waiting to make her sad.

I wrote a song about Jean, then later disfigured it with new lyrics when the affair between us soured. She'd flown out to New Zealand to see me, and my ex got jealous and tried to woo me back. I also had the flu. Seeing Jean again was a let-down for us both, and she wrote me a letter when she got back to LA, explaining how angry she was. She said she'd she felt like ripping her shirt apart like the Incredible Hulk. The song she inspired, which is directionless, guilty and half-hearted, is the worst song on the record.

We made *Blow* in LA with Paul Fox and his engineer Ed. We weren't ready to record, but we wanted to get it over with. I gave the songs my best shot but I had limited time, and it was the difficult second album—even though it was our third. We were so full of beans on album two it hadn't been hard at all, but *Blow* was a trial, and the band was losing its zip.

We were away for two and half months, staying in the San Fernando Valley, which had a nascent porn scene and nothing on its streets. We probably blew a quarter of a million dollars. A porn editor showed us outtakes of flies going up people's arses, and he said all porn was the same—oral, vaginal, and anal. It rolled out like a radio song.

On Christmas Day we drove around LA in our hired car eating Fatburgers and looking at other families' decorations.

My hands kept going numb during the recording. I'd been wearing a Les Paul, as heavy as a ship, for hours a day while recording. But, being a hypochondriac, I was sure I had a fatal disease. A doctor in Beverly Hills prescribed me blood thinners, and back in New Zealand the man at Dunedin Hospital said they'd operate for carpal tunnel syndrome but it might leave me with only eighty percent strength in my hands, which was bad news for the guitar player.

Eventually I found a physio who fixed me with deep tissue massage, mostly around the shoulders where the trouble was stemming from. I switched to an SG guitar after that, which was as light as a matchstick.

Rockin' Ron did a lot of speed while we were recording. In a photo he's entirely skeletal and wearing the red plastic bowler hat that he'd taken to wearing around the studio and our apartment, like a prospect for the gang in *A Clockwork Orange*. I remember David sitting in the shadows, his talk starting to garble. Sometimes his voice just flopped away in disillusionment, or because he'd lost his train of thought. He seemed to turn in on himself. He'd scratch his face in his sleep, so he had fresh wounds every morning. He met a promotions woman in LA—she was working with Radiohead—but towards the end she let him down, and when our plane took off for the flight home, he was crying in the seat beside me.

Paul Fox was an amiable guy and so was his engineer Ed. They smoked a mountain of pot—maybe too much—because they had no big hits after that. Paul had come in with a track record, having worked with the Sugarcubes, Natalie Merchant and XTC, and Arista had enough faith in him to give us the green light to record. They were hoping he'd knock us into shape because they didn't like the material. Chip pretended he did, but he wouldn't say much about it. Paul had some good ideas—it was Paul who did the arrangement for 'If I Were You', a song we'd originally called 'Nothing'. 'Nothing' had worked, but 'If I Were You' was better. Paul gave it a more supple structure with turns we hadn't thought of. I wrote the lyrics for 'If I Were You' in a single afternoon in my room in San Fernando Valley, proof of the effectiveness of a deadline. When I sang the new words in my booth the next day, Paul clicked into my headphones and said, 'You've really come through with this.'

But a lot of our relationship with Paul and Ed defined us and America. Too much talking across each other and never properly connecting. We were travellers on different ships. One day Paul was singing the praises of 'Tears in Heaven', a hit by Eric Clapton, a musician we couldn't stand. 'It's such a beautiful song,' Paul said, nearly choking up. There was a meaningful pause where we examined Paul's comment, then I think I changed the subject.

Blow was caught in a no-man's-land where the producer was trying to make a more commercial record that still had an edgy appeal. We just made a noise somewhere in the middle—two guitars on full, instead of one of them chiming. There's some good tunes on *Blow*, like 'Burn It Up'. The step up in the middle part of that song, where I'm muttering—*sazzafrazz, sazzafrazz*—is a potent chord change. And we were fans of a small song called 'Way', but no one else ever noticed it. 'Train' had a beautiful, hypnotic verse but I felt Paul made a wrong call rearranging the chorus, and when we played the song later we went back to how it was. 'Let It Blow' was another song let down by a one-dimensional recording. People didn't get the sarcasm of the 'La la la's in the chorus either, and they thought we were being serious.

The single 'Cat Inna Can' is annoying. I'd envisaged it as a glittery T. Rex number with a touch of Thinking Fellers Union Local 282, but it came out as a cowboy song with meowing backing vocals that AllMusic described as 'painful'. That song is a minor moment in my discography, and whenever someone in Australia tells me how much they love it, I think they're a bit stupid.

Andrew Dominik made the video for 'Cat Inna Can'. We

recorded it in a warehouse and I did a lot of spinning around on a playground roundabout. The video was stronger than the song. I may have been trying to 'project' in that video too, because Todd from Arista said I had to project more.

The rest of *Blow* lives in the dustbin of my mind.

The album came out and some American media said it blew and I walked out of an interview with *Alternative Press*.

Of course, every artist thinks that their latest piece of work—a record, a song, a book—is great, and when we made *Blow* we thought it was great. With *Blow*, we thought, 'Finally we have a record that rocks,' and that we'd promote it with devastating live shows and conquer the world, but in the northern hemisphere the number was up. The records under Mushroom were getting more ordinary. Big budgets and name producers and A&R intimidating us with their 'international standards'. Suddenly the Flying Nun movement wasn't as hip. A lot of bands were getting sucked in or confused, and we were becoming one of those bands.

That's the great commercial irony: you attract attention because you're different, but after that they want you to be the same.

At a bar in New York one night, I told Gerard Cosloy of Matador Records about our troubles with Arista and he just rolled his eyes. His whole demeanour said that me, my band, and our people, should have known better. Matador was then probably the biggest independent label in America, with bands like the Jon Spencer Blues Explosion, Pavement and the Breeders, so Gerard was used to having major labels sneaking into his warehouse and trying to nick his roster.

Bob Lawton, our American promoter, had offices on Broadway and he'd booked shows for Sonic Youth. We heard that Thurston Moore turned up once wearing a T-shirt for the *Done* EP, but I doubt he got the one for *Blow*.

Straitjacket Fits' first gig, on the trailer at Otago University. Richard Steele bides his time out the back. Dunedin, 1986

On the rooftop, Straitjacket Fits' first visit to New York, 1989

Straitjacket Fits prepare to play the Galaxy (now the Powerstation), Auckland, 1987

Publicity shot for *Hail*, 1988

The mullet lives. Filming the 'She Speeds' clip, Christchurch, 1987

PHOTO: JOHN COLLIE

Post-mullet, modelling a new jacket in trendy Chapel Street, Melbourne, 1988

Shayne Carter, Melbourne.

Freezing in the van, first European tour with Galaxie 500, 1988

Straitjacket Fits, 1988
PHOTO: KERRY BROWN

Recording *Melt*, Airforce Studios, Auckland, 1990

Lying down on the job. *Hail*
publicity shot, 1988
PHOTO: JOHNATHAN GANLEY

Hanging at the Grey Lynn shops, 1991
PHOTO: CHRIS KNOX

David Wood, Los Angeles, 1989

Radio One interview before the Flying Nun 10th Anniversary gig, Dunedin, 1991:
Robert Scott, Peter Gutteridge, David Kilgour, me, Martin Phillipps

Me and David making a pair at an airport somewhere in America, 1991

Hanging with Clive Davis after playing an Arista party, New York, 1992

Straitjacket Fits with Mark Petersen, 1993
PHOTO: DARRYL WARD

Lee's Palace, Toronto, *Blow* tour, 1993

Talking it up in New York, 1993

Dimmer in the 'Crystalator' era: the first line-up with Peter Jefferies and Lou Allison, 1995

With Carey Hibbert at his post-wedding party, Newtown, Wellington, March 2000

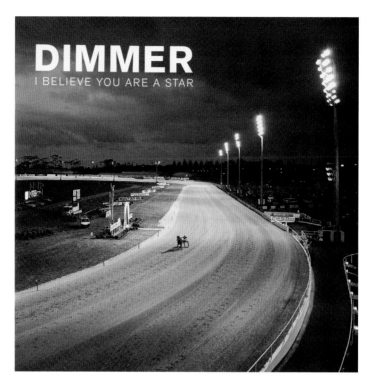

I Believe You Are a Star, 2001

Fake stage (and microphone) built in my backyard for the *You've Got to Hear the Music* launch party, Grey Lynn, Auckland, 2003

Dad at
Brighton, 1995

Me and Mum
before the
concert to raise
funds for Dad's
headstone at
Brighton, 2001

Mum, in
dressing gown,
with her kids
in the backyard
of her place in
Kensington,
Dunedin, 2005:
me, Marcel,
Mum, Kris and
Natasha

Nephew Tane stealing my thunder at a Dimmer soundcheck, Dunedin, 2005

Straitjacket Fits reformed for the 2005 New Zealand tour

With Helen Clark, winning the Lifetime Achievement Award at the 2005
bNet New Zealand Music Awards

Performing with Chris Knox and the Nothing, Laneway Festival, 2010
PHOTO: JACKSON PERRY

The picture they put in the paper. Singing with the Southern Sinfonia, Tally Ho Concert, 2017
PHOTO: GREGOR RICHARDSON FOR *OTAGO DAILY TIMES*

Getting Gone on it with reformed Straitjacket Fits and Dimmer, Dunedin, 2018
PHOTO: ESTA DE JONG

It was Bob who suggested, during the *Blow* tour, that I should do something else. We'd just played an awful show with Bailterspace and the Verlaines at CBGB, with hardly anyone there for our set. My amp blew up—just died in a frazzle. It felt like a mercy killing.

Later we played a gig with the Bats at Asbury Park in New Jersey, a dead beach resort town famous for producing Bruce, and the crowd was so sparse we got everyone to individually introduce themselves. Our enigma was falling away.

When Bob suggested I leave the band, he wasn't being devious—he'd said it as a friend. I'd stay with Bob sometimes in his apartment in the East Village. I liked to imitate his Massachusetts whine and the way he said 'Welllll, you knowww' through his nose. One night during that tour I went for dinner with Bob and some others, but I left before we ordered because I'd arranged a rendezvous at the same time, and I never went back to the dinner. I apologised to Bob for my rudeness later. But I was getting increasingly distracted. I was starting to flap about.

We were staying in an expensive hotel in the middle of the financial district, and the doormen in their royal red jackets looked as if they were dressed for Buckingham Palace.

Our last trip to North America, in July 1993, was part of a package tour with the Bats and JPSE. JPSE were on Matador, and the Bats were being put out by Merge in Chapel Hill, and, while we resented being lumped in together, I think we all thought we would benefit from a united front. These were the days of Lollapalooza and package tours.

A few weeks before, in Australia, our joint tour was called Beyond the Jangle. Whoever came up with that needed a talking to. The tour for North America was renamed Noisyland, but that was weak as well because there were far more noisier bands around than us. We were getting put into boxes by squares.

JPSE had travelled a similar path to us. They'd started out as the Jean-Paul Sartre Experience, then the record company thought an abbreviation would be more commercial. The general public wasn't interested in French philosophers. The Jean-Paul Sartre Experience had played the Flying Nun Christmas party in Christchurch in 1986, but the Dunedin crew got liquored on the way up so when the band came on I was conked out on a table. But JPSE started coming through Dunedin, and we got to know them better. They were Prince fans too. Dave and Jim could be foppish and announced their songs in a slightly camp way. They didn't care about being slightly effeminate or vulnerable—it was contrary to the New Zealand character and maybe they also figured that that would appeal to girls, the same way the hair metal bands had worked that out in Hollywood. They'd do a slow grind when they played, squirming on the mic.

The other guitarist, David Mulcahy, was more steadfast. He'd plant his feet and stay completely still all the way through the set. David had furious red eyebrows and he'd swear in his songs, which none of the others did, but his tunes were just as melodic as theirs. He wrote some of their prettiest music on their first EP.

The drummer, Gary Sullivan, grew up in Invercargill. The First XV had gatecrashed his fourteenth birthday party and as a birthday present their captain had punched him in the face.

Gary was a force in JPSE with his little skitters and shuffles. He did a lot to make them different. Gary could be loose wristed but he also kept a mean 4/4. I never listen to the drummer. You feel them instead. If the drummer isn't good then the whole deal is dead. Gary swings and he's funky without being Mr Funky. He's one of the best around, which is why I've played with him for the past twenty years.

The first EP by JPSE is a classic Flying Nun release. It tinkles along with a small sadness that gets more powerful the quieter it gets. However, JPSE got tougher with each release, maybe because they thought they had to prove that they could rock out too. Mushroom latched on to them and started getting makeup people for their videos. The clips the band made themselves in the backyard of their flat were always better.

America seemed to me a place of disparate states, a world of contrast, locked into itself and oblivious to the life outside its borders. In the middle of nowhere, the main street of a small town called American Falls was draped in flags, and the people there were hostile. The storekeeper rushed through an exchange, begrudgingly. There was no feeling of triumph in American Falls, only the mean scent of victory. Their stores had Operation Desert Storm bubblegum packs with cards with military themes—pictures of soldiers, machine guns, evilly gleaming rockets, maybe a map of Iraq. It was a couple of years after Desert Storm, so the gum was cardboard and stale.

In Chicago a businessman said to our soundman Rex in the hotel lift, 'I wish I could dress like that.'

I liked Chicago. I sat in its diners looking across the street, imagining gangsters up against the opposite wall, being mown down by Al Capone and his men with machine guns. Sometimes I'd have reveries about the size of John Dillinger's penis, which apparently was huge. Maybe I'd heard a rumour that they'd put the gangster's cock in a museum, the way they displayed Phar Lap's heart in Melbourne—well, even if they didn't do that, the penis, like Phar Lap's heart, was said to be a winner.

After soundcheck in LA, Dave Allen interviewed us, and I felt fraudulent; I was finding it difficult to back my band. Dave Allen had played bass in the Gang of Four, whose first album *Entertainment!* was a landmark, but Dave looked lost in the mainstream too. He had coke-style rings under his eyes, and I thought it was a bit tragic that someone from such an important group was reduced to asking us questions for a free LA rock weekly.

The American tour knocked me back, even if *Rolling Stone* gave us the best review and the *New York Times* called us 'the most abrasive band on the bill'. We weren't used to having to fight for ascension at gigs, or worse, to play to crowds that didn't even like us. They liked the Bats, and it was the Bats who would be offered tours with the Breeders and Radiohead. The JPSE and the Fits generally fiddled away with their steadily normalising rock.

One of our last American acts was on *Late Night with Conan O'Brien*, which is when I got Celia Mancini to courier over my brown polyester suit. Morton Downey Jr was a guest too—he was a cheap shock-jock TV host with a screwed-up, prejudiced face who was always harassing people on his show. His audience would howl and brawls would break out, and the cameramen transformed into security. All I got from those shows was how judgemental the audience were about the guests, because being superior made them forget their own lives and feel better. Downey had an ever-present cigarette and he was always saying something mean. Later on he lost all credibility when he made up a story about being assaulted by neo-Nazis and said his assailants had painted a swastika on his forehead, but it was on backwards, so you could see he'd painted it on himself in a mirror.

On *Late Night* we played a song called 'Brittle'. We'd worked on it in LA with Paul Fox—I'd had three days to write it on a stopover in Auckland—and recorded it in a wooden seventies studio. The heavy metal band Danzig were rehearsing down the hall. Glenn Danzig himself was a little man who wore leather and had dyed black hair and looked like he should be off burning churches in Scandinavia. I really like the video clip where he's insulting someone backstage and the guy knocks him out.

'Brittle' was a good song that got lost towards the end. Paul suggested the chords behind the lead break that soared, and he did a Star Trek speech, mixed subliminally, which added a Deep Space ambience. His idea for the outro was less funky, and 'Brittle' ended up two-thirds of the way towards being a classic.

We were nervous when we played the song on *Late Night*, and people noticed. We were getting more unsure of ourselves and it was intimidating to think we were being broadcast nationally. The old Straitjackets would have just gone in and killed it.

'Brittle' was recorded for an AIDS benefit album that Arista released called *No Alternative*. Benefit records were big then, because they were still selling albums, and *No Alternative* had all the major alternative bands on it, like the Breeders, the Smashing Pumpkins, Soundgarden and Pavement. The Verlaines and the Straitjackets were there too, waving coyly at the bottom like true New Zealanders. I always believed the Verlaines were there by credit while we were there only because we were with Arista. That didn't feel like a victory.

By this point, Arista were staging promotional competitions where members of the public dressed in a straitjacket and ran around a record store grabbing as many CDs as they could underneath their chin.

Europe was no better, although Roger Shepherd was in the Mushroom Records offices in London then, and he convinced them to give us a push. Roger was working with Gary Ashley, who was always a decent man. Gary died in 2017. We liked him better than Gudinski. Gudinski was more rock 'n' roll but he was patronising, used to being condescending. When we were in Australia recording *Melt* he said to John, 'So how is it in the big recording room?' like we were children playing in a sandpit.

In Europe we drifted about in winter on a bus that smelt like a toilet, a dozen and a half of us sleeping in tiny bunks that had seen a million lonely wanks. I'd lie there and think, 'I wonder if the singer from Wonder Stuff did this?' but that would put me off and I'd have to go back to reimagining the porno I'd stumbled across on American cable TV.

We broke down outside of Manchester.

In Hamburg, at midnight, when we were returning from a bar, a man with a strung-out look on his face crossed the road with a giant knife behind his back. Rex Visible hadn't seen the blade so he just laughed at the guy, which put the knife man off. He did a U-turn and walked carefully back across the road.

I scored some coke in London, an 8-ball, which put me off coke for good. It was obvious that it ate up people's souls.

Richard Pryor nearly destroyed himself with coke. I loved Pryor—his stand-up comedy, not his films, because in his stand-up he seemed like himself, while in the films other people were telling him what to do. In 1980, after days of freebasing coke, he poured rum all over himself and set himself on fire and got third-degree burns all over his body. He survived and kept on doing comedy.

Pryor looked like he might cry when he did his stand-up where he'd talk about the fire, but he always found a punchline because Richard Pryor was a funny motherfucker. He was the king of comedy, and tragedy too.

You'd do coke before a show and you could hear the music sink midway through the third song, the way a coke rant sinks in the middle of a sentence. You always needed more with coke, and in the end I didn't need it.

In Amsterdam we spent our time in coffee bars ordering buds out of the jars on the counter—thick, sticky stuff called Lebanese Crack You Up or Moroccan How's Your Father. Then, stoned, we'd wander past shops selling porno rags with women doing animals on the cover, or walk through men's only areas where sex workers waited. Often haggard and toothless, they stood in negligees behind glass shopfront windows, lit by lamps, beckoning you in with a finger. Before a show in Amsterdam we got ripped and the gig was a marijuana nightmare. I couldn't tell if I was in tune. I felt stolen from the band. When I was singing, I was thinking, 'Do people really need to hear this?' and then I'd decide, probably not.

Pot makes words hang in the air, so you can examine them for their stupidity. What a dumb thing to say, you'll think, as a sad line plops there limply.

After Amsterdam I gave up smoking pot before gigs, and these days I always play straight. Standing in front of people in a maelstrom is weird enough.

We set a crowd record at the Marquee, only because it was attended by every New Zealander in London. To balance this up, we played to the bar staff in Bremerhaven and tiny crowds in Hull, Southampton and Leeds. I liked traipsing around the outskirts of England though, because it was like J.P. Priestley's *An English Journey*, with its depressed industrial towns, stone cottages and people making crockery. It snowed in Hull. When you said 'Hull' like the English did, it sounded a bit like 'Hole'.

When our unsuccessful Euro outing ended, Mushroom made us go back three months later to do it all over again.

*

I knew my band was over, but I held off telling anyone for a while. We'd been in the same band for a few years now, and eventually you tire of running in a gang, or you want a new one, where you haven't become over-exposed to people and all their annoying weaknesses.

There's no place to hide in a band. All your failings are out in the open. You spend too much time in each other's pockets to keep up the pretence. You hope that in the end, you'll be able to forgive your bandmates' foibles, the same way they forgive yours, because you're family, and you can move on—and usually you can.

But we couldn't move on anymore. Disillusioned, feeling half molested, our foibles now stuck.

I suppose I was dreaming of getting new music together and going back to the US and Europe with something I really believed in, but I got stranded in Dunedin, where I signed up to the dole only weeks after being driven in a limousine to the Conan O'Brien show in Manhattan.

The man at Social Welfare looked at the address I'd written on the form, and then at my tatty hair, and he asked, 'Do you live in the halfway house down the road?'

One night later that week, a resident from that halfway house walked into our disused warehouse then into my room and stood at the end of my bed. When I woke up and asked him what he was doing, he said he didn't know, but that he'd probably be off now. He nicked my leather jacket on his way out.

We went out playing stadium shows, which suited us because Straitjacket Fits were a stadium-sized band. We were built for it. What could sound too much in a small bar made sense in an arena bouncing back over thousands of heads. It was wide open music, so it suited wide open spaces.

We played at the Mountain Rock Music Festival in horizontal rain in a paddock near Palmerston North. It freaks me out to watch a video of that show, because we're standing, wired up, in puddles. But the picture is heroic. When 'Dialling A Prayer' destroyed at the end, the crowd was a full can of worms. You can see in that video clip that we're good—strong and confident. I think we ruled back in New Zealand because we knew our own turf, and because we'd played countless gigs around the world and you only get good by gigging. Out on the road you hone your set and learn how to make it work in any environment. Somehow you don't get sick of your songs; instead you go further into them. When you only know how you sound in a practise room, a new space is unsettling.

It's a shame you can only play a dozen times a year in New Zealand before people get tired of you. Then again, in Australia you can play the suburbs so many times that you become a backdrop for beer-drinking, playing simpleton music for drunks.

We were invited on the Big Day Out tour around New Zealand and Australia. It would be Straitjacket Fits' last tour.

In Sydney I said onstage, 'Every New Zealander's nightmare: twenty thousand Australians.'

I meant it as a joke, but it was met by a long, heavy silence. One person called out, 'Aw, ya wanker.'

On the plane home I still felt proud that I'd said that to so many Ockers.

It was forty-three degrees in Perth and the Indian Ocean was warm at Fremantle. The day after we'd been swimming, a twenty-foot-long Great White zipped through the same waves we'd waded in up to our chests.

The Ramones were playing the Big Day Out too. Maybe they were a bit sad by then, and the drummer was wearing a Ramones wig, but they weren't to be messed with—because they were still the fucking Ramones. In Perth, while the Ramones were playing, some clown on stilts walked in front of the stage, showing off. The burly stage manager hauled him down off his stilts and gave him the New York bash. No one stilt-walked in front of Johnny and Joey when they were playing 'Judy Is a Punk'.

I sat across from Joey Ramone after the gig in Perth. He looked long and awkward, like a misplaced stick, and people were leaving him alone. Joey had his red granny sunglasses on, his leather jacket and his Converse boots. I only needed to lean over, stretch out my hand and say, 'Good on you, Joey Ramone.' But I didn't, because I was too cool and probably too shy. I always regretted that, especially when Joey died. It's good to acknowledge other people—it's not like you want to rob them. There's nothing wrong with telling someone you respect them or admire what they did, or how they made you feel inspired yourself. Being an artist is hard and too many artists get talked at by the wrong people.

Chris Cornell from Soundgarden seemed a bit scared of the Ramones too, because he made a big deal of big-upping them at his gig in Perth. Soundgarden played doomy Sabbath metal. Like Sabbath, they had some top riffs, especially the one in 'Jesus Christ Pose', but they often sounded grey and oppressive, like they were drowning in a bath of gravel. They made more sense in a smaller warm-up show, like at the Powerstation in Auckland, where they sizzled. Because of the perversity of some of their riffs, they reminded me of the Butthole Surfers.

Björk was probably the best act on the tour. She sang her odd, modern Icelandic songs like a boss. She was genuinely more out there and innovative than any of the guitar bands. In Adelaide, we were the only people in a field backstage and Björk looked over and seemed to wonder who I was.

Billy Corgan from the Smashing Pumpkins may have thought the same thing when we crashed around a corner of a tent and nearly bowled each other over. He did a little start and a Bryan Williams sidestep. People said I looked like Corgan, that we had a similar face, but I wasn't a big Smashing Pumpkins fan, even though I'd enjoyed their first album, *Gish*, with its dreamy, psychedelic songs and the burning guitars that I could relate to. In Australia, Corgan always wore a Superman T-shirt and whenever he busted out one of his seventies Boston lead breaks he looked very impressed with himself. Maybe a part of me knew that Corgan was about to sell ten million more records than me and I was just jealous, but it irritated me that the Smashing Pumpkins were placed higher than us in the touring hierarchy. Music promoters are into hierarchies.

It's just more control—'You can't do that because you're number 23 here and that band is number 15, so you're not allowed to talk to them or go over and eat their hummus.' I can't be bothered with that. And the bands generally don't care. All musicians start in their room, with their records, an instrument and a dream. The feeling is equal when you write a song.

I was addressing Corgan and all of his sycophants when I wrote the Dimmer song 'I Believe You Are a Star'. It was the first song I wrote after Straitjacket Fits.

I believe you are a star
Because you beam above my head
And they say you'll travel far
How you go a long way back
That you're brighter than you are
That you beam about the best
That you're going to linger on
That you're lonely on your own
But you're exactly like the rest
You're exactly like the rest

It was also a reference to Sly Stone's 'Everybody Is a Star', which I loved, because it was sung democratically by people of different genders and colours.

In Auckland one of the Deal sisters told me I looked like the actor David Carradine, and she wanted to know what I was up to. The Breeders were on a roll then, but Kim Deal wrote later in her autobiography that they were drowning in drugs and booze.

Straitjacket Fits played their final gig at Mount Smart Stadium in Auckland, at the last Big Day Out show. Because we were more popular in New Zealand, and because the promoters knew that it was our last show, we were given a plum spot between the Smashing Pumpkins and Soundgarden, late, when it had gotten dark.

We went on and I wrung stadium-sized feedback out of my guitar and we blew both those bands away.

*

I returned to Dunedin and went on the dole. I hadn't belonged in the world I'd got lost in but I didn't belong back here either.

I hid in freezing warehouse flats and hardly went out. If I did go to see a band I'd stay in the corner, feeling self-conscious. 'You can't go on hiding in a warehouse,' someone said to me, but I was sober and nobody else was. Dunedin had changed in the time I was away—with a lot more immigrants from the North Island, musicians and artists attracted by the recent boom. Everyone played free noise, although the 3Ds didn't; they played noise with naughty children's melodies. They'd recorded their last album with Tex in his studio down by the wharf, and it was a better record than our last one had been. They'd recorded it on a fraction of our budget, too, which convinced me that corporate rock and the people who played in it still sucked. I felt tainted by association, that I'd been in the wrong crowd. I'd been stuck in a box for Barry Manilow. Todd, Randy and Chip gathered as one to haunt me.

The publisher from Mushroom was now harassing me on toll calls with a nasty echo on the line. He was a guy who had once backed our manager Debbi up against a motel wall late one night in London, and another time he had stood up at a dinner and said, 'All I want to say is that I've got spots on my deeeck.' He said we needed to renegotiate. He hadn't heard any of my new songs, because I didn't have any, but according to him the goalposts had moved. One of his underlings rang me too, and I was hostile with her, and I later heard that people in the busy circles were saying

Carter had gone crazy. I looked to Roger for help, but he wouldn't take my phone calls. I still enjoy Roger's company, but we're awkward when it comes to business.

Instead, Flying Nun management in Auckland said to me, 'Don't forget you're thirty now,' like I was over, a dish cloth they'd almost wrung out. Thirty was the age of doom.

I spent my thirtieth birthday alone. I'd had an argument with my mother. Her and Tony were having crazy fights, and for a while she shifted out and behaved badly around town. Mutual friends said she'd moved in on their flatmate. She started getting involved with people on the periphery of my scene. For a while, Mum lived in a one-room cottage, but then she went back to Tony to reach the same old conclusions. The only time I heard her sound satisfied was when I told her over the phone that I felt depressed by the family messiness as well.

Her and Tony visited me separately to complain—Tony about Mum's drinking, Mum about Tony's violence. They were afraid of each other.

Tony attended a men's violence support group. While there seemed to be a lot of bonding and sharing of war stories over cups of tea and biscuits, I'm not sure how effective the group really was for Tony. I think people with those kinds of issues are usually convinced that they're in the right.

I got joy from my sister Maria's kids, three girls and a boy, cute wee Māori kids with ruddy cheeks despite their dark complexions. They thought I was pretty cool, although they were young, and they only knew I played some music.

Dad had helped set up a small village in old Air Force barracks out on the Taieri, cheap housing where he could gather the local Māori. Many of them were members of the Mongrel Mob—it was possibly part of Dad's personal marae fixation. Once, when I was staying there, a huge woman with no front teeth and tattoos came to the door and threatened to give Dad the bash. She abused him for being an arsehole while drunk, and Dad said, 'Hey, hang on, I've got my son here,' but she kept going.

Maria and I spent time together, but a lot of it in silence. Because Maria was adopted into another family the year before I was born, we had missed out on a lot of each other's lives and we didn't really know each other or where the other had come from. She had a better knowledge of the local gangsters than me.

Once I was getting to the car in Mosgiel, where Maria and Dad were sitting, and I overheard Maria say, 'I don't know what to say.'

I wasn't sure what to say either.

Maria was gentle and easy going, but maybe I was worried she was becoming Dad's new favourite.

Dad and her spent less than $20,000 on a house in Invercargill and had it cut in half and transported north. It was bunged on a property by the river in Brighton, just around from the boatsheds where fifties-looking rowboats bobbed in swampy water and duck shit. I gave Dad some money and said it had to go on the house. Dad joked with other people that I thought he was going to spend it on parties.

Later, after Dad died, I spent a month in his cottage beside the cut-in-half house, writing a new Dimmer record. I'd had my heart broken and I wanted to write a raw, spontaneous record, so I wrote in a trance in front of a pot-belly fire with the river at my back.

My sister Tash had moved out of a house in Andersons Bay, like the rest of us, as quickly as she could. That home was just around the corner from the Bains' house. The eldest son, David, once asked my sister Tash to the school formal, but she turned him down because he was weird. In 1993, someone slaughtered the entire family except for David. He was an immediate suspect. But David blamed his father, who he said had left a note on the family computer explaining that only David deserved to live. Not many people believed this.

It emerged that there had been a family meeting on the eve of the massacre to discuss the family's issues. David had convened it, presumably because he felt he was the one to take charge. I remember when Bain was eventually pardoned after a royal inquiry—how he stood on the steps of the court with his stooge, former All Black Joe Karam, and thanked all of his supporters and didn't once mention his family. In a documentary later, Bain sat around at smoko with his new factory workmates. He seemed to be bluffing in his new surroundings, pretending to be one of the guys.

Sometimes, I think people live for so long in denial or become so disassociated that they believe their lies are true. I read O.J. Simpson's *If I Did It*, a bizarre book in which he describes the murder of his wife and her friend in intimate detail, but with the disclaimer that it would have only have happened that way if he'd been the one who did it. That book is a narcissist's dream. O.J. complained that he was the victim, and he always had his wife in it, going, 'You know, O.J., you're absolutely right.' It's one of the most despicable documents I've read.

My fellow Kaikorai Valley High alumnus, Clayton Weatherston, was the same. He was a university tutor in economics who had an affair with one of his students, and, when she told him she was moving to Wellington for a new job, he went to her house and stabbed her 216 times, while her mother tried to force her way into the bedroom. His defence team tried to blame the victim, saying that she had provoked him, a slur so extreme that the law around using provocation as a defence was changed after that. Weatherston stood in the dock with his university lecturer's glasses and wavy blond hair, and he talked in words several syllables long and got into the courtroom banter. It seemed that the point of the whole exercise, to him, was to show how smart he was. A lot of people hoped he got what he had coming in prison.

There was a rumour much later that the cops had found a set

of song lyrics that had been pinned on David Bain's bedroom wall. The cops were able to decipher some of the words. They were Straitjacket Fits lyrics, apparently signed by some of the band, and the cops found the words so ominous that they thought, initially, that they were a confession. That's a wild story. If it's true, I like to think they were Andrew's words, because David Bain sang in amateur theatre groups and he probably would have enjoyed our more accessible melodies.

I walked past the mass funeral for the Bain family on a Saturday morning, at First Church in Moray Place. Five full hearses sat in front of the Edwardian steeples in the moist Dunedin gloom.

When I did go out in Dunedin, it was usually with Hearts R Us. That was a fake dating club that Roy Colbert formed when Lou Allison had complained about being single. Lou was from England, and among other things she drummed for King Loser. She'd only planned to stay in Dunedin for a day, but the place had lured her in. Lou was an artist and musician who'd grown up with punk like the rest of us. She'd taught scuba diving in the islands, and the English pop singer Samantha Brown was one of her oldest friends.

Hearts R Us had a membership of about a dozen, and some of its members were couples. Roy made a fanzine for the club every month. Some people criticised Hearts R Us, because it was a singles club that wasn't really a singles club and the supposedly lonely members were actually all good-looking. Really it was just an excuse for us to go out, and we did go out—to the straightest places we could imagine. Bingo and housie nights, go-kart racing and ice-skating rinks—none of them were safe with Hearts R Us about.

At the ice-skating rink, the Skate Inn, I met Terry, who had once worked with my dad at the Savoy. In those days, Terry was the best-looking man in Dunedin—he just was. He'd had luxurious brown hair, a beard, and milky brown eyes that pleaded and coerced. He had a way of talking softly so you had to lean in to hear him. That just made his whole routine even more seductive. Mum used to say Terry could park his shoes under her bed any old time, although she said the same thing about our doctor, Dr Moody.

At the rink Terry was playing seventies radio hits to four pimply kids who were in a huddle and ignoring him. Terry was now the resident DJ at the Skate Inn. A green light flashed behind him, protesting a little too much. How the mighty had fallen, I might have thought, but the same could have been said about me.

Terry seemed unselfconscious though, and he was pleasant, as he'd always been. He had impeccable manners. Before I left we said we'd see each other about, but we were both unsure when that would be. Europe's 'The Final Countdown' accompanied me out, drained of its previous glory.

In 1994, Straitjacket Fits were awarded some New Zealand Music Awards for our last album—the award for best band, and I was the top male vocalist—so Hearts R Us held a celebratory club night. Roy knew I'd be sitting alone in my warehouse otherwise. I wasn't any good at victory. I'd rather pretend not to care.

The *Otago Daily Times* ran a front-page photo where I look like an afflicted boy in a beanie with a teacup, waving a fist sarcastically like I've finally made the grade. But somehow it was a bit half-hearted. When my green perspex trophy arrived in the Dunedin post it had snapped in half, and the other one was knocked off the table on the night of the awards and broke.

In the photo I'm surrounded by Hearts R Us members who join me in in mock, or genuine, celebration. A big homemade banner behind me says 'Shayne—You're Our Top Male Vocalist!' and with me are my people—Tash, my cousin Terry, Martin Phillipps, Graeme Downes, Jay Clarkson, Christine Colbert, and Dick from Dick and Fanny. Roy was probably in hiding, or writing a scurrilous letter.

Three other people are in the picture, including someone who told people later that she needed to knife me. Over a period of years she wrote me anonymous emails, accusing me of being a wife beater. I'd shared a dinner with her once with the band HDU and Tash, where she was severe, flicking me with bits of her Indian meal. It turned out she'd taken a dislike to me after I'd flashed the lights off and on when she was doing a dance routine as part of a Hearts R Us talent show. I'd thought the effect was only enhancing her dance, but she didn't like me putting her in the dark. Roy did a magic trick afterwards, and everybody clapped. I didn't do a performance that night. I'd played my part with the lights.

I put down a song with Lou on the bass and Peter Jefferies on the drums. We recorded it with Tex at Fish Street Studios, down from my fridge by the water. Peter's beat was murderous and Lou played a single note. I was exploring a new minimalism, trying to boil the music down to a quintessential truth. 'Crystalator' is one of my favourite songs, even if it's an instrumental. In it, I hear anger, lamenting and a giant 'Fuck you' to Mushroom, Arista and anyone else who'd suppressed me.

I'll give you a radio song, a song that could be a hit if it was rerecorded.

On 'Crystalator', I used an Ebow. The Ebow is a handheld device that produces a guitar sound magnetically, so when you hold it an inch above the pick-ups it sounds like a cello or violin without any pluck at the front. It can make a guitar sound backwards. Apparently there was a six-string version called the Gizmo, which 10cc used on 'I'm Not in Love', a song I really rate.

I abused the Ebow in 'Crystalator' by bashing it directly on the strings, an approach they hadn't mentioned in the manual. It sounded like a predator. When you pushed even harder the string squeezed into the pick up so the whole guitar squealed. That sound became the basis of 'Crystalator', which we recorded live in two takes. Sub Pop released it as a single in North America.

The flip side was strong as well, even though with its hushed restraint it was totally the opposite of 'Crystalator'. The lyrics for 'Dawn's Coming In' have imagery I'm proud of, like the 'pin through her nipple', which could be a shaft through the heart as well as a trendy piercing, or the warning to not 'feed the illusion', as if the illusion was shut in a zoo.

Dawn could also be the name of a character or a dawning realisation.

I wrote 'Dawn's Coming In', I think, about my mother, who'd tried leaving home but failed. Maybe there was also something in the song about a friend who'd got a drug habit in New York and come home to clean up, and maybe there was a bit about me in the song too. Lyrics often turn out to be different to what you think, but that's the best part of creativity, when you ambush yourself.

She's back 'cross the water
Brought back something for ya
They'd asked her to stay—she didn't wanna
She's sick of that order
Dawn's coming in
She's got a pin through the nipple
That place sure undid her
Was just a slap in the face
Reality hit her
Dawn's coming in
Too many drinks, too many hugs
Invisible things can glow in the dark
Too many dreams pull her apart
Don't feed the illusion

291

Dawn's coming in
She gave it everything, but it wasn't enough, yeah
Dawn's coming in

'Dawn' was subtle, so it slipped by most people—something that happened later on with Dimmer too. There, I no longer wanted to advertise all my songs in big neon colours, because I discovered subterfuge and slipping in under the covers.

But if I have a masterful song, 'Dawn' is a masterful song.

I still wanted to rock when I formed Dimmer, because I needed to exorcise myself. I built a set of new songs with Lou and Peter. It's a thing with me to start from scratch with every new band. I have to contradict whatever I've just said and I also need to prove that I have somewhere left to go. It's an immature attitude, in some ways—you don't give yourself any credit and you don't enjoy the fruits of your work. It was a bit like when Straitjacket Fits stopped putting 'She Speeds' in our set because it was too popular. We wouldn't allow ourselves a simple victory.

The first Dimmer set was abrasive and deliberately uncommercial. I don't remember most of the songs, because most of them weren't written to be remembered. We may have had 'Seed' already, and that remained a cornerstone—a hypnotic, half Can, half Family Stone number that played on a single chord. Later, when we played 'Seed' in Dimmer, we could make it last twenty-five minutes.

My Bloody Valentine could do that with their song 'You Made Me Realise'. It started on fire, got boring, then lit up again after ten minutes. I liked the extended effect. Brian Eno's ambient music was similar, in that you could drift off and make a cup of tea but when you came back it was still sitting there, like a house you've only just noticed on a street you've walked for years.

I enjoy songs and movies that set their own pace, that let

revelations unfold in their own time. David Lynch did it with *The Straight Story*, a film that some people resented because it was too slow and not like his old stuff, which was something I heard a lot of as well.

The first line-up of Dimmer toured in New Zealand for the first time in August 1994. Straitjacket Fits had played their last show only five months before, so it felt like an achievement. I wanted to move on, contradict myself, maybe escape Dunedin. In Dimmer we played with conviction—but neither me, the band, or the material was ready. In Auckland, we slayed everyone by playing 'Crystalator' first up, but it went a bit downhill from there.

When we got back to Dunedin, Lou went back to England, and took Steve, the new King Loser drummer, with her. And maybe I decided I needed to cut the cord with Peter too. Peter was as talented as me, and just as strong-willed and opinionated, but I didn't want to share the table anymore. Peter went too.

In my freezing flat, I wrote twenty songs and put them on a cassette. They were early version of tunes like 'Seed', 'I Believe You Are a Star', and 'Pendulum', which all later ended up on the first Dimmer album. They were genuine songs with tighter structures. I thought they were money in the bank, but Mushroom didn't like them. The only reason they'd go on supporting me, they said, was because Roger thought they should.

I spent five years morphing and twisting those songs, first with bad-boy conglomerates in Dunedin and, later, on my own. It was hard to get them out of the corner.

The first versions of Dimmer were improvisational—we'd jam around the kernel of a song. It was different from how things had worked in Straitjacket Fits. Straitjacket Fits had felt like musical hopscotch sometimes: you skip to the top, turn around and do it again. I wanted to be more liberated than that. None of the musicians I played with in Dunedin were scared of improvisation, but often the core of the song would get lost. It's hard to find the centre in a sea of free expression. I've always been respectful of the song and a song has to know its own mind if it's ever going to work.

The baddest early version of Dimmer was with Chris Heazlewood, Robbie Yeats and Cameron Bain. I like a bit of lip, and those three gave me plenty.

Dimmer got bottled at a festival in 1995, somewhere in a rural hellhole, by a lubed-up crowd who were all there for Johnny Diesel. We responded with a ten-minute version of Donna Summer's 'I Feel Love'. We killed that song while the crowd tried to kill us, although there was a gang member, with a patch and a moko, who pushed out his lips in a Māori way and nodded along, because he liked our confrontational attitude, and he also liked 'I Feel Love' by Donna Summer. I just focused on that guy and played the song to him.

The only recorded evidence from my Dunedin stint is a three-song single from our failed attempt at an album. The album didn't work because we were generally playing a different song—Robbie out the back and Cameron, Heazlewood and Carter pulling their pouting, naughty rock boy moves along the front. We recorded with Tex in a space beside the church where the Bain family funeral had been held.

I liked Cameron. He'd come down from Auckland with his mate Roddy Pain, and they had a band called Constant Pain. Cameron looked one part Elvis one part Jon Spencer; Roddy just looked like a slob. Cameron learned Russian while Roddy cooked food at a local café, which worried everyone because he had such disgusting fingernails. But Cameron and Roddy both loved electric guitars, boozing and Hank Williams. Cameron died in his sleep in his early forties, and Roddy died of liver disease two years later.

There is a photo of them standing at dusk in silhouette and holding their guitars out like *Star Wars* lasers.

Flying Nun released the single called 'Don't Make Me Buy Out Your Silence' from the Dimmer sessions. I listened out for it on the Campus Radio Top Ten the week it came out, but it didn't even enter. People were too busy dancing to records that sounded like Les Mills gym workout music, or the hideous helium inflections of happy house, where fans sucked lollipops and wore school backpacks and pretended they were twelve—they'd been lobotomised by too much E.

'Don't Make Me Buy Out Your Silence' was partly inspired by Tricky. I enjoyed the paranoia in his music, like he was too scared and stoned to answer the phone. 'Don't Make Me Buy Out Your Silence' was also something Joe Pesci might say before he baseball-batted someone in *Casino* or kicked their head in in *Goodfellas*—it was a warning to shut your trap. People were gossiping about me in Dunedin, envious folk, men usually, spreading rumours that I was a junkie with AIDS, or that I was crazy, or screwing somebody's girlfriend. Dunedin could be so small that you felt like there was a special bulletin board about other people's activities pinned up in the Octagon.

I felt a bit paranoid, like Tricky, while I was there. I'd hide from former schoolmates by crossing the road or going into Arthur Barnett's or joining a different line at the supermarket. I was well known, although not as well known as I was later, when I'd been about longer. That's when they call you a 'stalwart'—just someone who hangs around.

The main benefit of fame, I learned, is that people watch you buy toilet paper at the supermarket or look disinterested but surprised when you go by on the street. I guess there are added benefits of fame, like free jeans, and women wanting to talk to you, but that's about it. You become a magnet for opinions, resentment and gossip.

Don't Make Me Buy Out Your Silence was the last record I released for five years. The struggle continued after that, until it ended with balloons dropping from the ceiling and people patting me on the back. Then the balloons popped again, and after that I went back to struggling.

I played with many different musicians in Dimmer, because I saw it as an umbrella with me as the common denominator. I wasn't interested in being in a gang anymore, and I wanted an out if people got troublesome or annoying. So I flew solo for a while, sustaining myself on stubbornness. But you need other people eventually, because other people lift you and make you better.

*

Somewhere through this period, I thought I might give up singing because singing was too much like Bono, some self-anointed preacher convinced that he knows best. I did solo gigs with a loop pedal, and I sometimes lost my way.

The B-side of *Don't Make Me Buy Out Your Silence* was an instrumental song, almost techno, that I called 'Pacer'. Dimmer always has good instrumentals—go on, tell me I'm wrong—and they work because they have a structure while sounding like an improvisation. Each section of 'Pacer' was the right length. Instrumental music articulates the unspoken. Also, I got sick of hearing myself complaining into the mic.

In the mid-nineties I was impressed by the democracy of dance music, possibly naïvely so, as the superstar DJs were worse than Bono, because instead of lecturing at a lectern they were just playing other people's records. Still, the releases by electronic acts like Autechre and Aphex Twin were crushing in a way rock no longer was. Guitars are dead, in fact, said the press, although they'd been saying that for years. But rock in the nineties was meat and potatoes, retreads by thickos like Oasis, and whoever the other one was. The only Britpop record I really rate is *This Is Hardcore* by Pulp, because it's about the end of Britpop, and Jarvis is an excellent lyricist. The band behind him were average, pies with peas at the pub.

Because I'm so obsessive, I started a nerdy swot about electronica, rhythm, and the people who'd been the historical forerunners. Some sang, some didn't, but I became aware of the continuum that ran through the hard Payback funk of James Brown and the Germans who did a stiff-kneed Euro version of that, like Can. It was all the same voodoo, the way Thelonious Monk sounds like late Franz Liszt, or how Kraftwerk went to Detroit and turned techno, or how one long note by Miles Davis stretches out like an ambient Eno record, and you can hear the same iron fear and dreaminess. I fell asleep to Eno's 'Ikebukuro' and 'Thursday Afternoon' for about ten months.

I like to go in deep. My nerdy swots are private, and personal. Music is so infinite you'll never find the bottom.

In 2002 I played Thelonious Monk for a year, mostly his solo records. The record he made on his own in a hall in San Francisco, when he thought his wife might be dying, is celebratory and regretful. He makes the sweetest sounds, but with a lemon tang and surprisingly small fingers.

There's an extended jam of 'Round Midnight' on the solo record *Thelonious Himself,* where you hear him musically think out loud, as he tries and abandons sketches of his most well-known song. He'd been playing 'Round Midnight' for years then, but he always played it different. No back and forth in the tired old way; he didn't do musical hopscotch. He dips in then dips out, and has a word with the engineer. Then he ducks back in again and turns it inside out. He doesn't need to be singing, because Thelonious

297

Monk already is.

The swot I'm in now has run for nearly five years, but this time with a different form of instrumental music. I knew nothing about classical music, so I listened until I did.

Musicians and artists feel the same pulses, whether they're in Dunedin, Vienna or Harlem; whether it's 1880, 1996 or 2019.

They're the magnetic fields we all feel, like pain and loss and love.

Part Three

Getting What You Give

I think I've had about twenty people in Dimmer—I'm not totally sure, because I've lost count. One of them was Matt Middleton, who Heazlewood brought in to play drums in my icebox flat in Dunedin. Matt was an escapee from Invercargill. He'd get drunk and smash restaurant windows, but he also put out a series of near-genius cassettes under the name Crude. On the cassettes Matt squawked and ferreted in a thicket of synths and drums. He honked a sax, abused his guitar and, although he was barely past twenty, he'd sing like a grizzly old man. Matt was a tower of nerves. He'd sometimes make little Mr Magoo noises, as if he was searching through the jumble in his head.

I once interviewed Matt for a magazine that had asked musicians to interview other musicians they rated. I asked him if Crude was the sound of mental unwellness, and Matt said that it could well be, but that the sound of mental wellness was actually rather boring.

When I asked him whether a song should ever be used for revenge, he said you can't stab someone with a song.

He thanked me for asking him interesting questions.

Matt didn't last long in Dimmer, because Matt couldn't sit still. He went to Melbourne, where he's given up music, because no one understands him.

301

*

Basketball sustained me when I was back in Dunedin, and football did as well, even though there was one time when a man I didn't know tried to snap my leg. Playing sport made me feel free; I could let go of negative energy. I played pick-up basketball games with some guys I'd made friends with shortly after my return.

Jeff Wilson was at the gym where we went for basketball, playing with some other people at the other end of the court. He was a double international in cricket and rugby, and someone said he was a fan of Straitjacket Fits. The All Black Josh Kronfeld may have been one too, because I saw him at the kebab shop after one of our gigs.

Wilson's spiritual inheritor is Ben Smith, a fullback who also plays for Otago. Smith is the same as Wilson—surprisingly pacy and skilful for a Pākehā. I saw Smith play a game a couple of years ago where people bashed the shit out of each other for eighty minutes, and Smith still acted like he was trimming the lawns by the Victoria statue down at Dunedin's Queens Gardens. When his team scored a crucial try he walked before the main stand and did a little thumbs up, a shy one that he held down by his navel. Despite his win, Smith didn't get carried away.

I woke up in my icebox for my second winter in Dunedin, and thought maybe I should move on. The punishment of the year-round freeze had got too much. Maybe I also needed to escape my family.

I returned to Auckland, because Auckland had an easier climate and more than a dozen people wandering down one street. You could find your own space in Auckland—a corner for a nerdy swot. But there was a lack of community there. No rallying point, no common thread, no friends to casually visit who'd show you a book or tell you about a good idea or take you next door

302

for a jam. I enjoyed the cosmopolitan mix in Auckland and the colour in people's faces, but a lot of Aucklanders ponced about and placed great importance on the buck. Its winter could get you in a more insidious way. The Auckland sky was a flat grey slate, unlike the more honest freeze of the south. Still, I lived and worked in Auckland for twenty-five years.

At first, I was broke and I often had nowhere to live. I owed the record companies money from records that would never recoup, so I'd be sent statements showing astronomical amounts that bore no real relevance to my life.

For a time I slept on cushions at my sister Tash's house in a block of council flats. Another time, before the first Dimmer record came out, I slept on cushions at a football friend's place. He was a driver for a brothel where his girlfriend worked. Each day he'd take half-hour showers, as if he was trying to scrub the thought of that away.

After my father died, I was still homeless and destitute, this time freshly kicked out by my girlfriend. I was grieving. And I was also concerned about a hole in my ear. The specialists were investigating for cancer, because eardrums shouldn't have holes. At the ear, nose and throat clinic, I'd lie on a chair while the specialist poked at my ear. These visits were deathly, even worse than visits to the dentist.

I got depressed and watched pornographic gifs on slow dial-up internet and thought I'd probably die.

That's when I started drinking again.

I tried seeing a therapist because I was barely hanging on, but I couldn't connect in any real way with him. The therapist got angry when I made a joke about cancer. He'd lost a friend to cancer in the ear. He dropped me off in his car afterwards and we never reconvened.

It was when I was sleeping on cushions and had a hole in my

eardrum that I had to go back out again to promote myself and my forthcoming record.

I Believe You Are a Star was a three-year battle that I won, but I hurt myself doing it. I ran myself in circles, and eventually into the ground. At one stage I got a testicle infection and had to go to hospital, where I clawed at a metal bedframe in agony. I'd had sex with my girlfriend and when I pulled the condom off it was filled with blood. That shouldn't be there, I thought anxiously. The next morning my right testicle blew up to the size of a grapefruit and it felt like I was constantly being kicked in the balls. I was immediately put into hospital. My doctor suspected cancer. They ran tests but I was eventually cleared, as I'd been cleared with my ear, but neither infection was ever fully explained.

The one bonus of my hospital stay was that they gave you these special mesh undies to hold up your balls, because it was too painful letting them hang. I grabbed several pairs to save a few bucks.

I made *Star* in a Portacom building that Sony paid for and had lifted into the backyard by crane. The crane driver told us his name was Michael Jordan. Rent was expensive in Auckland and it had been difficult finding a space, so this way proved to be more economical. Our flat was in Ponsonby, and it was owned by Paul McKessar's parents, and when the shed was eventually lifted out the lawn underneath it had died. Mrs McKessar cried when she saw that, but my dad had just died, so I thought she was overreacting. But I was sorry about her lawn.

The Portacom shed had aluminium walls which I left blank, like a canvas I needed to fill. There was a harsh natural reverb as the sounds bounced off the walls. The desolation of that reverb— abrasive, cheap, with a subtle edge of nastiness—is all over *I Believe You Are a Star*; it colours all the tracks. I worked on the album for hours, days, weeks, months, and eventually years. It was a serious length of time. Sony spent a tad over six figures on *Star* in the end as I sat there shifting sound files around by a tenth of a second. Of course, I would have to pay Sony all of that money back. As I worked on the songs, morbidity climbed through the window. Sometimes, I thought I might die before I finished my work. But then I'd sigh, and go, 'Ahhh well,' and pack another pipe.

In between recording, I started reading the website run by the Texas Department of Criminal Justice, where they listed the last meal requests of the condemned.

I've always been obsessed with mass murderers, reading books by Colin Wilson and upsetting myself. As a boy—perhaps like most boys—I went through a phase of reading a lot about Nazis, but you reach a point where you can't handle one more tale of someone being taken away to be shot in a pit.

On the Texas website, I'd study the backgrounds of these people and the crimes they'd committed, and try to correlate that with their preferences in food. The beans, cheeseburgers and fried chicken seemed so trite compared with the gurney just next door. Some of the prisoners turned their last meal down. Some made no final statement.

When I got back to Auckland, I'd started jamming with Gary Sullivan and we developed a new way of playing. I knew Gary from the JPSE days. We had a series of photos from the tours our bands did together in which the pair of us were shaking hands in a variety of international locations. We called these the handshake photos. They were deliberately Kiwi Gumby. 'Aw g'day mate, we're not that good, are we?'

Gary and I were both sick of rock music—the glory and predictability of it all. I liked Eno's ambient records and empty electronica, and Gary liked all that stuff as well. We swung all the way to the opposite end of the spectrum, and we'd play so quietly in our practice space sometimes that we could almost hear each other breathing. It was a completely new dynamic for us. Instead of lifting for the big pay-off, the music just fell away. Gary would do a little tap on his hi-hat, and I'd lightly touch a string. 'Ooooo, that sounds good,' we'd say, and then we'd play nothing again.

We learned the true beauty of space, of silence. We learned that there can be an eloquence to shutting up. It was educational, refreshing, and against the code we were known for. Another contradiction. 'Fuck you,' it said, but quietly, with a slither of wah guitar.

Gary was by my side for most of *I Believe You Are a Star*, although he had to walk away in the end, because my obsession was driving him nuts and he couldn't face listening to a track just one more time, and then another time again. I sat in the shed and shifted tracks around by a tenth of a second, forgetting to come in for dinner, staring at the flickering screen until my eyes filled with grit.

One of our favourite tracks in our early recordings was a fart one of us did that we'd managed to capture. Sometimes, if we were getting bored with a song, we'd just drop it into the middle of the track. The fart was quite long, and it went through several key changes without ever pushing too hard. We called it 'Empty Fart', because it was an empty-sounding fart, and we'd dress it up in delays and dub riddims, and then we'd laugh even harder. It became our friend. It sounded powerful slowed down. People would ask me how the recordings were going, and I'd say, 'Yeah, good.'

There was a little shelf behind the speakers where I put up four carved letters made out of wood that spelled out the word GONE. Gary had made the letters at art school. GONE became our philosophy. We wanted this record to be gone—woozy, stoned, with a stagger in its step. The wooziness was aided by the fact that

I was working on Pro Tools, the recording system that everyone uses these days. I didn't really know how to use Pro Tools. I couldn't be bothered wading through a manual, so my knowledge never went beyond 'record', 'play', 'add new track', and 'delete'. I did a lot of deleting.

I also didn't discover the Bars and Beats function where you can shift blocks of music about in measured increments so that, no matter where you put them, they'll still fit. I calculate I added nine months to the project through repositioning elements by ear. Many parts of the record are slightly out, but I think that adds to its feeling of gone-ness. True funk lives off the beat. I saw D'Angelo play once, and his band was so far off the one, their rhythms were like a buckled wheel. It was the hardest and meanest funk I've ever seen.

It's rock that keeps in time. In this age of sheeny, processed music, where records are quantised into perfection, the best thing you can say to some musicians is, 'Hey, I enjoyed your record—it's really in time.'

I'd left Flying Nun because I felt like I'd become a drag, someone distracting them from their real work whenever I went to their office. Also, I was now over thirty.

It was when I was working on my early Pro Tools experiments that I ran into Malcolm Black in the record store Beautiful Music on K Road. Malcolm, Sony's A&R man, was someone I knew from Dunedin—in fact I'd slagged off his band the Netherworld Dancing Toys in the university paper *Critic*. Malcolm wrote their hit 'For Today', which made him a lot of money. People were always singing it at the Sevens rugby tournaments.

I was looking good when I saw Malcolm in the record store, in my nice white short-sleeved shirt, tanned and trim because I was playing a lot of football and was still off the booze. When I told Malcolm I had some new tunes, he said he'd be interested in having a listen. So I sent him some demos, but he never received them, because one of his staff thought they'd come from a bedroom hopeful. I concluded that Malcolm didn't like the demos. He thought I'd never sent them. Eventually, when he did get to hear the tunes, he liked them a lot.

Malcolm became my main man, my ally, all through the making of *Star*. He was warm, encouraging and patient, which was just as well, because if he hadn't been I would've thought he was just another record company wanker. Malcolm was respected at his work, and I think he was allowed Dimmer as a sort of personal indulgence. Sony usually dealt in glossy, processed stuff with catchy choruses, and Dimmer was its goofy puppy with a wrong-shaped head. But Malcolm backed me all the way. He never questioned my direction, which was important to me, because Arista and Mushroom always had.

Beautiful Music was run by Gary Steel. Gary was a music critic and he pissed off some people with his snooty reviews, but his writing didn't disturb me, because Gary was well informed. I liked that he wasn't afraid to go against the grain. To me, it was a sign of passion.

Beautiful Music had a lot of records that fitted my new continuum. In the minimalist techno from Berlin and Canada, Gary Sullivan and I could hear people emptying music in exactly the same way we were doing. But they used 808s, while Gary tapped on his hi-hat. They used washy synths, while I got gone on guitar.

Gary Steel's shop had a lot of outsider music, and one of the best records I discovered there was by Mark Hollis. Hollis was the singer of Talk Talk, and the only solo album he did was a masterpiece. It was pitched at such a low level you had to bend in to hear it, the same way you had to with Terry back at the Savoy. Hollis was equally seductive.

A band backed Hollis, but barely, like a phantom band, with a series of soft jazz chords, while Hollis sang in a quivering croon. He sounded a bit upset, disconsolate, like he was singing himself to sleep after a particularly trying day. I liked his tone of resignation. I liked the fact that the music was so withdrawn, that it had an inverse power beyond the average rocker. His album was concrete evidence to me that my fresh way of working was right, that quietness could be just as effective as bashing. Quietness was like a person stealing into your room.

Another of my favourite purchases from Beautiful Music was a collection of mysterious recordings from shortwave radio stations—'numbers stations'—called *The Conet Project*. These are encrypted messages transmitted by European intelligence agencies, using secret frequencies. Amateur radio enthusiasts would stumble over these recordings; there are so many that *The Conet Project* goes on for hours, over four CDs. Male and female voices reel off strings of numbers and innocuous-sounding phrases. Sometimes it's just tinkling music-box muzak, but the music has a code. It's an ambient record but, with its lack of warmth and humanity, in places it becomes ominous and threatening. I played it a lot when I was doing the vacuuming around my flat.

Eighty-three . . . zero one one . . . twelve . . . four . . . Yankee . . . foxtrot . . . hotel . . .

Tinkle tinkle tinkle.

I met Steve Braunias for the first time at Gary's shop. Steve would later write that when he saw me in the store he thought, 'Yuck, there's Shayne Carter', but he also said that he liked me as soon as we talked. I enjoyed Steve too. He's my favourite journalist in New Zealand. He's into Brian Glanville and Graham Greene, and when

309

his columns first appeared he called people out in a way no other New Zealand journalist was doing at the time. He wrote about sitting around on the dole in old lady cafés, eating pastries and pink lamingtons and enjoying an honest pot of tea. Then he'd take out some bureaucrat for being such a loser.

'Oh, you're the soccer guy,' I said to Steve the first time I met him, because some of his columns were about being a not very good junior soccer player in Mount Maunganui, where he'd always avoid the ball. He played out on the wing like I did but saw a lot less action.

When he was young he'd collected *Tiger and Scorcher* comics and dreamt of being Roy Race's teammate in Melchester Rovers. I'd had the same comics—Blackie Gray and Hot Shot Hamish, with the cartoon swoosh behind the ball. The foolishness of the idiots in the pages of *Whizzer and Chips*.

The day we met, the first thing Steve did was take me back to his place and show me his soccer books. He had an enthusiast's collection, many of the books old and mouldering, about men named Tommy who'd played centre forward for Wolves in the fifties.

Steve was my friend from that day, even if he can be overly sensitive to criticism. He's the classic 'give it but can't take it'—like Roy Colbert, and probably like myself.

When I was back on the booze, I'd join Steve for endless Friday night drinking sessions at the Alhambra, a tropical-themed upstairs bar at the north end of Ponsonby Road. The Alhambra attracted various miscreants, like Marx Jones, who'd dropped flour bombs from a plane during a 1981 Springbok test; the poet Bob Orr; and Rufus, the in-house piano player who'd once been in the Quincy Conserve. Rufus was Māori, and one night I tried to sing 'What a Wonderful World' with him, but I was so drunk I couldn't remember any of the words. Rufus just looked at me wisely and asked me what tribe I was from.

'What a Wonderful World' is a genuinely spiritual song. It's message is populist but profound. 'The bright blessed day, the dark sacred night'. You could describe a lifetime with that.

I Believe You Are a Star is my best record. Every song is strong, apart from 'All the Way to Her', but nothing's perfect. I had a point to prove, and I didn't let it go until it was right. It was a record I made to be a record, unlike most of my other ones which were often tempered approximations of a live sound.

Because I didn't know how to use Pro Tools, I did things you weren't supposed to. The record is littered with scruffy interjections and random flotsam, stray strands of guitar and keyboard hums in inappropriate places—but it still made a painting. Pro Tools meant I could spend time on my record instead of rushing it through in a couple of weeks. I got better at Pro Tools later on, but that just meant that sometimes I squeezed too many of the pips out of the music. Sometimes it's better to leave them alone.

I played nearly every instrument on *I Believe You Are a Star*, including the unconvincing keyboards and shonky bass. I stacked up a lot of vocals and duetted with myself on disturbing verses. I even shook a shaker, even though I'm a useless drummer—I'm a guitarist, and I'm sloppy and I play all around the beat.

I ended up working with four different engineers or co-producers on the record. I needed assistance because my recordings sounded shitty, and even though I often liked that, it was frequently too tragic—a dude forgetting to flick the switch, or not even knowing the switch existed. All of the people I worked with were non-rock, or, if they were rock, it was from a warped perspective. Nick Roughan had been the bassist in the Skeptics. When he helped with *Star*, he was working with hip-hop people like DLT and making his own electronic music. Nick was over rock. He hadn't been into it to start with. He was never a conventional pop person, either. If I played the Beatles, he'd go, 'Ewww, I can hear the mould growing.'

Andy Morton was hip hop, and he'd had a lot to do with the excellent early singles by King Kapisi. He'd probably never touched a guitar in his life. Angus McNaughton came from dub, and I doubt he had a lot of Dunedin Sound records in his collection.

The other engineer was Dale Cotton, who was my sister Tash's partner at the time. He'd recorded the surrealistic early HDU records and had worked a lot with Mink, an eccentric Dunedin art-pop collective.

All of these people brought their own spacey vibe to the record and helped me finish it when I was staggering down the home stretch with drink breaks at the hospital.

With Pro Tools I found a new way of singing. When you're developing music in the studio, you don't have to shout over a band. When Frank Sinatra made his studio recordings with orchestras he discovered this too, that you didn't have to push—that you could insinuate, or whisper, make statements under your breath. Frank was the stranger at the cocktail party, with a little piece of lemon skin on his lapel, acting as seducer. Or the rejected lover standing alone under a streetlamp at night, smoking a cigarette, chastising himself, a secret agent of love. The series of albums Sinatra released in the fifties after Ava Gardner broke his heart—*Only the Lonely*, *No One Cares*, *In the Wee Small Hours*—are classics of noir romance.

'Drop You Off' was a whisper, a sequence of shadowy threats. It opens the Dimmer album with a shuffling drum loop that Andy Morton made. I'd based the song on James Ellroy's book *My Dark Places*, about his search for the person who'd murdered his mother when Ellroy was ten years old. She'd been abducted, driven off and killed. It was a clammy, claustrophobic work. A lot of Ellroy's novels have a screwed-up detective in them trying to save a woman.

I'd also just broken off a relationship, so the lyrics told another story too—but both stories came back to betrayal and how you can be sitting with a secret that the other person is completely unaware of. We made a video for 'Drop You Off', and the best shot was the camera looking up at trees from the perspective of someone lying on the floor of a car.

The video had a shot of a letterbox with no number on it, so I asked the production people to draw one on. When I watched the rushes later, I saw they'd written the number 42. That was the number of our old Caldwell Street address in Brockville. Dad had just died, and I thought it was another one of his tricks.

Weird the way it falls
How you don't see it at all
Questions that I'm never gonna hear the answer for
I'm not your friend, I'm a stone cold traitor
Getting ready to, set or not
Getting ready to
To drop you off

The song ends with a plonky acoustic and a sample that sounds like baying hounds.

'Seed' is a classic. Everyone likes 'Seed'. I sang it a bit like Damo Suzuki. That may have been one of the vocals that made the General Manager of Sony tromp around his office complaining, 'But he can't sing.'

'Seed' has a train-like rhythm. Miles Davis liked train rhythms. He used them on his album *Tribute to Jack Johnson*, about the black American boxer. Miles Davis thought the movement of a boxer was like a train. One, two, three—pop; one, two, three—pop. Boxing is another elemental rhythm, like breathing, walking or fucking.

For the song, Gary made an animated video clip where a train goes through a surrealist landscape and, at one point, runs through a blow-up image of my head and explodes it into bubbles. Maybe this was Gary's payback for the trials I'd put him through.

On a record that has no hits, 'Evolution' should have been a hit. It doesn't miss a step. The lyrics are like a series of slogans or catchphrases that roll all the way to the bank. It felt like an injustice that it wasn't a smash, when bands like Nickelback have them all the time.

Gary and I were big fans of the song 'Smoke', which was small, vaporous and hazy. The breakdown to the struggling lead break is one of my favourite Dimmer moments. We recorded a rainstorm on the roof, and, when it rained down on the song behind the guitar, it became the real accompaniment.

Star has three instrumentals, because that was a part of where we were at. Saying it without saying it. Josh Frizzell—Dick's son—made a video for 'Drift', the first instrumental, by filming his father in time-lapse as he did a painting of a ship. The video was never publicly broadcast, but the image of a ship chugging through waves suited 'Drift' perfectly, as did the bit where Dick wanders off-camera to take a phone call while the tune keeps humming.

The middle section of 'Drift' empties out to a scratchy loop of an out-of-time bass. I loved how the album led up to this moment—that this was its sort of summary, and what it all came down to. One dumb note. A void, clumsy clang.

The song 'I Believe You Are a Star' was another big hit although, of course, it wasn't a hit either. It had a ride cymbal in it like the one in 'You Caught Me Smilin'' by Sly Stone, and I sang it in a sweet soul falsetto that undercut the meanness of the lyrics.

The glitchy electronica I'd been listening to, and *The Conet Project*, helped shape 'Pendulum'. I'd originally tried it as more of a rock song in the sessions with the bad boys back in Dunedin but it hadn't worked then. It did when I made it glitchy. One of the best sounds on it was a keyboard going through an effects box with its

314

battery going flat, so it sounded like something dying. It wasn't a sound they'd put on the radio. It was the static on the line from a call from a public telephone box, from someone harbouring bad intent, a call that neither I nor Tricky wanted to take. 'Like that minute where I passed you, and the next one you passed me,' it said. 'Pendulum' was about the power swings in relationships.

Nick recorded the sounds of birds in his backyard for that song. When they come in at the end, they sound like Hitchcock birds.

The most rocking instrumental on *Star* is 'Powercord', which was a good title and a good instrumental, almost techno—but techno made in real time, on real instruments, by two losers in a shed. One of my favourite bits, after the breakdown, sounds almost like Aphex Twin. 'Rer rer rer rer,' it went. Gary and I recorded the song in a practice room, when we weren't recording empty farts.

Andy helped me retrieve 'Under the Light' after Gary and I had backed it into a corner. I played him 'Mother' by John Lennon, where Ringo is back on level one, so Andy put on a similar plodding kick drum and dragged the music behind it, so it was funky like D'Angelo or King Kapisi. 'Under the Light' had started out close to a folk song, in that you could play it on an acoustic guitar, but Andy pushed it far away from that, to somewhere nearly electro. I'm not a fan of folk music, and I can't stand Joan Baez. I do like Judee Sill, but she goes beyond folk, a naughty Valley Girl disguised as a librarian, doing her version of Bach.

Star ended with 'Sad Guy', an instrumental with Gary telling a story on his drums. 'Sad Guy' sits in a mist of Ebow loops recorded on the loop pedal that I'd thought had been made in Salt Lake City by Donny Osmond. Bass donks in sparely—but only once or twice. The music finds its own way, and is better for having no map, so it wanders around, a bit lost, a sad guy finding a new path to fail on. Gary thought it was the best piece of music he'd recorded.

I knew I'd made a great record. But Sony were confused by it, and I'm sure they didn't see the purpose in 'Sad Guy'. They never released the album outside New Zealand. They ended up dropping me instead, which is a shame, because *I Believe You Are a Star* can stand in any canon, and it's a record that was apart from, and ahead of, its time.

I Believe You Are a Star won me the award for Most Outstanding Musician at the bNet Music Awards. I gave my trophy to Gary to look after on the evening I received it, and he lost it. I was disappointed because even though the last thing I wanted to be was a muso, or an outstanding industry figure for that matter, I was chuffed to have my skills acknowledged.

Star got unanimous five-star reviews, and the *Listener* said I was New Zealand's greatest rock star, and I was given various other awards. I'd be at these functions expecting to win, and I often did. 'Thanks,' I'd say into the mic.

I'd often get drunk at the award functions and have foolish conversations with people I respected, and some I didn't. Not of all it was foolish—a lot of it was well-intended. I congratulated the Dawn Raid guys once, because I was happy for their success and even though they were dealing in South Auckland hip hop, I could relate to their outsider battle. They gave chances to people who ordinarily weren't given chances. Sometimes, all a person needs is a break.

Despite the plaudits, being dropped by Sony made me and my album feel like a failure. Suddenly I was trapped in New Zealand in a limited, conservative market, and Channel Z, the rock radio leader then, decided whether or not you would eat. Once, I said in an interview that I didn't make music for Channel Z listeners, because I didn't, and the station yanked my record off their playlist. Later, I apologised to the programme director of Channel Z.

Apologising to that guy is one of the biggest sell-out things I ever did. As if I had to kowtow to that jerk. He still came to the release party for my follow-up record, but I didn't have anything to say to him, and he might have left early, but I wasn't watching. But these were the rules now, and this was my battle for survival.

I was hurt when, after Sony dropped me, Malcolm said I should consider doing something else with my life. It felt like another abandonment, like a father telling his daughter she should give up acting. I'm sure Malcolm meant to be supportive, and that he meant, commercially at least, that I'd just missed the boat. Malcolm is sensible, logical, and possibly a millionaire.

But music can't be dropped as easily as that. Not for me. It was my blood and my self-definition, an outlet for all the bad things I felt, and, sometimes, the good. Leaving all of that to push a pen, or a lawnmower, or a shitty product onto someone, was my idea of a nightmare. Music kept me sane, even if it could drive me insane.

*

Dad died when I finished my record in 2001. He was fifty-seven. Steve Braunias was at my door when Mum rang with the news.

I was on the phone to Steve fourteen years later when I got the message that Mum had died too, so I asked Steve to stop doing that.

Mum was a bit drunk when she called me about Dad, and she told me it was a heart attack. I later found out it was an aneurysm, but it didn't matter, because Dad was dead. He'd been feeling unwell and had asked Maria to take him to the hospital for a check-up, although he may have been feeling poorly for a few days, and maybe he was getting freaked out, because later one of his friends told me he'd found an empty whisky flask on the floor of Dad's car. It makes me sad to think of Dad feeling that sort of fear.

When he was taken to hospital they did some cursory checks

and gave him the all-clear, but when he was bending down to tie his shoelaces he just fluttered and passed away. Maria was there, and she said it was gentle.

Dad had his tangi in a Mosgiel community centre, the base for a local Māori education trust he'd helped to set up. A man called Boogie swung a pūrerehua around my head as I sobbed before my father's coffin. Dad looked absent and waxy, but he had a Jimmi P. Carter disco push to his lips, and I was glad the mortician had put that on. The pūrerehua made a woolly sound as it called up ancient ancestors. I heard my guitar in the pūrerehua too, and my relatives.

I believe in residual energy, and in having dreams dreamt by other people, and in memories you may have inherited.

We all slept together in the hall. We had to keep Dad there for five nights, because the grounds were too hard to bury him in. There were out of season frosts and, between those, grievous downpours. Five days was too long, and Dad got waxier and, even though it was cold, the insects started buzzing around. After five days, it was time for him to go, in his box full of trinkets and mementos.

Cousin Terry said he saw Dad standing over the people asleep on the floor one night, and I believed him because, at a tangi, you believe in those sorts of things.

Losing your father is a profound, religious experience. The agony and the loss, and the realisation that you've assumed their position in the world; you look into a mirror and get a fright, because you've turned into them.

We cleaned up Dad's place after his burial, and that's the saddest thing I've done. Handling the pieces that were special to him when he was special to us.

We burned his clothes in a pile down by the river, and sorted through his folders of information. I found a diary from the year when I was fifteen, and I sneaked a quick peek at it and on one page he'd written, 'Saw Shayne today and he's great . . .' I wished he'd said that more often to my face.

He had a battered Māori dictionary which I took, along with his yellow hairband and a rook from his plastic chessboard. I also claimed two patu that Dad had carved and stained. Materially this was all I inherited from Dad, but it was enough.

I played 'Evolution' to him one night at his tangi, and accidentally mispronounced the name of the Māori minister. When a squeal of feedback came through my amp, Dad's adoptive sister Mary let out a cry of fright but I just shook my fist because I'd called in the spirits, and everyone else there laughed.

When I finished my song, a man stood up and said we shouldn't be sad, because Dad lived on in me.

The best part of the tangi was the response of the children. Dad had taught them about Māori at their school and wrote Māori songs for them that he played left-handed on his upside-down guitar. The kids liked Dad, and a lot of them were upset when they came by to pay their respects; that is, when they weren't having a sneaky poke at his corpse and going 'yuck'. But children are barometers of truth. Their regard for you may be mute—but that doesn't mean they can't see you.

When I spoke, I said that Dad had been troubled by his lack of identity, by not knowing where he was from, but that the response from the young ones had told us who he was.

A bunch of us were sitting outside in the courtyard one night, and a bottle of whisky went around. I took a swig, my first in thirteen years. I was wearing trendy Manchester jeans with ridiculous flares at the bottom, because they were big in Auckland at the time, and someone there was having me on about them.

'Don't believe the trousers,' I told him. One slug of whisky led to another.

There was a beautiful Māori woman there called Pam. Whenever someone said something suggestive, she said, 'Hah, here we go . . .'

Pam had two teenage daughters, but she hanged herself a few years later. That was becoming a thing around Brighton. There was a string of copycat hangings, by teenagers mostly, who were impressed by the attention other dead teenagers were getting at tangi. Several teenagers died by suicide around that time.

Marcel came back for Dad's tangi too, his first trip home in ten years. I sat with him one morning outside the hall in a car with fogged-up windows, and I told him that I got the deal with him and Dad, how they'd never had a chance to connect properly. Marcel didn't say much back. He wore a suit at Dad's church service, when everyone else went casual. I'd come straight from the tangi and hadn't bothered with my hair.

We played 'Red House' in the church, because that was one of Dad's favourites. It sounded out of place with its talk of whorehouses, but somehow that made it appropriate too. Marcel picked Fleetwood Mac's 'Albatross' as his tribute.

Dad's coffin was too heavy when we lifted him out. Young men did a haka.

Mum was miserable. She'd always said Dad was her best friend, from the time he'd rescued her at the party where they'd first met. They saw a lot of themselves in each other, even though he was black and she was white.

She'd called Dad Jimmi, and Jimmi called her Rick. He was always turning up for family occasions like birthdays and Christmas, carrying poorly wrapped, cheapish, eccentric presents in a banana box—stuff he'd picked up at secondhand shops or something of his own he thought he might pass on, because he never had much money. Both him and Mum were happy he could be there, and Dad would make a joke.

Mum smelt jasmine in her car two days after Dad died. That was his favourite flower. It had grown in pale budding bunches around his cottage.

A bird came by Mum in her sunroom, and she thought it was Dad.

The last time I saw Dad, he'd come to see me off at Momona Airport when I was flying back to Auckland. He was on time for once—usually he was an hour late. You could set your watch to it.

He was annoyed, because I'd played a solo show in Dunedin and he hadn't seen it because he couldn't afford the petrol to drive from Brighton, so he was mad at himself. He told me he was sick of poverty and that he was trying to get something done, so he'd invented a new carving instrument with individual finger blades on a glove. When he told me about that on the phone, I was only half listening because I thought it was just another one of his stories. That annoyed him, so he told me again with exaggerated patience. The last image I have of Dad is him looking a bit forlorn at the airport.

Someone at the tangi said fifty-seven was too young, but the Māori man who'd played guitar with Dad in the Tempters said Dad had made his journey. I believed that too. Dad had connected with his Māori roots, studying the culture on his own in his cottage that smelt of firewood and patchouli, and he even did a version of the language, which, although it was his own take on te reo, he made sound convincing. He'd cleaned up a lot too, although he'd sometimes have a puff before he went to extrapolate in front of his students in Mosgiel. 'Extrapolate' was one of his favourite words. He'd often put it in a sentence close to another word four syllables long.

I believe Dad found some peace. Living with Maria and his mokopuna made him happy, although he could still narrow his eyes and deliver a surly growl.

Maria's children still believe he's around, rattling the ledge outside their bedroom window or shifting their toys to somewhere where they can't find them, playing his tricks.

I wrote to Dad once, several pages, after my therapy at the rehab place. I was still haunted by the look he'd given me in Alexandra.

His pain was his, he said, in a reply of extraordinary honesty, where he left nothing covered up. I still have that letter, but it's too painful to ever read again.

Dad loved me, and I loved him. He was proud of me, and I was proud back, because he was kind, funny, and not afraid to be an original. He was a man of his convictions.

When I was living in Dunedin in the mid-nineties, Dad came around to record one of his children's songs on my cassette portastudio. It was a song about the Māori origins of Saddle Hill, which he called 'The Saddle Hill Taniwha Song'. When he came to my place to record it he was a bit shy, so I left him on his own once I'd shown him the recording basics. Later, when his students performed his song at kapa haka events in the Dunedin Town Hall, I found that Dad had listed me as a co-writer in the programme, but I'd had nothing to do with writing his song.

Saddle Hill is a monumental feature rising over Mosgiel in the shape of a saddle. Cook made special mention of it in his diaries as the *Endeavour* ran down the coast of Otago. The best view of Saddle Hill is from the other side, where you can look down from the peninsula. It ends the scene majestically, like a giant exclamation mark behind the city. But the front part of the saddle is being ruined now by companies that mine it for roading.

A similar desecration happened with the spectacular basalt rock formations down from Brighton that grew out of the ocean at Blackhead Point, in symmetrical, God-designed, grey and black pillars. Mining ravaged them too, and the sight of both these assaults drove Dad crazy as he went past them in his half-broken car.

Dad's song has a couple of big clunks where he's dropped in to fix up a couple of vocal bits, but he doesn't fix very many. He sings a bit like Damo Suzuki, in a half-gone voice, and you can hear him stomp his foot like John Lee Hooker to a riff that reminds me of the one in 'Seed'. The song is infectious, playful, and he's a good storyteller.

In the dawn of time on the Taieri rise
When the dinosaur and taniwha reigned
There came to this place a most fabulous race
Here's how the Taieri got its taniwha name

Wae ka nui honu Taieri Paranei
Ko na ika o te Matamata hei
Wae ka nui honu Taieri Paranei
Ko Meremere taniwha hei!

Well they romped and they stomped
And they wriggled all around
And they flattened that hilly terrain
And there before us stood a wonderous sight
And they called it the Taieri Plain

Hei—hei—hei!
Wae ka nui honu Taieri Paranei
Ko na ika o te Matamata hei
Wae ka nui honu Taieri Paranei
Ko Meremere taniwha hei!

Well the hills they blew and the lava flew
And the taniwha tried to escape
They climbed up the fill and they formed a hill
And in the saddle you can see their shape
Hei—hei—hei!

When Dad died, even though it was unseasonal, it snowed. Then, a freezing wind blew up from the south and brought in heavy showers. We were standing outside the tangi when the rain stopped, and a huge rainbow broke out, right there, in front of us, over the immense hill.

*

The decade after *I Believe You Are a Star* was often a battle, because I drank through a lot of it, and smoked a lot of pot. It was my mid-period slump. Pot makes music sound good, and gives you tangential ideas that you have to grab quickly before they evaporate and you eat a box of biscuits. But pot is terrible for prolonged concentration, and for answering the phone. It makes filling out government forms awkward. Meeting people becomes a problem and it's better to avoid them. Your comments might seem tragic in the air.

The most striking feature of pot is that it makes being alone bearable, and being alone becomes your preferred state. When you abuse it, it's not good for relationships. You're on a flat, far-off level then, and your take on things is skewed.

It scared me to hear reformed heroin users say that the worst thing about smack was that it made you feel good for no reason. I didn't even feel any good. I'd be in my room pushing audio tracks around and obsessing over the clashing factors in songs that weren't actually clashing. I squeezed out a lot of pips. All of the Dimmer albums that followed *Star* had class tunes, but they had a few that were average. My recordings sometimes became overworked and withdrawn, probably because that was the way I was feeling myself. At times the music may have sounded a bit defeated. Pride made that hard to admit. The last time I saw him, Peter Gutteridge told me there was something dark surrounding the Dimmer project.

His comment caught me off guard, but Peter was insightful.

I felt disillusioned. I'd given *I Believe You Are a Star* everything I had, and I knew it was a brilliant record. To have it come out and then fade out hurt. I'd had a rock band that was one of the best around, and that hadn't worked either. My reappearance with Dimmer had given me kudos, but I never talked to the people who were impressed by Dimmer because I never went out. I stayed home, pissing into the wind and going in tiny circles. In the end it felt like it didn't matter.

I completely disassociated from rock music for the second Dimmer album, *You've Got to Hear the Music*. I thought of that phrase after Dad died.

On *You've Got to Hear the Music*, I explored introverted soul with cloppy beats, because I was into Marvin Gaye, D'Angelo and Al Green. They were my new continuum.

The Belle Album is the best Al Green Album there is. Al Green made it after he cut ties with his producer, just after an incident where a rejected lover poured a pot of hot grits over him. He was right on the ledge between damnation and God. He played acoustic guitar on it. I found a DVD of Al Green performing live on a regional TV show in America, and when he does the song 'Belle'—looking cool in a tartan suit, fro, and a scarf and big orange sunglasses—he gets so carried away he has to run out into the audience and do a little victory lap. The crowd claps and moans as he flits around their seats. Then Al gets back on the stage and throws directions to his band, who play with such an emphatic thunk you wonder who they are.

At the start of 'Belle', Al turns to the drummer and says, 'Ssshhhh . . . pleaaaase . . .' turning him down with his hand, because the drummer is too loud. Al knows you can't start at the roof, because then you've got nowhere else to go. 'Sssshhh'—

because then, when you come in, it counts for double. Al Green sings the blazes out of 'Belle' and that's why he's a master. I saw him play a live show at the Civic Theatre in Auckland, when he was in his seventies, and I cried when he came out and sang 'L-O-V-E'. He could still sing, although you could see him bending over in the wings at the end. When he sang a fragment of 'I've Been Loving You Too Long' by Otis Redding, all the stars aligned.

Marvin Gaye was another big influence for me—the way his songs were so yearning yet erotic. A sadness floats all through his music even when he's underselling major grooves with titles like 'You Sure Love to Ball' and 'Keep On Gettin' It On'. Marvin's lyrics could sound empty, but his music wasn't. He was a major league sensualist. In all of his songs he just wants to feel good.

There's a disturbing photo of Marvin sitting with his dad, the cross-dressing minister who was always jealous of him and who would later shoot and kill him. In the photo Marvin looks nervous and stoned, his hands placed defensively under his arse, sitting on a brick wall, and his father is beside him, peacocking in full pimp regalia.

Marvin's dad, Marvin Gaye Sr, wanted to be the star. He looked after the trimmings and kept on telling Marvin that what he was doing wasn't any good. I could hear that all through the music—the search for self-justification and purpose, for a shoulder rub, for the blessing of a woman who'll make everything all right.

The wordless outro to his song 'Come Live with Me Angel' is possibly my favourite passage of recorded music. After a standard three minutes, the band veers off in a whole new direction and then they go twice as long. A little clavinet is doing a stinky groove in a far-off corner, and everything else—the keyboards, horns, guitar, drums, percussion—has a perfect response.

The best part of that song is Marvin's wordless improvisation. He is a harmonising Jedi. There's a part in the vocal, a little bit like the 'Drift' throb on the Dimmer album, that says it all, about everything Marvin—and you, me—has ever felt. He dips into a minor scale just as his bassline does, and sings with himself. And even though his part sounds simple, even obvious, it's only because he's made it sound that easy. Marvin calls on the ghost of his affairs. A woman who has been moaning sexually at the top of the section—a seventies soul staple—vanishes in a glaze of spectral doo-wop and becomes a kind of mourner, as if she's the connection between sex and death. The outro to 'Come Live with Me Angel' is my definition of a deep groove.

Marvin's soundtrack album *Trouble Man* has very few words too. It's full of haunted vocal ensembles and savvy finger clicks. His early seventies records—*Trouble Man*, *What's Going On*, *Let's Get It On* and *I Want You*—are a remarkable sequence.

Marvin was terrified of live performing. There's a video of one show he played where he looks nervous in the first song, but he soon relaxes and by the time he gets to 'Let's Get It On' he's taken his shirt off. He's getting a little flabby, but the women scream and he's still doing things in their pants. Poor Marvin. He was in his forties when he was murdered, just like Lennon was, and Elvis only made it to his forties as well. For a while I thought I'd die in my forties too.

*

The strongest song on the second Dimmer album is probably 'Getting What You Give', with its Sly bass homage and Al Green vocal. It's about how what you give comes back to you. I saw that with the kids at Dad's tangi.

Gary made another animated video for the song. It has blank, white, human figures picking along in a zombie rhythm on their way to an airport, where they all hop on a plane. Then the plane takes off.

When I was recording that song, I was living in Mount Eden with Nick Roughan. We spent about a year crying over our respective relationship bereavements, drinking too much wine, and playing Dr Dre's instrumental album at a house-shaking volume. Then we'd put on an Eno ambient album and play that loud as well, until it sounded like Motörhead. P. Diddy's 'Bad Boys for Life', with its perverted riff, became our national anthem. Then Nick would go out and cook a delicious steak on his barbecue, with a lovely corn salad that had a dash of coriander.

Sometimes we could hear each other sobbing in the next room, and we'd fall into a harmony, like on a Marvin Gaye record. A dark pool of tears stained the woolly grey carpet.

When I was making *You've Got to Hear the Music*, an electronic artist called Burnt Friedman (a.k.a. Bernd Friedmann) approached me about doing something together. He was from Cologne and his album *Golden Star*, under the name Nonplace Urban Field, is a modern classic. I was psyched Burnt wanted to work with me because he was highly regarded. I'd met Burnt earlier, but it was only after he heard *I Believe You Are a Star* that he noticed me, and then he came up to me at a small gathering and apologised because he hadn't been aware of what I did.

He worked on a track I called 'I Wanna Go Driving With You and Listen to Marvin Gaye', which wasn't a great title, but something I really wanted to do. I'd said that to a woman I was falling in love with. She was much younger than me, which had become a pattern and a problem, because young people are at a different stage in their lives, attending to matters you've already attended to.

When I sent the song to Burnt he put on masterly touches, but he also added a guitar with chorus on it, and a mystery woman backing vocalist who sang about the snow. I don't know where the snow came from, unless it was interrupting our drive. I wasn't feeling those factors so our collaboration ended there.

The cover image of *You've Got to Hear the Music* is an empty cinema and a blank screen with red curtains and darkness surrounding it. I liked the implication of the ambient spaces, which was a look I used on all the Dimmer covers: an empty racetrack, an empty movie theatre, a statue standing with hands cupped, a shot of the moon surface with an astronaut on it. A Dimmer compilation put out by Rogue Records in Australia had a picture of an empty, rainswept street, and it was called *It All Looks the Same at Night*.

With many of the songs on *You've Got to Hear the Music* I wanted to write small, funky, campfire tunes that groovers could sit around and clap their hands to while boiling up the billy—something more down-home and human than many of the automated sounds around me. But when I was writing I got sucked into the internet as well. I'd waste long hours on not believing What This Child Star Looks Like Now and reading reports on executions from Texas. I even watched a video clip of a prisoner being beheaded in Iraq and it was the worst thing I've ever seen.

I wrote 'You're the Only One that Matters' for someone, because that's what I felt. She was moved when I played her the song, and she sat with her hands clasped between her legs, with tears in her eyes. She loved me after that, although I wondered whether I'd got the middle-eight right.

A video was made for 'Come Here', but I didn't like it because they used a group of models in it, which I thought gave the video a sort of superior beauty fascism.

The best part of *You've Got to Hear the Music* is the bonus acoustic disc that came with it. The versions of 'Case' and 'Lucky One' are better than the album versions. Anika Moa sang with me on those. She played live with us for about a year, although she doesn't put that in her bios. Anika shifted into our flat for two days before she shifted out again, because Anika was a wanderer who never stayed in one place. I related to Anika because she was a bogan part-Māori from the South Island, and a pure musician. I also identified with her battle in the recording industry, because they wanted her to be pretty and wear lots of makeup. They would have freaked if they'd discovered she was gay.

Anika was part of a growing brown contingent in my band. Willy Scott was on drums and Ned Ngatae was on guitar. Gary had gone to Australia to do computer animation. But, in the wake of Dad's death, I wanted to play with some brothers. Ned said to me once, 'I'm going to say one thing—*Band of Gypsys*,' which was the album Jimi made with his own brothers.

Some of the acoustic tracks were recorded at a gig we did at the Grey Lynn Bowling Club, and in the middle of 'Seed' someone poured a shed-load of bottles into a bin, but the song was cooking at that point, so we left it in.

Because I was drinking, I could sometimes get rude to the band. I'm usually respectful with the people in my bands—I don't stand over them and scream like some other people do. But a couple of times, pissed out of my mind, I let that slip and the group started dividing and people felt put down.

One night, drunk after a gig in Christchurch where we'd done tequila shots on stage, I was rude to Andy Morton—he was playing keyboards in the band at that time—it was something about him and me, another blurry episode involving a woman we'd both liked. I relayed this story in an unkind way, and my girlfriend, who was trying to sleep in the next room, said to me the next day, 'I heard all of that.'

She left for New York shortly afterwards and never came back.

I was in love with her, as was half of Auckland, a brunette with memorable eyebrows and eyes like Natalie Wood's. She had an engaging laugh, a knowing half chuckle that came from deep in her breast, and when she laughed, she meant it.

When she played in her band, she wore retro clothes, sixties get-ups like Suzanne with the Chicks, always immaculate. We went to an awards show once and, while everyone else was hiring their clothes from Kate Sylvester, she went to a material shop, bought a length of blue satin, and wrapped it around herself like a gown which she held up with several safety pins. She was the sassiest woman there. I remember Nicky Watson looking perplexed.

She had a methodical, analytical intelligence. Her mum and dad were teachers who taught sciences and maths. She once made me up a jigsaw puzzle of the famous trotter Cardigan Bay, and I couldn't work out how she'd figured out all the different shades of blue sky. She probably worked me out as well, because she went to the States with her band and that was the end of that.

When we first met, we'd hold hands on my secondhand couch and stare into each other's eyes for minutes. I believe in love, and I'm a romantic—once incurable, mostly cured these days by long stretches of reality—but when you feel love strong enough to stare into someone's eyes and not be afraid, or challenged, but accepted and reciprocated, you feel like you've known that person before; maybe you've loved or fought alongside them in another time or place. Their soul is familiar—so you look, hoping to rediscover the person they once may have been.

I've had that a few times. With the sweet girl I met in the early 2000s, a person of innate goodness, who I saw for two years. The Brazilian woman who I met twice, kissed once, and wondered about forever. Teresa from Atlanta, a gorgeous tall blond woman with a big burn mark on her wrist, whose 'y'all's were always killer. The German woman who I once met on a flight to America and never saw again. I would have fallen in love with her, but I couldn't arrange a stopover in San Francisco, so she left me at San Francisco

Airport with a broken shoe, because the sole had come off at the front, and even though I tried chewing gum to stick it back on again, it didn't work, so my shoe flopped around like a puppy with a chewing gum tongue.

Kathia laughed at that.

I believe in love—how inexplicable it is, indefinable, like soul, or a rock star, or deep, like a song. I also believe in beauty, which was probably what led my therapist to describe me as a collector, but I see beauty in all forms—a wave, a football pass, a row of zeroes and ones, how the scraping sound in 'Crystalator' kicks fucking arse. I've been lucky, because I could be with smart, beautiful women. A good deal of my songs are about women, which is a pop cliché, but these are the people who've made me feel.

The downside is that I've often been attracted to damaged women. I have an unerring radar for them, because they're the people I'm familiar with. My antenna goes up, and without exchanging a word I'll find them on the other side of a full room or in the middle of a stadium. Oh, she seems screwed up, maybe I'll be with her. Crazies are my kin.

It's the squares that scare me, because I can't relate to their aspirations, like the necessity of a mortgage, or satisfying the boss, or voting in pillocks like Key.

The only squares I enjoyed spending time with were some of the people I played soccer with. Football kept me connected to other people and the outside world. I'd go and kick a ball with ordinary men under the floodlights at Western Springs or on a mucky field down by Cox's Bay. There, I was surrounded by peers who looked after themselves and who dealt with the everyday as a matter of course. Some of them were impressed I played in bands, but most of them didn't care—you were just another bloke puffing and badly misplacing his passes.

I'd often smoke pot before games, which could work at indoor soccer and the casual Sunday kick-arounds, but it didn't work so well in competitive matches where the players really meant it. I would drift out of the action sometimes, go a bit awol, like I sometimes did with my music.

I did score some pearlers though. I'd skip past several players on one of my slalom runs, using the old Stan Matthews in-and-out, and the one where you pull the ball back and it disappears before you find it again, because only you know where you've put it.

It was at Debbi Gibbs' fortieth birthday party, at her father Alan's art farm north of Auckland, that we had the idea to reform Straitjacket Fits and do a New Zealand tour.

Gibbs Farm is an incredible place. Near the Kaipara Harbour, it has hundred-foot-tall sculptures by world-famous artists on the hills, and all manner of animals wandering about: yaks, Texas longhorns, llamas, ostriches and zebras—they've even got two giraffes. There's a Wild West street down in the bushes in a town called Grief, and it's not made up of facades but real buildings—a church, a blacksmith's, a saloon—which is a real saloon with a boudoir—and Grief moonshine behind the bar, and the lopped-off heads of animals staring off its walls. With their frozen half-grimaces it looks like their lives ended in pain.

Sometimes Debbi's father drives through the town in a tank or one of his jeeps with the anti-aircraft artillery gun on the back, and there'll be paint-gun fights in the bushes where people dress as soldiers and became very serious and committed to shooting people. Debbi's father sometimes gives people a fright by setting off explosions.

A chef prepares elaborate meals which they place on crisp white linen outside that somehow stays spotless, despite the dust and debris blowing down the main street of Grief.

Alan has spent time in Detroit developing amphibian vehicles that Richard Branson once demonstrated by driving across the English Channel. The kids play on one of those now in one of the artificial lakes. Down on the flats, the series of soft hills is a real-life sculpture.

Alan has reclaimed a large area of land down by the water, reshaping the estuary leading into the harbour, and it's like he's parted the water.

We played at Debbi's birthday in one of the barns. When we performed the Straitjacket Fits songs, they locked in straight away. The music lives on in your tendons. It was liberating for us to play with no consequence, without someone sitting there judging us, or Todd at Arista saying we should project more.

Because no one said we couldn't, we toured. The Straitjacket Fits tour was triumphant and the band burned. Good music sounds good no matter where you put it. We reminded ourselves that we were Straitjacket Fits before each show, and then we went out and did it.

I cried at soundcheck in Christchurch, because I was still upset about my girlfriend in New York. After the show, the Christchurch musician Roy Montgomery came to our motel. When someone asked me how I was doing, Roy laughed darkly and said, 'What do you think?'

We finished our tour playing to eleven hundred people at Sammy's in Dunedin, and I gave that show everything I had. 'Cast Stone' went to a painful and gracious place. 'Train', one of the let-downs on *Blow*, had the understated drama we hadn't been able to find in the studio. 'Burn It Up' was incendiary and 'Life in One Chord' scoured the roof. We pulled them all out. Mum and her new partner Laurie were sitting on the balcony, and if she hadn't drunk so much Mum would have been proud.

*

I wrote all the songs for *There My Dear* in about a month, mostly in my father's cottage at Brighton with the fire in front of me and the river at my back, the scent of my dad around me. I wanted to write quickly, to capture an acute and miserable time. I liked that *There My Dear* was one-track and miserable—I wasn't afraid to let that out. Get right to it and put it in their faces. I couldn't be bothered pretending, because pretending never works.

Dylan's *Blood on the Tracks* was an inspiration, because that was about a relationship break-up. It's my favourite Dylan record, along with *Time Out of Mind*—'Not Dark Yet' on that is a classic. Mum used to listen to that song in her car parked by St Clair Beach, one of our favourite spots.

My girlfriend rated *Blood on the Tracks* highly too. Someone told me she had gone to a Bob Dylan concert with her man in New York, and that had been the clincher. He was a *Rolling Stone* journalist with a famous rock star father. He also took her to see Al Green, and introduced her to Al afterwards.

She looked at her lover's phone eventually, and found out he was cheating. I said to her, things usually end the way they've started.

Marvin Gaye's *Here, My Dear* inspired me, too—so much so that I almost stole the title. *Here, My Dear* is known as Marvin Gaye's divorce album, because half of the royalties went towards his million-dollar divorce settlement. Marvin recorded the record, all about his break-up with his wife Anna Ruby Gordy, then said, 'Here you go.'

Although I enjoy parts of *There My Dear*, I don't listen to it very much. Some of the songs still make me feel sick the same way they did when I wrote them. A lot of the songs are true, sometimes too true. But that's better than being a fake.

'You're Only Leaving Hurt' came out in less than half an hour, the quickest song I've written. It trickles like liquid and it reminds me of Roy Orbison, in that it has an Orbison strum and charts an entire universe in a matter of minutes.

Gary did another video for 'You're Only Leaving Hurt'. It's one of his best—an old sailing ship tipped up at sea in a storm, and someone leaving a light on in a wooden hut in the middle of the woods. Immigrants trudge wearily along a road. At the end, a New Zealand flag flaps limply on a flagpole. Good on ya, Kiwi, it seems to say desultorily, and although some people thought the flag was random, I knew what it meant—stoking the old home fire, brave and philosophical, going, 'We're not that good, are we?' and doing a little thumbs-up.

I like 'One Breath at a Time' because the woman it's about guested on it, and it feels eerily abandoned, with its edges curled by sex.

'Scrapbook' has a rhythm that sounds like a band skidding on dirt, kicking up dust and struggling for momentum. I wrote it about my girlfriend almost getting Female Fox at the bNet awards, and how perhaps she'd got a little sucked in by the hype, reading her scrapbook a bit too closely.

You're building a dream house
A state of the dream house
You're building your dream house baby
The state of the dream now
If you wanna believe your own scrapbook baby
If you wanna believe your own scrapbook

'Mine' is a beautiful song, like something off Neil Young's *Harvest Moon*. At a party at the Gibbs' farm once they played *Harvest Moon* at dusk, and it was perfect. At first 'Mine' made me a bit embarrassed because it's so naked and revealing, but Don McGlashan made me pull it out at a show we did together, later, and I believed in it again.

336

The singles we put out were the weakest songs on the record—half-jolly efforts where I was trying to be optimistic or strong, but they don't reflect the album. Half jolly doesn't do it, because in music half anything isn't any good. But the record company always encourages you to put out the peppy ones, because bleak songs put people off.

When Nick and I went to deliver the record, all proud after so much hard work, the record company offices were empty. The lights were off, even though it was only 4:15 in the afternoon. Nick and I peered in with our faces pressed against the glass door, with our hands across our foreheads like we were doing a salute.

'Ah, ya fuckin' losers,' we probably said.

I'd spoken to the A&R guy earlier that day, but he'd forgotten we were coming in.

My favourite song from *There My Dear* is 'What's a Few Tears to the Ocean', because it moves me. When we play it live, it gathers like the sea.

Bic Runga, Anika and Anna Coddington do backing vocals at the end, and they float about like sirens.

I'd written the song when I was in Mahia, with Bic, Anika and Anna, on a singers' bonding trip before we worked on *Birds*. Bic had buried her father in the hills at Mahia just a few months before, so the place, already resonant, ached even harder. We could feel the ancestors looking down from the hills.

Late one night Bic and I were on the beach, which was covered in driftwood. The sea waved in, oblivious to witnesses, making its own arrangements on shore. The stars were unencumbered by city light, and I stared out beneath the canopy, over the water, thinking about that girl who broke my heart.

In the dark, a short distance away, Bic cried out my name because she was seeing bodies in the driftwood.

We both agreed they were probably there.

We left the beach and walked up a path through a hill. It was past midnight, and when Bic said 'Shall we turn around and go back now?', it made my skin prickle because I could feel exactly the same vibe.

On our walk back I said to Bic, 'Has anyone had a song called "What's a Few Tears to the Ocean"?' and she said not that she was aware of, which was a pity, because it was so good someone should have thought of it.

We went back to the house and played table tennis, because table tennis was reassuring, although I did several smashes and made Bic go get the ball.

'What's a Few Tears' is a strong lyric. Possibly my best. It has ambiguity and total depth. You can tell a decent lyric just by looking at it on the page, because it'll make an ideal shape—it'll look correct, somehow. You can see it even without reading any of the words.

What's a few tears to the ocean
It's only one night on a beach
Bitter's the salt that I'm crying
That's hitting the foam at my feet
You can't change the forces around you
Give into them first to be free
What's a few tears to the ocean
It's just the order of things

The song repeats 'We're living beneath our dignity', which has two possible meanings—how demeaning poor behaviour is, but also how the stars are a dignity we live under.

Bitter's the salt that I'm crying
And vast is the space in your wake

What's a few tears to the ocean?
And the moment it takes

I played the song to a friend who had terminal cancer—Rachael, Terry's second wife, who'd been brought home to her parents' to die. I travelled up to Wanaka to play her an acoustic set when she had only a few weeks to live. She was in her early forties. Her and her closest made an audience of six as I played her some of my tunes.

Rachael was brave, scared and philosophical, and it was strange when I hugged her goodbye, because I knew I'd never see her alive again. I went back to her parents' place two weeks later, and there she was in a coffin.

When I played Rachael 'What's a Few Tears', it touched her. She said she hadn't realised that so many of my songs were about mortality, and that maybe she was just projecting—but she wasn't.

It made me feel content that she was moved, because it was the best, and only, gift I had to give her.

*

The Straitjacket Fits tour brought me back to guitars and the power of live performance. I convened a new band for the next Dimmer record—a band not as commanding as Straitjacket Fits, because it hadn't been together as long, but the musicians poured themselves into it.

I drafted James Duncan in on second guitar. Gary had recommended him. It was a bit awkward between me and James at first, because we'd had the same girlfriend and he was still seeing her, so when we were alone in a room there'd be a telling silence.

But James locked in. He's been playing with me for over ten years now. James is a cerebral, skilled guitarist. He's not afraid to give it a twist and he always makes class moves. When Straitjacket Fits formed again in 2018, James filled in on bass, then he went back to playing top-level guitar, because he's capable of doing that. James also looks good—he's tall, with a floppy fringe he's always flicking. He may have been a model at one point. When Vaughan Williams played bass with us a few years later he and James made very appealing bookends.

James and I have this thing that has to do with Billy Joel. When we're driving in his car in Auckland, he has it tuned to Classic Hits. No matter where we are in Auckland, no matter what time it is, Billy Joel will come on in James's car—all the stink ones, like 'Uptown Girl', 'We Didn't Start the Fire', and 'In the Middle of the Night'. I'm a bit partial to 'Piano Man' because it's so depressing, but the other ones are irritating, with Joel doing his poor man Frankie Avalon and the Four Seasons impression. Apparently Elton John got upset on a 'Piano Man' tour they did together, because Joel was often drunk.

Recently, James and I pulled up outside the rehearsal room, feeling let down because we hadn't heard any Billy Joel yet. Then, when I was in the middle of a sentence, James put his finger in the air: 'Wait.' The song 'It's Still Rock and Roll to Me' had just come on the radio. We high-fived.

We dial up Billy Joel like miracle workers.

When I rang James a few weeks ago, him and his mum, Carol, had just been talking about me. I was stoked because it made me feel like they'd tuned me in like Billy Joel.

Dino Karlis drummed with us on the third Dimmer album *There My Dear*. Like Gary, Dino is very music literate, and he looks good too—he's part Greek and has a suave Mediterranean disposition that Mum was swift to point out.

Dino had drummed in HDU, one of my favourite new Dunedin bands. HDU were a heavy trio with a charging, surrealist sound.

The guitarist, Tristan, looked like he was pushing out one of Rosemary's Babies whenever he kicked in another worrisome chord. They played with Steve Albini's band Shellac once, and Albini got up after the HDU set and said someone had just melted his face.

Dimmer played a show with HDU at the Auckland Stardome, in the planetarium, a dark shell with a fake galaxy on its roof. When HDU played, I leaned back in a rich, thick armchair and entered a parallel universe.

Justyn Pilbrow played bass on *There My Dear*. Justyn is motivated and clever. He was in the pop-punk band Elemeno P, a commercial group always on Channel Z, and he wrote all their songs. I knew he had serious chops because I'd seen him play bass in a progressive jazz band on TV, and he did it as free and easily as the bare feet he was wearing.

Nick fiddled on the soundboard. We'd always greet each other with a half-choked 'Good on ya mate', because someone in a Speight's beer ad said that to their mate as they handed him a fresh one.

When we toured *There My Dear*, we found a new bass player. Justyn was busy with Elemeno P, so we added James's bandmate Kelly Steven, from Punches. Kelly is similar to James, clever but distracted, an appealing space case, and I could just picture their Punches practices where they'd um and fidget, and say 'I'm not sure . . .' and stare off a lot, and do a lot of hanging over thoughtful pauses. Kelly looks like that person you saw in that film who you're sure you've seen before. She'd been to art school, where she did paintings. Kelly was also younger than me, as were Dino and James, and I looked on her as a sister, maybe even a sort of music pupil that I could help show some things to.

We were touring around the West Coast of the United States

with the Brian Jonestown Massacre. Their guitarist Ricky Maymi had asked us along because he was a Flying Nun fan. He'd said that a late Straitjackets set he'd seen had been an influence.

Ricky was a globetrotter who popped in and out of the various pop centres, both with his band and on his own—London, Liverpool, Sydney, Auckland, and later China—and he was always hooking people up. Through him, we met Pete Kember from Spacemen 3 and Spectrum and a raft of switched-on Americans. I appreciated how Ricky introduced folk to other people they should know—it helped foster a community of people who probably felt on their own.

The Brian Jonestown Massacre were big then. They were a bunch of good-looking American men playing massed guitar, turned out just right in quintessential late-sixties gear. They had a tambourine, so people said they were psychedelic.

When I walked in on the Brian Jonestown Massacre soundcheck in LA, the singer, Anton Newcombe, was shouting at his band and making them start a song over, about two dozen times, even though the first ten seconds sounded exactly the same each time.

I thought, these guys must really want to be in this group, because I'm sure I would have walked across and twisted Anton's nose.

The Brian Jonestown Massacre had been made famous by a documentary called *Dig!* When I saw that documentary I recognised all the characters in it, even though I'd never met one of them personally. The onstage brawl the band has at their million-dollar industry showcase is classic, as is the moment afterwards where Anton says, 'Someone broke my sitar.' Anton was the star of *Dig!*, because he was a bit demented. He'd spout off like American rockers can do, lavishing himself with praise. But at least he meant it.

I liked Anton. He was a wounded child, always damaging

himself and indulging in self-sabotage, but his eyes lit up when he heard his own song playing back. He was realer than the Dandy Warhols, who had become the BJM's foes. The Dandy Warhols were more calculating and, in conventional terms anyway, a lot less screwed up.

The documentary shows Anton roller-skating around outside a Dandys show, even though he couldn't roller-skate very well, and giving away copies of his new single, 'Not If You Were the Last Dandy on Earth', to the Dandy's punters.

'Oh, awesome, Anton,' one of the Dandy Warhols says in the back of the van, in a trembling voice, after Anton mails them a bullet.

I talked to Anton on the phone before the tour. He said he loved *I Believe You Are a Star*, and wanted to release it on his own imprint. Despite his shambolic nature, Anton could be a savvy businessman. He was one of the first to realise that a band could build a following by giving their songs away for free on the internet. But he said I should change the cover for *Star* because no one was going to understand a small man sitting in a cart behind a horse; at least, he didn't, although he'd heard it had something to do with my childhood. He argued that the image wouldn't make any impact on a collector flicking through millions of records. I disagreed philosophically, because I like the symbolism of the image. But Anton is right, and that's probably why he's sold many more records than me.

Anton got obnoxious after one of our phone calls. He wrote me a drunken email, threatening me and saying that maybe I needed to find someone else to help with my 'new gold dream', like I was one of his sycophants who'd come up to him after a show. I wrote back and told him he must be confused, because I didn't ride on anyone's coattails. He respected me after that.

Although Anton was nice to us, he was a mess on the tour.

He was doing bottles of vodka a day. Kelly didn't like him being in our van because he smelt and didn't make coherent sense. People came to the gigs to see the side-show and would egg Anton on—which worked, because every night his set would end an hour early. He was usually sweating, topless, in white trousers with a tasteful buckle, screaming at the stage crew and his band, telling them he was a professional and that they were lucky to be there, that if they were only there to pick up chicks then they should pick up their sticks and leave. One night in Seattle, he stood in the door of a hotel room with Ricky, shouting, 'But I want pizza!'

I think Anton found it off-putting that we seemed impervious to all the shenanigans and that we steered clear of them, usually from the back of the hall, where we threw metaphorical paper darts, as Kiwis often do. When we saw Anton, we'd just say, 'How's it going, bro?'

Dimmer also ripped as hard as the Brian Jonestown Massacre.

The tour ended in San Diego. Anton, drunk again, started bad-mouthing a mutual friend we had back in LA, who'd once pushed Anton, who was on his computer at the time, into a hotel swimming pool. I stuck up for my friend and told Anton he was a wanker, because it was the last show and I felt like I could say that. Anton walked off in a huff, muttering away, but he was sweet the next time I saw him.

We opened for Pete Kember at the Echo in LA, with another LA psychedelic rock band called the Warlocks who looked like they'd stepped straight out of the film *Monterey Pop*. In LA the look meant as much as the sound.

Kelly got high later and asked Pete if she could look through his bag because he might have grabbed the Ebow I couldn't find. Pete was taken aback, and a bit offended, but he laughed when I said that I knew that he'd taken it.

Pete had played in Spacemen 3, who I once said weren't as good as Snapper, but they were as good as Snapper, and their first album *Sound of Confusion* is a classic. Pete wasn't so much a musician as an organiser of sound, and he did that on his own now, oscillating his synthesiser and little druggy nursery rhymes.

He was tall and dressed cool, quietly, and sometimes he'd wear moccasins and a multicoloured rugby jersey because he was from Rugby, Warwickshire. Pete could get away with sartorial elegance. He talked a bit like Peter Jefferies did, all about equipment and where he had put the mic on a certain recording. Pete was into gear. I once tried to discuss a relationship issue with him, and although he did his best to be polite and nearly care, I could see his eyes glazing over. He was more comfortable discussing a reverb unit.

We toured Australasia with Pete and his partner Sam for about three weeks. Sam seemed to have to put up with what a lot of partners of well-known people put up with—others talking over them, or being nice only because they want to get to the person they're with—but Sam brushed it off, because she's her own woman. She'd have to be, knocking about with Pete.

I enjoyed Pete because he was different and a bit of a visionary. He didn't worry what people thought, because he knew he was right. Sometimes he'd be rude, but only because he genuinely hadn't taken the other person into consideration.

Pete was always being hassled about football when he went on tour. Everyone took it as a given that, being English, he'd be into it. Pete wasn't into it. He loved it when I told him that the name some New Zealanders had for soccer was 'kick 'n' kiss'. He chuckled away on that for minutes.

In Australia, Dimmer formed a backing band and played some Spacemen 3 songs with Pete, which was cool, because these were important, seminal songs. When we played with him, he said I should turn my amp up.

After the Brian Jonestown Massacre tour, I went to upstate New York to produce an album for Die! Die! Die! I was into being a producer, because I didn't feel like I had to put myself all over the record; instead, I could help make the songs better. That's easy when you're a step away from them.

I'd seen Die! Die! Die! play a show at the South by Southwest festival in Austin, Texas. The guitarist, Andrew Wilson, had his broken wrist in a cast, so to cover for it he'd make some shrilling loop on his guitar and then he'd roll about on the floor. There were only about twenty people in the audience but they dug it hard.

That show helped create an idea to make the Die! Die! Die! like a drum and bass album, with spare guitar over the top. Die! Die! Die! had an excellent, aggressive rhythm section. The drummer, Michael Prain, Andrew's less brash partner, was good at pushing Andrew's buttons in a clever, experienced way. The bassist, Lachlan, was lovely—a lanky twenty-year-old Australian who played big bass and always let the other band members load the speakers on top of him when they went on one of their long drives.

Die! Die! Die! were from Dunedin and had been managed by my little sister. Albini had recorded them in Chicago as well. I remember them as fat little schoolboys in the band Carriage H— well, Andrew was; Michael was skinny—and whenever Carriage H supported my band I'd call them 'mate', 'dude' and 'bro', because I couldn't remember their names.

Die! Die! Die! toured internationally, sleeping on couches, loading the speaker on top of Lachie, and getting into trouble in New York. I respected that they did all of that themselves. They were driven and had contacts all around the world.

They gave me a demo before I left and I knew there were some changes we could make, small things like having a breather between the vocals. Singers often feel like they should be filling up a song, especially when they're sitting at home singing along to a backing tape. You get bored and think you should say something.

I thought they could repeat some of their refrains too. In your bedroom you sometimes get sick of them, but some things are better said again, and they become a hook. Die! Die! Die! sometimes blazed right by their hooks.

We met in LA for pre-production, in the space where I'd once seen Danzig, and because Die! Die! Die! had never had someone else in their practice room they were a bit unsure at first, but they relaxed once they saw it was working.

We travelled to upstate New York to a studio in a barn outside New Plaza, an uptight college town by Wizard of Oz paddocks. It felt foreign, conservative. I pictured Amish people walking around in bibs, or witches going on trial in a court with a dust floor, then being turfed into a river.

Lachie had a 4x10 stacked on top of him for the drive.

The studio was run by a conspiracy theorist who didn't like it when I touched his equipment. In the end I had to tell him I was there to produce the record, so he did a big Rathbone sigh and rolled, begrudgingly, out of the way. But he couldn't help himself. After we left he added his own touches to the recordings, including an ugly, completely random pan on the opening—the first thing you hear on the record—that was so abysmal I could only put it down to idiocy or malevolence.

We lived at the barn for twelve days and didn't leave much, although we'd sometimes go to the conspiracy theorist's place and have conspiratorial showers.

One night a storm came in that threatened to blow us all the way back to Kansas, a huge, ungodly event with silent lightning on the horizon and clouds thick and billowing like an upside-down ocean lit by sizzling colours I'd not seen in a sky before. Electrical purple, yellow, a queasy version of green, an entire spectrum that lit up the fields like noon. At first there was no sound.

I thought it might be the end of the world, the one I'd pictured on my porch back at Brockville. Maybe a bomb had gone off over American Falls and it was taking all night to reach the coast. As we waited, the storm seemed to mock us with its grave quiet.

Then there was a blast. The barn rattled and screamed and nails shook and the tin on the high roof groaned. It only lasted a couple of minutes, but the place lurched about for an eternity. Andrew was in the next room doing a vocal and he probably thought it was him shaking the building.

Promises, Promises is a great punk record—boisterous, lean, smart, with riffs, and most of the songs burn. I liked how it was Andrew and his band's blues. He had been doing things he regretted, like getting banned from venues and possibly ruining relationships, but it gave his songs a wound that he plastered with self-righteousness and a sick-sounding guitar.

I took care assembling Andrew's vocals. By then I was skilled at shifting audio around by a tenth of a second, and I made his singing more fluid and got most of it in tune.

'Blinding' had a line that I thought was one of the hooks they'd missed: 'I could never forget her if I tried.'

I suggested repeating it at the end, and in a review later, the *Guardian* wrote that the line should be dumb, but in Die! Die! Die!'s hands it wasn't. No, that line turned it into a punk shoegazer hit, even if it wasn't a hit in the end. The *Guardian* gave *Promises, Promises* eight out of ten.

No one has asked me to produce their record since.

When I finished the Die! Die! Die! record, I impressed the conspiracy theorist by getting Howie Weinberg on the line and asking him if he could master this little punk band.

Howie Weinberg is a mastering sensei. He has mastered all the big rock records, like Nirvana and Metallica, and whoever else that kid plays when he pulls my stolen SG out from underneath his bed. Mastering is a mysterious sprinkling of cookies and cream. I'm actually not sure what it is. It's all secret handshakes, a Masonic process involving knobs I don't understand and frequencies people usually don't hear, but dogs do, and some musicians as well. Howie did genius things in a small dark room, but I never met him. Apparently he always had food on his sweatshirt.

I'd learned the value of mastering when Howie had mastered *I Believe You Are a Star*. Sony offered to fly me out for it, but there was no point because I'd just be sitting there asking what that button did. But the record came back sounding about a quarter better. I'd got Howie cheap, because he was married to someone I'd known at Arista. He liked Straitjacket Fits.

He mastered Die! Die! Die! at a cut rate, because he liked that album too.

I was in a destructive relationship at that time with someone from a similar background. Because of this we'd thought we might help each other but we just tortured each other for ages instead.

I remember my first sight of her—an exceptionally beautiful dark-haired young woman wearing a white dress. She was intelligent and pulled out a bewildering array of facts in our games of Trivial Pursuit, a game I didn't like because I didn't know any of the answers.

Once, when it was her birthday, I cooked my girlfriend breakfast in bed and gave her some guitar pedals as a present, because she wanted to rock her guitar. But she felt upset that I hadn't wished her happy birthday on Facebook. She was someone who shouldn't be left to guess. To be fair, because of our issues I was distant and afraid of commitment. So she did have to wonder. We lived in separate houses for close to five years.

Another time, I told her she was one of the most beautiful

women I'd seen, which she was. But she told me her former boyfriend had told her she was the most beautiful woman he'd seen, which was representative of the losing wicket I was on.

It became tumultuous and very messy. Maybe at one point it helped crack me up—but I'd learned that my role was to save her, and as far as I could see that was the responsibility of all the men in her life, but it didn't do any good. She'd become a habit I found hard to give up, but we eventually fell apart.

I still remember kissing her at night, beside a mossy pool, with flax, to a chorus of ribbiting frogs.

The energy of Die! Die! Die! gave me a lift for my next album, *Degrees of Existence*, which was the last album I made under the name Dimmer.

The title track wasn't friendly. It had zinging guitars and a big thumping bass played by Kelly. Dino did a mantra in the middle. The song was a finalist for that year's Silver Scroll songwriting award, and Demarnia Lloyd did a superb version with just drums, bass and a small vocal ensemble, and when I heard the words come out of someone else's mouth I realised the lyrics were right and that I could allow myself some credit.

The song 'Comfortable' is another highlight for me, because it's small but deep and has a similar minimalism to 'Dawn's Coming In'. Later, I deconstructed that song for some school kids I was mentoring, to explain why it worked. I'd given the song instinctive touches, like sections sometimes shortened by a bar—seven instead of eight—to make the shift to the next part swift and unpredictable.

I hardly ever use rhymes in my lyrics. Rhymes like 'rain, pain, Spain' can make a song boring. Instead I repeat assonances and consonances. It's always better when words rub up against other words they shouldn't rub up against, like poetry.

Graeme Downes explained 'She Speeds' to me once, because he

teaches it at a university. He said the non-repeating verses and the chord changes made it 'unexpected, yet inevitable'. The lyrics to 'She Speeds' are included in a songbook called *Nature's Best*, a collection of sheet music for New Zealand's thirty greatest songs as voted by members of APRA, and 'She Speeds' was in the top ten. But almost every word in the *Nature's Best* version is wrong. It's like the lyrics have been translated by a baby or a monkey or whoever was banging the wrench with Charles Prod in the garage. They've taken all the lines phonetically and none of them make sense, which is disrespectful, because they could have just called me up. That book sits in schools and public libraries now, so people think it's true.

Graeme orchestrated a bunch of Flying Nun songs for a couple of concerts with the Dunedin Symphony Orchestra at the Dunedin Town Hall, which was a Herculean effort on his part. The concerts were called Tally Ho, after the Clean single. Some of the songs he arranged sounded better than others, but I could hear the Otago Peninsula in all of them. Jay Clarkson and the Verlaines' 'Dirge' was the best. There were two shows, and the second was dedicated to Roy Colbert, who'd had a lot to do with the original concept.

Some people didn't like the orchestration, saying it was desecration, but I liked it. It was fun, and not trying to be definitive. Also, singing with an orchestra is a kick. I felt like Frank Sinatra.

I sang 'Dialling a Prayer' there, although the conductor was flustered and forgot to cue me in, so eventually I wandered up to him as he sweated with his baton and said, 'Shall I come in now?'

A young student of Graeme's named Molly belted out a Shirley Bassey version of 'Randolph's Coming Home'. We'd told her not to over-sing it, and she didn't, although the last 'home' landed like a bombshell. I watched her from the back of the Dunedin Town Hall and found her performance extremely touching.

An opera singer called Anna Leese did a version of 'Waiting Game', and even though it had horns, and sometimes covered gaps

I'd deliberately not filled, she found her own message and delivered.

After such a long time up north, I felt valued by the community when I returned to Dunedin. The chief executive of the city council gave me a little badge with 'Dunedin' written on it in trendy Gothic letters. They use our bands as a currency now, because they're aware of Dunedin's strengths.

It was ironic to have our music given a standing ovation in the town hall, when as kids it got us beaten up in the street. That's the respectability of age, and time proving you were right.

Probably because of our first two albums, some critics had given Dimmer the label 'soul rock', which made us seem like one of those weak, genre-straddling bands that didn't know what they were doing. But we were sure when we played live, and never limp. With its guitars, and Gary and Dino, Dimmer was visceral and exploratory.

I've always done it live. Recording is anal and full of small tensions but the stage is my domain. I'm always confident on stage because I come prepared, even for the bits I'm making up.

'Fuck you,' I think, squeezing my eyes, discovering the subject. These days I'm generally more pleasant to the audience. They like to laugh and have a good night too, and I know they respect my music. I think they appreciate having me around.

It's easy to be famous in New Zealand, and because of that I turn a lot of things down, like going on game shows or comedy quizzes, and being everybody's friend. I don't need to be New Zealand's friend. I learned early on that the last thing you should do is run over to anyone who doesn't like the expression on your face, and say, 'Oh, please don't think that.'

I think sometimes people prefer it when you say you're not nice. Most people have to go around pretending they're nice all the time, which is an effort.

Degrees of Existence has a song I called 'Dark Night of Yourself', about a leader who was out of control. The title was inspired by something Chris Morris said to Peter Cook in their classic radio show *Why Bother?*, a series of spoof interviews that they made a year before Cook died. Chris, as the interviewer, refers to the 'night of wanton destruction' in which Cook's character, Sir Arthur Streeb-Greebling, took part in the 1992 Los Angeles race riots after failing to assassinate Eric Clapton. 'That was reported in one of the Sunday papers at the time as "The Dark Soul Of Sir Arthur Streeb-Greebling",' says Morris.

When Morris asks him about Eric Clapton, Streeb-Greebling says, 'I mean—having to play the guitar all the time—must be absolutely awful for him. Yes. Eric is a pathetic individual, really.'

Streeb-Greeling's night of wanton destruction ended, he says, when police found him in a McDonald's sharing a Big Mac with Rodney King.

Cook never lost it. You could see what a brilliant improviser he was in *Derek and Clive*, his talk show appearances, and even the phone calls he made to a late-night radio show where he'd pretend to be a Norwegian fisherman named Sven. Cook was at his best when he was thinking on his feet.

Chris Morris went toe to toe with Cook on *Why Bother?*, which made it better, because Cook had someone standing up to him. I liked Chris Morris. He made squeamish comedy that often didn't feel right. He covered taboo subjects in ridiculous ways, like the world's thickest person and children murdering adults. He even put his own warped electronica on it.

We'd play *Why Bother?* in the van on tour. We also liked *Shut Up, Little Man!*, a series of recordings of arguments between two alcoholic roommates in San Francisco in the late eighties. Their neighbours recorded the arguments by hanging a microphone out of their window in a bucket, and gave out copies to their friends.

There's a lot of pain between the funnies, and the arguments were freewheeling and disturbing—like *Derek and Clive*, maybe even like the Dead C, and probably like Little Richard too.

'Dark Night of Yourself' was empty and discordant and I enjoyed every line, especially 'You're just a natural naughty boy,' where the music stops and holds its breath.

I was knocking at the door while you were shouting out the chorus
Saying they better get it better, yeah you sure put 'em in their place
And every morning you wake up to another night of horror
And all the bits of shrapnel that came falling from your face

Who's gonna be left, who's gonna hang around and help you get through
The dark night of yourself
Yeah who's gonna be left and maybe hang around and help get you through
The dark night of yourself

All the crashing and the banging just means people cease to hear you
It's just crashing, it's just bashing, you just become a bunch of noise
A ruckus in the playroom who bust all the things about him
A ruckus in the playroom—yeah, I guess you're just a natural, naughty boy

Then the guitars resume their struggle for equanimity.

In June 2009, Chris Knox had a bad stroke. His partner Barbara found him lying unconscious on the bathroom floor at home.

Dimmer went to America in 2010 to do a fundraiser for him. It was amazing that the créme de la créme of American independent music played that night in New York, and they raised a lot of money.

Jeff Mangum from Neutral Milk Hotel played a set, his first one for years. He'd got freaked out when their album *In the Aeroplane Over the Sea* suddenly sold nearly half a million records. After the show I talked to him a bit drunkenly and said I knew how that stuff could screw you up—not the selling of that amount of records, because I'd never sold that many, but the inappropriateness of many industry demands.

Mangum was treated like Jesus at the gig. The Americans all swooned. A lot of the tunes sounded like the Tall Dwarfs, and, later, Mangum said he'd been influenced by them because their music sounded like it had been made with pots and pans. He hadn't known that you could do that.

The Clean were in New York too. They played the songs they used to play at the Coronation Hall, and the music still charged you up in the same way.

As well as Mangum, lots of other well-known folk contributed to a benefit album for Chris: Will Oldham, Yo La Tengo, and Jay Reatard. They each played a cover of one of Chris's songs, and the songs all stood up—although Chris told me later that his music could have been better. Every musician thinks that.

On the way to New York we played a show in Los Angeles. One night Gary and I drove down Sunset Boulevard in an SUV, thinking we were really fly. The hire car only had a radio and it was playing a limp country and western song that sounded disembowelled because he couldn't find the control for the bass. We also couldn't work out the volume, so the song played at a level where you could hardly hear it, tinnily. We rolled down our window anyway, pissing our pants, shouting 'Yeah boi!' to the boulevard, because we really were that sad.

Around that time, I was asked to contribute to the soundtrack for the film *Black Swan*, made by Darren Aronofsky. The music director knew me because she'd been in New Zealand working on *The Lord of the Rings* when she heard Dimmer. I actually can't stand *The Lord of the Rings*. It's bits of CGI running around having medieval battles and it's as touching as a brick. I fall asleep in blockbusters and can never tell what's going on, because I don't care. Equally, *Star Wars* mystifies me—everything about it. Before *Flight of the Conchords* came along, people in the States would hear my accent and say 'Hey—*Lord of the Rings!*'

The music director of *Black Swan* played *I Believe You Are a Star* to Aronofsky, and I was invited to the Brill Building in Manhattan. They showed me a scene from *Black Swan* in which the characters have taken ecstasy and are misbehaving in a club. It was brilliant straight away. They said they wanted the music to reference Tchaikovsky's *Swan Lake*, and they left it at that.

They realised that when you bring in someone to do the music, you let them do it: that's the reason you asked them in the first place. Earlier, when trying to make a soundtrack for a New Zealand TV series, I'd had ten people giving me various opinions, so I failed. I didn't know what they wanted in the end—I was just guessing.

I worked on the *Black Swan* music when I got back to New Zealand. The music director loved the first thing I sent—she said it made her bop around the office doing a Charlie Brown dance— and Aronofsky was impressed as well, especially with a noise I'd made on guitar and reversed by pushing a button on Pro Tools that said reverse. Aronofsky said he could use that sound elsewhere.

But my music never made it. I'd worked on an extended version of one piece of the puzzle, but I did it on pot, which I'll always regret because I didn't undo the puzzle. They used the Chemical Brothers in the scene instead.

Black Swan was a top-class film and it had a lot of Academy Award nominations. It could have given me a foot in in the film arena, but I didn't take my chance.

I did score a film called *For Good*, which was about a girl who is abducted, raped and murdered, unfortunately a commonplace New

Zealand scenario. It was made by Stuart McKenzie, now Miranda Harcourt's husband. I suggested they play 'I Need Your Love' by Golden Harvest in a public bar scene. That's a classic seventies song by a Māori band, one of whose members played electric guitar with his teeth.

For Good's music had jazz shuffles, regretful interludes and a drum clatter inspired by the film *Belle de Jour*. I wrote the haunted main theme as soon as I'd read the script.

I made bleak noises as cicadas chirped outside in the sun, to images of a girl being pushed through a forest while crying and holding her bunched clothes in front of her.

Around the same time, I was approached by Brad McGann, the director of a film called *In My Father's Den*, which also featured kidnapped children. Obviously I was the musician film directors turned to when they had a film about abducted, murdered children. 'Oh, let's get Carter, he'd be good for that.'

In My Father's Den was a powerful film, the only one Brad made before he died of cancer. I didn't do the music in the end, but I remember Brad as a modest, pleasant and purposeful man.

Sometimes you wake up at night and you've written a song in a dream. You're all excited and you moan it into a dictaphone, because you know you'll forget it by morning. I come up with a lot of music in dreams: it's like you're solving songs in your subconscious, the same way you solve other everyday problems. I sometimes have a dream that I'm back at school, playing a song but I can't remember how it goes, and I've got no pants on, and the drummer is fiddling with his ride cymbal because he can't remember how it goes either.

In New York in 2010 I walked around with a dictaphone, thinking I might make an urban album next, full of big city rhythms. I'd hum into the mic on the street, thinking I was on to a real winner. It was like walking around in a dream. But often it was just me repeating what I'd heard coming out of a clothes store, going 'Uhhhh-ahhh-ahhh' like a zombie who isn't singing a melody.

I went and saw jazz groups in Harlem and walked across the Brooklyn Bridge. A chiropractor called Lila cracked my back in Wall Street, and I could breathe again. Pete Kember played at the Knitting Factory and I may have been rude to his bassist, and some Australians too, but that was because I was drunk. A wolf in lamb's clothing, an Australian woman called me.

I went and saw New Zealand draw with Italy in the soccer World Cup, and I was the only person in the bar, drinking Bloody Marys and eating over-fried onion rings at five in the morning. New Zealand went undefeated in that tournament and drew all their matches, which was a remarkable achievement for a country so small, but they always say that about New Zealand. We didn't earn enough points to get through into the next round, which reassured us that we weren't actually that good.

Mostly I enjoyed New York, because it's the Big Apple and you just have to hit the street to stay entertained. I drank a lot, and had a mixture of a happy and miserable time.

When I returned to New Zealand from America, I went back to being a caregiver for Chris Knox at Hakanoa Street. I did it for two and a half years, working ten hours a day, for five days a week at first and then three, because it got too exhausting. I did it because I had the time, and I loved him and his family. I thought it might be good for me to be out of my room as well and do something for someone else for a change. Maybe I could still hear my mother accusing me of being selfish.

With Chris, I was just sitting around, at the kitchen table, or on the couch watching an old movie, or going for a walk, helping him on the computer, assisting with his stretching—but it was intense, and continuously serious, and it affected me far more than I knew. When each day was over I couldn't leave it at the door, because he was my friend. Combined with my bad relationship, my pot and my drinking, it probably did me in.

Initially I thought I might help make him better, but he didn't get much better. Not really.

I saw a scan of Chris's brain once where you could really see the damage. Violent white rectangles sitting on grey. Still, Chris always seemed present, and I recognised him, even though I could see holes in his cognition and comprehension, like a block of Swiss cheese.

His stroke was a shock, with its suddenness—how extreme it was, and the way it took his words.

Don McGlashan and I went in for Friday night jams with Chris soon after his stroke, when he was in recovery at the rehab place—sixties songs mainly, like 'Baby I Love You' and 'Waterloo Sunset'. We tried some punk songs, like 'New Rose' and Proud Scum's 'I Am a Rabbit', but they sounded a bit inappropriate. We thought the music might help Chris's brain to heal, but when I asked him if it made any difference, he shook his head: he just liked the songs. He'd scrunch up his nose and join in sometimes, singing his nonsense words.

Back at Hakanoa Street, Chris would sometimes have epileptic fits, juddering ones, and I'd have to watch in case he hurt himself. Him in his chair foaming at the mouth, me hoping it'd soon be over. I told Chris that while his fits were terrible for him, they were terrible for me as well. I'd give him anti-seizure medication if I could see him about to go, but it usually didn't help.

Chris could get bossy sometimes, probably because he wanted to feel in control, and also because he's bossy. I'd tell him, 'I'm not your fucking slave.'

Barbara would hear me say that but she didn't mind, because

she knew I was there for her and Chris and their whānau.

Usually I communicated well with Chris. Even if I could finish some of his thoughts, I'd leave them, because it was important he practised expression that was valued. He had a couple of words: 'Yes', 'Good', and mispronunciations of some names. The only time I felt really sorry for him was when he fell over when we'd been out walking and his hand landed in a pile of dog shit, and he couldn't move it because his right side was weak. But Chris never complained.

He remained disciplined. When he was told that sit-ups could help improve his condition, he got up to 350 sit-ups a day, and we got worried and told him he should relax, even if I squished on his feet as he did it. He'd leave the oven on, but then again I did too, so that made a pair of us.

Chris was obsessive about keeping his objects—hundreds of DVDs, CDs, books and artworks—in perfect order. He didn't like me rearranging his things. A lot of his art had a homemade feel, and was usually subversive and darkly humorous. Some of the stone sculptures were Barbara's.

Chris had an excellent selection of films and a screen as big as a cinema's, so we'd hunker down with tea and biscuits and the curtains drawn, in the room where we'd once filmed the Doublehappys clip. We watched C-grade horrors mostly, or forties noir and European obscurities. He seemed to know what was going on, although we'd watch only the foreign films dubbed in English because he couldn't read any subtitles.

'Good,' he would say at the end.

One day Chris was trying to tell me something by drawing it. Even though he's lost his words—aphasia, it's called—he can still draw really well. He draws with his wrong hand, because the other one's in a splint. He kept drawing the same picture and going 'Ahhhh' and crossing it out. After about twenty minutes, I finally got what his point was—that he'd had his first shit in five days and that it felt amazing. We nearly shat our pants laughing.

As well as his drawing, Chris still has his sense of melody. We did an incredible gig with him at the Laneway Festival in an Auckland carpark in 2010. He had no words, but he just screwed up his big nose and went for it. The songs hadn't been properly arranged either, because Chris wouldn't remember, so everyone went by feel.

The stage manager tried to stop us after four songs. I turned my palms up towards him and said, 'Come on . . .' Then we played a fifth.

It was one of the bravest performances I've seen. All of Chris shone through. It was a real testimony.

Warren Ellis, the violinist from the Dirty Three and Nick Cave and the Bad Seeds, watched that set. Warren is a dude and I spent all day keeping a respectful distance until I was drunk enough to call him over.

'Hey Warren,' I said, waving an arm, 'I'm Shayne and I played in Chris Knox's band earlier.'

'I know who you are, Shayne,' Warren said, in his dapper Bad Seeds suit. 'I used to go to your shows in Melbourne.'

It was a real kick to discover that someone I'd approached as a fanboy respected me back.

I asked Warren about the fiery mini-guitar he played in Grinderman, and we talked about Chris, and the 1950s crime novel *The Killer Inside Me* by Jim Thompson, with its spare way with words. Of course we discussed Elvis too. Warren was chewing an apple. He was teetotal now because he'd drunk enough for several lifetimes.

The next time the Dirty Three played Auckland they dedicated a song called 'Everything's Fucked' to me. It's beautiful and Warren is always rapping some quasi-tragic tale before they play it. Warren is softly humoured and humble, and he does good karate kicks when he's getting into it. He played with Grinderman at a Big Day Out a year later, and they made everyone else who played that day look like pre-schoolers farting around with blocks. Grinderman were bluesmen who'd lived every word. Primal Scream were on before them, playing their third-division Stones, and they were dire.

Barbara was amazingly loyal to Chris. She's stayed at Hakanoa Street since the stroke to help protect Chris. They've both got new partners now, which in Chris's case is something—he's currently engaged to be married to a lovely woman who's a librarian. But he's always been a charmer, even with two words and a splint. Very determined. 'Yes,' he said, when he told me of his impending marriage. 'Good,' he said after that.

Barbara's new partner is a Labour Party MP named David Parker. David is a lot straighter than Chris, a lawyer, and these days he's the Attorney-General. I like David, because he's from Dunedin and a bit of a Southern Man—he's happiest when he's tramping. David's decent and he makes Barbara happy too.

When there was a General Election, there were a lot of nasty rumours that painted a picture of David and Barbara getting frisky by Chris's frozen body, which was sick, but politics makes people professionally mean. A reporter from the *New Zealand Herald* contacted me to ask about David and Barbara. She said, 'There are many people out here who care about Chris,' and that they were worried for him, so I told her to fuck off, and how dare she try to get her sleazy story under the auspices of caring.

Barbara was Jacinda Ardern's right-hand person, so I saw Jacinda, at events or Hakanoa Street, quite a bit. Barbara worked out of the Ponsonby office that arranged Jacinda's affairs. Jacinda was a List MP when I first met her, and even though she'd just lost Auckland Central, she was appealing, because she was genuine and had charisma, and in her late twenties she was already being shaped as a leader. She was like the nerdy student council leader who always swotted constitutions, with statistics and facts to back up her argument. She knew what people were up to in the corners I never looked at. When we talked about the Gibbs Farm, she didn't seem impressed by the embarrassment of riches.

I'm glad Jacinda's our leader now, and I don't like the fact that people make a big deal about her being a woman and a mother in office—it shouldn't matter. The fact that people like Jacinda and Barbara are in the corridors of power gives me hope, unlike those other arseholes who stayed in for nearly a decade. They just made me feel disenfranchised. People in sleeping bags outside Lamborghini dealerships—that's the evidence of their work. The rock star economy, they called it, even though they were all hopeless squares. 'The rock star economy is at the bottom of a pool in Parnell,' I wrote on Facebook after the Nats crashed out—one of my better posts.

I hope Jacinda doesn't get disillusioned by politics, like David Lange did, because no matter what environment you're in, it seeps in by osmosis, like major record labels do with their compromise and cynicism.

Sometimes when Dimmer played, we had Jacinda, David Parker, Barbara and Grant Robertson dancing up the front. Grant is from Dunedin and a Flying Nun nerd.

David would do a pogo, so we called him Dave 'The Pogo' Parker. I doubt anyone in the press gallery ever calls him that.

He pogoed furiously to 'Crystalator', which I hadn't figured he'd like.

Barbara pogoed too, because she'd made an aesthetic decision to reduce her dancing to its most primal level, which I respected, because I'm really into minimalism.

You'd never see Gerry Brownlee, Paula Bennett or Simon Bridges pogoing to Dimmer.

On the night of the APRA Silver Scrolls in 2010, Jacinda and I were sitting at a table together in the Auckland Town Hall. It was the year when the Naked and Famous won. I saw Ray Columbus in the foyer and he asked after Chris. Ray had had a stroke too, and he showed a tender concern.

Malcolm from Sony saw me at the urinal, and he might have done a double take because I was looking so terrible. Fiona from the Headless Chickens said that I looked dreadful that night as well. Another friend said she'd driven past me and Chris on the street, and wondered who was looking after the caregiver.

At dinner, I drank glass after glass of wine, although Jacinda was more circumspect.

It got darker later that night, when I was absent but still walking around. We went to a club where a friend plied me with rocket-fuel cocktails that added nothing to my condition, which was paralytically pissed.

The publishing guy who'd tried to screw me was there, and of course he was a greaser.

I went to another club at the top of Symonds Street and careered towards a landmark disaster. I only have shreds of memory, sad little pictures, like talking to Pip Ladyhawke about how we hadn't done the cover of the Crocodiles' 'Tears' that we'd planned. I was sure we would have killed it. 'Tears' was a genius song. I'd congratulated the guy who'd written it in the town hall bog earlier.

There's a mental photograph of Tiki Taane coming up to me at a table, probably where I'd been abandoned, and handing me another drink. I skulled it and probably muttered, 'Who gives a fuck.'

Sometimes, a thought can pass through a person's mind, like: I wonder what it'd be like if I stepped off this cliff, or if I walked out in front of this bus, or if I chopped my hand off with an axe? But only the drunken or severely disturbed would ever express that thought.

And at some point I thought it'd be a fine idea to grab Julia Deans' arse.

I don't know what reaction I expected from Julia, because I wasn't capable of rational thought.

Julia was standing in a circle with several other people, including her boyfriend, who may have been holding her hand. Perhaps I'd thought Julia would say, 'Oh, Shayne, I've always felt that way too.'

Julia didn't say that. She said, 'Heyyyyy,' with a force that still cuts like a machete through my amnesia.

I still feel sick about it—and I was the perpetrator. I did something similar to a male friend about the same time, and he told me, 'I don't usually let people do that.'

I never apologised directly to Julia, because I was humiliated and I couldn't face her, although I did say sorry through her boyfriend, whose email I had, and that was fucked as well.

I went on to play with Julia in a band, and she's a friend—a person and musician I really respect. She never said anything about it.

Julia, I'm sorry.

Around the same time, I went to a party at the author Emily Perkins' house with Steve Braunias, where I got drunk and broke down in the backyard in front of the entire Auckland literary establishment. This was around the time of my girlfriend's affair—she'd gone back to Australia to revisit the guy—and I'd sit at home in front of my computer writing sick, abusive emails to him, which my girlfriend told me to stop doing, because it was demeaning for me. His name was Bobby and he told me my music was no good.

At Emily's, the photographer Jane Ussher said she was concerned about me. Barbara gave me a hug. I may have talked to Emily in the kitchen, about how hard it was to sustain a relationship as an artist, although she seemed to being doing okay with her husband, the painter Karl Maughan, and their children. I might even have tried to hit on Emily—I thought it, so I probably did—and then somebody called me a cab to get me out of the house, and I left in the pouring rain.

After these incidents I gave up drinking again, mortified by my behaviour.

I played with Julia soon afterwards in a band called the Adults, which was Jon Toogood's solo project. He brought in a variety of New Zealand musicians to help and I co-wrote a few songs. I'd first seen Shihad at a Big Day Out back in the early nineties, and they made a noise that sounded like a fascist death squad marching into Poland. I could appreciate that he might want to kick back.

My favourite tracks from the Adults sessions were the improvisations that Jon recorded with Gary Sullivan and me at the Lab. We set up the studio in the recording room, so we didn't have to listen back through a funnel of speakers. Ladi 6 sang on two of those tracks, and they're the best tracks on the album. 'Nothing to Lose' was a single, and 'Please Wake Up' was a lyric she'd written about her cousin who had died. Ladi sang it in a voice with a woodfire crackle, like she'd smoked too many cigarettes, but the cracks were real emotion.

My other favourite track had the working title of 'Matty Johns' Room'. We should have kept that title. Matty Johns was an Australian rugby league player with the Cronulla Sharks, and him and a bunch of his mates had got into trouble after an incident with a woman in a hotel room. I played a horrible, squelchy synth to depict his personality.

When Jon asked me if I wanted to play in a touring version with the Adults, I said yes, because I like Jon—he's open and gregarious, and has an infectious enthusiasm. I was also broke and needed a gig.

I liked the people in the band, although I wasn't so fond of some of the material—they were other people's songs and not really my style. Bic said to me, 'I could never get up and play a song I didn't like'—but I'd plod along in the Adults, on the bass or on a one-note synth, stage right, while Jonny jumped over the monitors.

Once when I played at an awards show with Jon, I found that the road crew had written 'Stage Right' on all of my gear. Jon's equipment was labelled 'Jon'. I described myself as 'Stage Right' for a while, and decided that if Stage Right ever wrote his autobiography he'd call it *Someone Told Me*.

My favourite venture with the Adults was a summer winery tour where we played to middle New Zealand. I'd virtually be carried on to the stage by Pos, the big guitar tech, then lifted back to the catering tent where there were mountains of food. We made a band pact to go swimming wherever we could, because I was always either with Chris or shoving Pro Tools around in my room, so we went to wild beaches, glorious lakes, and once a clean, deep river on the West Coast. Like the food in the catering tent, it was absolutely delicious.

I'd sometimes ask the kids lined along the crowd barrier if they knew who The Man was. Most of them didn't. They thought it was Dad, or the guy who'd let them in.

The Adults did a couple of pop concerts with an orchestra, too— the APO in Auckland, and the CSO in Christchurch. Usually I'm not a fan of crossover concerts, because often it's just a band playing major chords with a bored-looking mob behind them, but I enjoyed the lushness and sensuality of the sound.

I was starting to get into classical music. It had become one of my nerdy swots. The size of it was intimidating—it was a mountain, but I knew there was gold there. I bought books from overseas, including encyclopedias and biographies of composers, and I played the music until I felt I understood it, which took many, many months. But the investigation was worth it, because the best art never reveals itself easily. It lies just underneath and takes its time. Beethoven sonatas reached out and touched me across a bridge of hundreds of years. The clarity of Mozart blew me away. I liked Schubert as well, with his honest, hummable melodies.

One of my favourite Schubert songs is 'Der Doppelgänger', about a man who stands outside the window of the house where his lover once lived, even though she's long since moved on. One night he sees another man standing there, looking tormented— and when he turns around, the first man sees that it's his double. I love that image of a man haunting himself.

When I played pop with the orchestras, I'd say to the pianist, 'But what about Chopin?' They'd be bored by that, because they'd been playing him since they were seven. Sometimes the orchestra looked bored when they performed too, or overly serious, like they were taking a test, or examining a trucking magazine in a petrol station. Sometimes I'd think, 'Loosen up motherfuckers, it's music, and you've got to kick out the jams.' But I'm sure they enjoy themselves.

The classical trip informed my solo album *Offsider*, which is the last album I've recorded. I don't know if I'll make another one. The industry gives me the shits and Spotify means I make even less money—but I always wonder whether I'll make another album, the same way I wonder if I'll ever be capable of writing another song. It usually sneaks up on me.

For *Offsider* I used my own name, Shayne P. Carter, because I finally felt comfortable enough to use it. The 'P' was a tribute to Dad and his Jimmi P. Carter Disco. Even though Dimmer was essentially a solo project, I'd always felt a compulsion to hide behind a moniker. Also, a solo name had seemed too singer/songwriterly, or folk.

Offsider was another contradiction, because I wrote and played it on piano, which was also another complicated victory. I'd never played a piano before. I bought a book called *Easy Piano for Beginners*, but it wasn't easy. I couldn't even play 'Twinkle, Twinkle Little Star'. The book got chucked.

When I'd started the project, I was fresh from the 2012 Laneway Festival, where I'd played a thundering set of hits from Dimmer and the Fits. I'd even played 'Randolph'. I could have capitalised on that by doing a rock record, but of course I didn't—I sat at home instead, for years, struggling on amateur piano. But I thought that naïvety might lead to fresh directions in my songwriting. When I threw my fingers at the keyboard I never knew what sound would come back, whereas with guitar I always did.

I still like *Offsider*. I wrote it in Te Atatu, and most of the songs were about a woman, although I purposefully didn't mention her. Inspired by classical music, I wanted the music to sound timeless and out of touch. It has three out of five on AllMusic, but that was all trainspotters still sobbing over Straitjacket Fits. I wanted the words of *Offsider* to sound timeless too, a bit nineteenth-century, and I used simple words to make the lyrics feel more meaningful. Every song tells two stories, because little words have different definitions. Long words just have one.

Steve Braunias lent me a mother lode of poetry. I was never a big poetry fan. Like folk music, it often seemed self-important— someone on a soapbox, pressing you with lyricism in a soft, affected voice. I appreciate lyricism, but I get tired wading through colourful stanza after colourful stanza, and I usually give up. I don't need to hear your internal dialogue; I've got one of my own. It's the same reason I hardly dance—I've made my own contribution to music.

But I discovered some impressive poems. There were original arrangements of old feelings, with the wrong words rubbing together. A friend caught me reading a book in a food hall, and when he saw it was *A Hawk in the Rain* by Ted Hughes, he said, 'Nice.'

Possibly my favourite song on *Offsider* is 'We Will Rise Again'.

Just when you thought we'd grown silent
Gone quietly—finally
Just when you thought we were buried
Covered at last
We will rise again
Hard to put off, we keep coming back
Backbone built kick by kick, brick by brick
I don't know if you know
Don't know if you know
We will rise again
So count us out at your own peril
A tap from behind—oh look, it's who you'd expect
Yes—we will rise again

I also like the song 'Mat', because its desperation is real and it has bleak chords like 'Der Doppelgänger'. Julia Deans is my siren on that, and I play a crumbling lead break on the bass.

'I Know Not Where I Stand' is about Dad and his children. The title explains itself. The music has a gallop like Schubert's 'Erlkönig', which I always mispronounce as Eric Nog, but you can't be a winner at everything.

I played 'Just a Moment' at Roy Colbert's funeral. It's the record's gentlest song. It's about the transitory nature of life, and how each instant, good or bad, will soon pass.

When I was nearing the end of recording the songs, I'd make trips to Wanaka, to Nick Roughan and Ange's place, so that Nick could help mix the album. I'd got my driver's licence. The wait was worth it, because the South Island is spectacular. I'd travel through the moonscape rocks of Central Otago and sometimes kill my car. Mum had just passed away so a lot of the drives I took were reflective.

I'd drive around the empty spaces of the South Island, gaping at its sunsets and vast, monumental beauty. Bach keyboard concertos rotated symmetrically on my car stereo. I had a lot of rookie driver scrapes, and I ruined three cars. Top up the oil and the water, and look to the rear when you reverse. I got stranded in the Cromwell Gorge once, but someone rescued me because South Islanders are friendly.

Nick and Ange have a small dog called Stan who's the worst-behaved dog I know. Ange lets him lick her plate and he barks outside the neighbour's bedroom at three in the morning. Once, at a show Don McGlashan and I played in the Luggate Town Hall, I slagged off Stan through the microphone. I could hear the howls of indignation from Nick and Ange's boys in the middle of the crowd. But I was only joshing. Stan is my mate.

I took Stan for long walks to the top of Mount Iron or by the Clutha, with its unfathomable blue water. I was grieving. I felt that Stan could feel my pain through his lead, and if I stopped, he'd pause too, and he'd turn around and look up at me with his soft brown eyes. He'd be patient and stand guard, and when I was ready he'd lead us back up the track.

The last song on *Offsider* is called 'Carried Away', and it reminds me of the Clutha, as well as David Wood, who'd died.

David died in 2010. I talked to him on the phone shortly before-hand. We'd discussed a Roxy Music concert where Straitjacket Fits were being offered big money to support Roxy and get the chance to ask Phil Manzanera about his guitar pedals.

One of the last things David said to me was, 'If you're a band, then you should play.'

He still thought Straitjacket Fits were a band even when we weren't, and at first I found his comment obtuse, but David was right, in his own angular way.

I told Chris Knox that David had died, and we sat together on Chris's bed and cried.

At his funeral David looked small in his coffin, as everyone does.

I gave a speech, which was heartfelt, because I'm okay at speaking in public when I care what I'm talking about. Then we played 'If I Were You', although the bass was missing.

*

I had to get out of Auckland, away from the pretensions and the diminishing space. Auckland was obscenely expensive, and, because I was too proud to go on the dole, my income dribbled in in tiny, uncertain amounts. The reports I made each year to the accountant were ugly, and I felt a bit ashamed—it wasn't a big-time look for a rock star. I'd wake up in the middle of the night, stressing.

A friend had let me live cheap in an outhouse in Grey Lynn, a space like a ski lodge, with beams and stained wood. When I was there I could picture myself living in the mountains, dressed in an alpine jersey and holding a third of brandy in front of a fire.

At one point I earned change teaching guitar to little children at a primary school. It was like trying to encourage lambs through a hoop. The strings hurt their fingers, and one boy would put down his guitar and walk over to the wall that had woolly Velcro on it. He'd rub his face up and down on the material and sigh with extreme pleasure. I'd let him fill his boots, then say, 'Come on, son, about that D.'

At the end of 2015, after Mum had passed away, I packed up and left Auckland. I wanted to return to the source and spend time with my family.

Things picked up for me in Dunedin. I left my mid-period slump. Maybe I entered the late period, where all the classical composers did their best work. Offers for projects started rolling in, and it felt like the community was rallying around me. Back home, I was no longer a stranger, but a boy from Brockville who'd gone and shown those North Islanders.

I became healthier in Dunedin too. I jogged and I didn't drink, and I gave up smoking pot all day. I hadn't done that for years and I felt clearer, more appreciative. Every morning I'd wake with the gratitude that I was in a world that still interested me, knowing there was a lot I'd never uncover.

The guy at the gym store gave me a treadmill for cheap, and I'd run on it even though I had some of the world's best scenery outside. Another mutual acquaintance gave me her bach in Aramoana to write this book. At first she charged me a hundred dollars a month, for power, and after a year she apologised and said she might have to put it up to one hundred and fifty.

Having my driver's licence was liberating. Last December I drove the length of the country to pick up my books from Auckland. I nearly killed myself when I got caught on the outside of a truck on a blind corner near Napier, and the image of that still shakes me up. But I was soothed by the terrain, the streams in the shingled valleys, the bushes busy on the ranges—it made me happy and also a little sad. Melancholy is a delicious, lonely feeling.

Atamira Dance Company rang me up and asked me to tour with them through China, Taiwan and Korea. Moss Patterson was their choreographer, a Māori man who'd grown up in Alexandra who was a fan of my guitar. Moss is married to a Farry, the well-

373

known Dunedin Lebanese family, and her father was once the managing director of 4XO. Moss said to someone in Auckland that he wanted a guitarist like Shayne Carter for a show, and she said, 'Why don't you just ask Shayne?'

In China we were put up in five-star hotels. I liked how the elderly could be seen in the morning in the park, doing t'ai chi, instead of rusting in old people's homes. I liked that I couldn't tell sometimes if a building was a shop or somebody's home. But in China there wasn't much personal space and you were always being pushed out of the way. Taiwan was friendlier, and entire families went about on scooters with the littlest one at the front, often poking at an iPad or a tiny computer. We were in Korea when the North Koreans were lobbing bombs over Japan, which added an edge.

The six dancers in Atamira were beautiful, chiselled young men. At first I thought a couple of them might be vain. Then, once I got to know them better, I found that they had their own insecurities that drove and tortured them, too.

James Webster accompanied me with the music. James was a musician, a carver and a tattooist. A Māori renaissance man. He played taonga puoro—traditional Māori instruments that mimic the sound of the natural world. I related to all of James's parts and found it easy to sit in with him, buzzing on my guitar as he called up the ancestors, and the click of insects, the call of birds, the water from a shingled valley.

On our travels, wondering where we were, we'd look out for one another and do little check-ins. 'All right, bro?' we'd enquire.

When I was asked to be the musical director for the Silver Scrolls, held for the first time in Dunedin in 2017, I brought in James and some other taonga puoro artists to cover a song. They performed a firm, dignified version of a single written by a young metal band who sang in te reo—Alien Weaponry, from Waipu, who'd written a song about the land being stolen. It was surely the first time the Māori flag has covered an entire wall in the cream-coloured town hall.

The Clean were inducted into the Hall of Fame too. I found Hamish Kilgour wandering around backstage, lost and eating an apple, while the rest of his band was onstage.

I did a tour with Don McGlashan which was one of the most enjoyable tours I've done. We went to towns I've never played before, like Staveley, Luggate and Kerikeri. Don was more well known to the rural folk, but they enjoyed my stuff too once they'd had the chance to hear it.

I like and respect Don, because he's a bard who writes literate, considerate songs. We chose numbers from each other's back catalogue for our show, and it was interesting having another songwriter pick your set. I went for a lot of Don's more obscure ones, avoiding the hits, and he picked those of mine with a tune. We played as a two-man band, but our sound was full because we took a shitload of instruments with us—keys, guitars, a euphonium, drums, and Don's French horn.

It was a different dynamic playing as a two-piece. We weren't solo and we weren't a band either, but once we knew where to pitch it, it worked.

We'd always rib each other onstage because we liked each other enough to do that. The only gig Don got right on top of me was the first night in Dunedin, at the Fortune, where, confronted by an audience who knew me, I felt oddly shy, like a twelve-year-old in the playground surrounded by peers who knew he couldn't fight. But I felt more comfortable on the second night, and I totally destroyed Don.

I went back to the Fortune Theatre in 2018 and backed Michael Hurst in a play called *An Iliad*, an update on the epic poem by

Homer. I gave myself room to improvise with the music, using live loops on a Moog that I'd shadow with guitar. I used Ebow with a slide, a combination I hadn't heard before, and tried to make the music sound timeless, like the nature of war. No matter what the setting is, war never changes, and it's always pride, greed and stubbornness, or sex, that kicks it off. But there were honourable attributes in the play too, like loyalty, bravery and family—so it was a mess, like everything human.

Opportunities still arrive. More tours to Asia with Atamira, shows in Australasia, and possibly Europe, with my band. An artist's residency in Bangkok. Arranging my song for a choir. Solo shows in Australia. A tour with a chamber trio. Writing a book.

I'm happy in my hometown, although I don't go into town very often. Maybe I'll go to the cinema and be the only person there. I have a secret romcom fetish, even though most of them are crap. *Serendipity*, *When Harry Met Sally* and *About Time* are all good ones. It's something about the wish fulfilment and the happy ending. Being the only person in the cinema is better than one other person being there, though, because that's weird and you feel like you have to keep an eye on them. When I saw *About Time* in Auckland, there was only one other person in the audience, a man, which made it worse. We sat at opposite ends of the cinema and I left before the lights came up so he wouldn't recognise me on the street.

I drive around Dunedin a lot, and when I first got my licence I'd do runs up to Brockville. I don't do that so much now, because I know it's there. All my nephews and nieces are different and have their own kinks, and they think Uncle Shayne's pretty cool, even though, with his Jimmi P. jokes, he can sometimes be a bit of a dick.

I'll visit Dad's grave under Saddle Hill on the way to Brighton. 'A gentle spirit, a special soul', it says on his stone. The kids have placed little toys around the grave, similar to the ones he's still shifting around at their place. I recognise a lot of names in the urupā, like Kenton's sister from Caldwell Street, an old school teacher, Tom the artist who lived in Brighton, Pam from the tangi, who killed herself. Dead people I have known. Celia Mancini called me up when I was in Korea last year, the night before she died. She sounded bright and we had a giggle.

I'd visit Mum in Dunedin, but there's nowhere to go, because Laurie has her ashes.

*

Mum.

She was eighteen years and two days old when she had me. She used to click her fingers through her hair when she was reading, or drawing her little doodle of side profiles of attractive ladies with big bouffants and top lips that curled up like hers. She looked so young that a lot of people thought she was my sister.

When she was little, living in foster homes, she'd sometimes be relocated to farms with horses. She'd ride them and sing at the top of her lungs, because she loved music.

There's a hand-tinted photo of Mum where her cheeks are especially ruddy. She has tight blond curls like Shirley Temple's. She's probably three and her innocence peers out.

In the foster homes, Mum was abused by predators who came into her room. She once talked about it on National Radio, and I'd thought she'd given too much away, because Mum could be a bit self-involved at times—but that wasn't right, because it was her story, and that story needed to be told. The government gave her and my Aunt Helen $10,000 each for the sexual abuse they'd suffered. It was hush money, bureaucratic and shameful, because after that no one could make another claim.

377

Mum got lost in alcohol and it turned her mean and nasty. She'd get narcissistic. Perhaps her self-importance stemmed from her early life when there'd been no one around to help her, to save her—so she had to battle on her own, feeling unimportant.

Mum would call me on the phone to tell me how selfish I was. But in her words I could hear her self-loathing, like she'd cut herself down, or off, before anyone else had the chance. She'd circle over the same subjects, her Easter Island rocks, and keep coming back to them, using exactly the same words every five minutes. I could put the phone down and go look for something, and when I came back she'd still be talking about the same thing. I took those calls for years because I thought it was my duty.

Once, at a gig in Dunedin, she was playing up in the audience and the whole crowd was watching me for my reaction as I stood in the spotlight.

I was hurt when Straitjacket Fits played their big gig in town in 2005, and she was too drunk to remember. I'd wanted her to really be there.

The most painful part about existing with an alcoholic is that you love them and you wish they'd change.

When I was still talking to Mum, I'd stay with her and Laurie in Douglas Street in South Dunedin, and she enjoyed having me stay, and she'd always bring me in cooked breakfasts and fluff up my pillows when I sat up, and I could tell she was pleased she could do that for me and that I was there. She gave me rings about my eating, always prolific, but brought in extra biscuits with my tea.

If I was out in the garden having a cigarette, Mum would look out her kitchen window and say to me when I came back in, 'I watch you out there sometimes and wonder what you're thinking.'

When Straitjacket Fits were inducted to the Hall of Fame in Auckland in 2008, Mum walked up the red carpet with me and squeezed my hand. She didn't drink, after I'd asked her not to. She enjoyed the night. She was impressed by Tiki Taane's song, but then she'd always liked the brown fullahs.

When I wasn't there, Mum would drink and do the damage she couldn't remember, and then she'd go on with her caring jobs like nursing, or assisting at an old people's home, or cleaning, or driving around old friends who were too unwell to drive. She took in her two handicapped cousins for a year, and scrimped and struggled to bring up my brother Kristen on her own after Tony abandoned them and went off to make money in property. She dealt with Kristen's myriad health issues alone, and they became loyal to each other. Their worst house was in Kensington—a dive—but Mum was impoverished.

Two years before she died, she took a computer course. And she bought a bike after I told her about my own bike-riding by the Northwestern Motorway up in Auckland, where I'd do little skits in a variety of silly voices that made me laugh out loud as I passed other cyclists. She didn't ride her bike much—later she found it difficult to even walk beyond her gate, because the outside world could scare her, so she'd stay in and garden, and pat her cats, smoke menthols, look out for Laurie. At five o'clock she'd go again.

I felt for Mum and her struggles, even if she was always advertising them. There was a remorse that no one else could solve.

She was afraid of the world, but she always stood up to it, because she had backbone. She could be fiery and feisty. I always admired her resilience and her pride, even though she continuously denied herself that pride.

Mum would hear I was in town in those last two years—I usually stayed at the Colberts'—and sometimes she'd send me a text message that said, 'You're probably on the plane now . . .'

She was upset when I played with the orchestra at the town hall and they put a picture of me performing, in colour, on the front page of the paper. Maybe she thought I might have invited her, because it was an important concert, and maybe it'd be a way of making up, but I didn't.

The text messages withered and died. I think our last exchange was a vile pair of emails that made both of us madder. She just dug in harder, because she had only herself left to protect, and I despaired further.

I refused to blame myself over staying away from Mum, although I'm still tempted, because I had my reasons.

She had her reasons too.

I hadn't talked to her for two years before she died, and on our last birthdays, two days apart in July, we didn't even contact each other, so I knew then it was serious. It was my last attempt at emotional blackmail, trying to shock her into sobriety by denying her what was most important to her—her children and our love.

Tash did that too. She intermittently blocked access to her two boys because she didn't want them to see Granny pissed.

That would have hurt too, because Mum loved her grandchildren. When they stayed, she didn't drink, and instead she gave them lollies. She was a lot more proactive with them than her mother, my grandmother, had ever been with me.

The day before she died, I walked past her street and kept walking, feeling disconsolate and heavy. Then I flew back to Auckland and it took them twelve hours to find me and tell me the news.

Mum died of a heart attack in 2015, six months after Tony died, also of a heart attack. They both bumped their heads when they fell, and got bruises. Laurie heard Mum cry out from the bathroom— she was scared of death, so maybe she had a second to be afraid. There was nothing Laurie could do, and even though a passing fire truck stopped and the firefighters attended to her in the hall, there was nothing they could do either.

When we reclaimed Mum from the undertaker, we took her on

a drive to Brockville and North East Valley, her old family homes. We were driven in a van by Hiliako, the partner of Pip Laufiso, our Caldwell Street friend, and he is a beautiful man. We were doing thirty kilometres an hour on a main route into town on the day of Mum's funeral, and someone drove by and yelled, 'You have to go faster than that around here mate.'

I wound down my window and said, 'We've got a coffin in the back.'

We kept Mum at Tash's place, in the lounge, in the days before the service. Having her children around her was all she had ever wanted.

We held the service at the St Clair Surf Life Saving Club, because Mum loved the promenade we'd often visited together. Sometimes she'd go alone to the beach and listen to 'Not Dark Yet' by Bob Dylan. The club was a peaceful setting and, through the windows, the waves gave us gentle, ongoing support.

Wiremu presided over Mum's service, a Māori minister who'd also done Dad's service. He'd been a close friend of my father; they'd shared some of the same eccentricities. Wiremu said he'd speak some Māori at the service, because Mum liked that. She always pronounced 'whānau' and 'koha' correctly.

I played 'Love Letters', which Mum had sung at Dad's graveside. We both adored that song, especially the way Elvis did it. When Mum recorded the song for her own album, I said, 'Just imagine you're whispering it into someone's ear.' I adore her version as well.

I forgot everything about the Sandie Shaw song I was going to play at the service, and someone said they felt for me. 'I Had a Dream Last Night' seemed so appropriate, but it disappeared as soon as I hit the first chord.

They played Mum singing the gospel song 'Stand by Me' at an incredible volume, and Laurie left the room. It's a towering hymn that Elvis recorded. His mother had loved him performing gospel, and that was the genre he really was into, singing songs of reconciliation and redemption when he ended up finding neither.

Then we took Mum up to the Andersons Bay crematorium.

She was always really proud of me, Mum. That I was a singer.

Mum was a singer too.

Tony didn't talk to any of his kids for twelve years before he died. He said people weren't acknowledging his feelings, which I thought was odd because that would have involved all the children, including Kristen, who was eight, getting together and saying, 'Right, let's not acknowledge Tony's feelings.' It was his own pain and stubbornness. None of his sisters and brothers spoke to each other either.

Tony still carried around a bone carving of Dad's on his car dashboard, for years, thinking that if he ever saw me or Maria he could return it. When he saw Maria, he gave it back. He told her he hadn't been aware Dad had died—he'd found out months later. But his absence was noted at the tangi.

I visited Tony for the last time when he was running a storage space in Andersons Bay, and when I rang him up to tell him I was dropping in to pick up some old boxes, I asked if he still had an orange car. The phone went silent. He hadn't expected to hear from me. He hadn't heard from me for years.

He had remarried. His new wife seemed to be a drinker, and maybe there was some hitting too. He was still the same sentimentalist, and his eyes filled up when he told me how much he loved his new wife.

He was probably still in love with Mum.

His tattoos were gone now. He'd made some money in property, and had them lasered off.

I went up to our old house that day, in Andersons Bay, and removed some other boxes from a flooded basement with the water above my shins.

Then I went to say goodbye to Tony, and the last thing I said to him was, 'I love you,' and he said he loved me back.

Mum made an album three years before she died, *Reconsidered*, by the Erica Miller Experience.

The idea had been floating around for a while. Mum had sung an Elvis song for Dad at the cemetery, and Gary Sullivan and I backed her at a benefit concert in the Brighton Community Hall, where we raised money for Dad's headstone. David Kilgour played at that too. Performing again reminded Mum of the kick of it and the gift she had.

It was Tash who convened the crew to make a record with Mum. It was a family effort. Dale produced, Tash managed, my cousin Terry made the record cover, I produced Mum's vocals and sang with her, and Kris made a seven-minute documentary we put up on YouTube. My girlfriend took the cover shot of Mum looking glam in front of the red velvet curtains at the playhouse where Christine Colbert did her plays. The cover was empty and resonant, red and black, a bit like a Dimmer cover. A green exit sign glowed.

Laurie put up the bucks to fund the recording and the tour that followed. I think he blew most of his pension. He drove around with boards advertising Mum's album stuck all over his car, and he'd roll down his window and play the record loudly whenever he drove through the main street of town.

I'm glad Mum had Laurie around in the last ten years of her life, because he loved her and treated her respectfully. He was a bit older, a former seaman troubled by rheumatism, but Mum loved Laurie back and looked after him too, puffing up his pillows. Laurie coped with Mum's drinking because he saw her through the day and he could drink as well, long glasses of warm white wine from a cask in the kitchen, but he was more placid than Mum and he'd usually just sink into the couch.

Tom Healy, the partner of Hannah who sang the backing vocals with me, was a star in the album sessions. He played all the guitar and the bass parts with an inordinate amount of skill. Tom plays with Tiny Ruins and Bic Runga these days. He's tasteful, but he digs in where it matters.

The other musicians were people who Tash and Dale knew. And there was also the drummer Marcel Rodeka. Marcel was a founding member of Mother Goose back in the seventies, and now he's a session player who's sought after for his drum lessons. His son is a top-level football player.

I love *Reconsidered* because Mum totally gives it up. Even though the songs are cover versions, I can tell what every song is about, because I know my mother. She claims every song. I can smell the crates of beer, the fondue sets, the violence in the kitchen. I hear her love for Dad.

They were all songs that Elvis had recorded. There's an Elvis thing in our family, and since Elvis covered the American songbook, the choice of material was limitless. I picked a lot of the songs, some that Mum didn't know, like 'Stand by Me' and 'Long Black Limousine'.

She was intimidated by 'Long Black Limousine' because it was an epic about someone finally getting to parade down the main drag—but in a coffin, because they've been killed in a car crash. Elvis sang a lot of songs where he was a stranger in his own hometown.

Mum nailed that song. She went 'Oh yeeeahhh' several times over and, on our backing vocals, Hannah sounds like a big black woman, although she reverts to being a little white woman on her harmony in 'Don't'. Hannah and I worked studiously on the backing vocal parts, because there were a lot of them and nearly all of them were killer. We were Mum's ghost choir and went just as hard as her.

Universal ended up releasing Mum's record, because it was

good, although the obvious selling point was that it was Shayne Carter's mother. I came up with the title. But it's Mum's album. All of it is her.

We did a tour afterwards, and not a lot of people came, and I had to warn Mum before the last show in Auckland that she should slow down her drinking, although I said it by saying she shouldn't smoke so many cigarettes. Mum shone at every concert. She was just as big a ham as Dad was, and she loved it, in her cabaret shawl, trying to be foxy, pushing out her lips as she faded on a note. Her seven-piece band loved it too, because we knew it was for real.

In the documentary Kris made, there's a scene where Mum is doing her vocals in the lounge of my tiny flat in Sandringham. She'd come up to Auckland because I really wanted to produce her vocals. I thought I knew how she should sing—even though she already knew—but perhaps I could help her on technical issues and encourage her, because I cared about her record. Mum listened closely and respected everything I said about tension and release and holding back so when you kicked in, it really counted. But then, Mum knew about tension and release. She'd hear me while clicking her hair through her fingers, like she did when I was a kid.

There's also a scene in Dunedin where Mum and the rest of the family are bawling with laughter, our hands on our knees. Despite our troubles, our family has a large absurdist humour and we've always been able to laugh.

My favourite part of the documentary, although I didn't realise it at the time, is towards the end, when Mum has just finished a take and I've played it back at a punishing volume on my Genelec speakers and it sounds fantastic.

I watched that bit after Mum died, and it made me feel so much better.

We're both chuffed, and we're standing just around the corner from the lounge in the small enclave where my speakers and bed are.

I hug my mother and she hugs me back, because together we've made an achievement, and it's special because we're flesh and blood.

Then we turn our separate ways, and go back to whatever it was we were doing.

*

Aramoana is a village by two beaches where the Pacific comes into the harbour. I came here to write this book.

Dunedin is twenty kilometres away, down a seriously windy road. Seals loll on the Aramoana Mole, which runs for 500 metres out into the sea, and seagulls bomb at the end to protect their nests.

Aramoana gained a black reputation in the early nineties when a local man went mad and gunned down thirteen people, including young boys and girls. He'd had an argument with his neighbour and then he went next door, shot the family, and set their house on fire. When people came to look at the blaze, including children on pushbikes, he murdered them too. He shot the cop from Port Chalmers in the sand dunes, after pretending to give up. The next morning he was killed by the police, when he ran out from a crib, waving his gun, yelling, 'Kill me ya bastards, kill me.'

The cops shot him up real good and left him to bleed. He died on his way to hospital.

My bach is three houses down from David Gray's, although his house was burnt down shortly after his crime, and someone has built a jolly adobe house in its place. The cartoon doesn't quite do it. I'd look down our street and picture bodies still lying in it.

There are memorials down by the beach, two of them—a plaque on a big stone in the carpark, and a more private space in the bushes, with shells and soft toys sitting under a sculpture behind a list of the bereaved. Time has washed the toys of their colour, and the scene is leaden and still.

At first I didn't like being in David Gray's street. I'd imagine him roaming my property. Then a friend who had spent family holidays at Aramoana said, 'You can't let someone like that claim the place.' When she said that, I was relieved. You don't have to look far to find blood in New Zealand, because it's all through our soil. The bay just around the corner is called Murderer's Beach.

I got over my dark fixations. I didn't want to haunt myself anymore, because it was a cheap kick I didn't need, and I figured it was like the people who annoy you or the places you shouldn't be. So you go the other way. You go somewhere else, somewhere that offers you more light.

Acknowledgements

I'd like to thank the members of my whānau, and extended whānau, who supported me through the writing of this book, especially my sisters Tash and Maria who at various points provided shelter, washing machines and meals to help tide a brother over.

Large gratitude to Steve Braunias who trudged through the 150,000-word first draft and gave me golden advice throughout. Similarly my editor Ashleigh Young steered me to a place of clarity and conscience after wading through the early work.

Thanks, too, to Fergus, Kirsten, Jasmine and everyone else at VUP .

Thank you Nikki Brown for your amazing generosity and the crib at Aramoana. Ten kilometres from the nearest shop, all but cut off from the internet, surrounded by mist, seals and sea—there couldn't have been a better environment for writing. Thank you Joan and Robbie for hooking Nikki and me up.

Love to Ange and Nick in Wanaka, and to Jaime for the road trips and river walks.

Thanks Margaret Gordon for support and feedback.

Thanks Aaron and Tony for keeping your car crashin' cousin on the road.

The following people assisted with photographs, copyright material and/or research: John Collie, Jeff Harford, Fraser Batts, Jeff Batts, Terry Moore, Lesley Paris, the Kenton family, Tommy Duff, Wiremu Quedley, Francisca Griffin, Bruce Mahalski, Kat Spears, Helen Middlemiss, Brent Williams, Sandra Nevill, the Estate of Peter Howard Gutteridge, Robert Scott, David Kilgour, Graeme Downes, Hamish Kilgour, Barbara Ward,Catherine Povey, Debbi Gibbs, Chris Knox, Jackson Perry, Greta Anderson, William Daymond, Jonathan Ganley, Ebony Lamb, Esta De Jong, Heazlewood, Darryl Ward, Craig McNab, Jan Hellriegel, Simon Grigg, Timothy Vaughan-Sanders, Matthew Davis, Jeremy Freeman, and Gregor Richardson. Thank you one and all.

Copyright Acknowledgements

Index